Which One Am I?

Thomas Smith & James Darrell Williams

Which One Am I?
Copyright 2012 by Thomas S. Smith & James Darrell Williams

All rights reserved. No part of this book may be reproduced or transmitted in any form or by any means without written permission from the author.

ISBN-13: 978-1479120772
ISBN-10: 1479120774

Introduction by Mary Barnick

Edited by Kathy Jones and Erika Compton

Cover Design: Thomas Smith
Back Cover Author Photo: Jana Pendragon

Back Cover Collage Photos: Mary Barnick, Scott Barrett, Michelle Crispin, Robert Dann, Martha Faye Joshlin, Gregory Scott Largent, Jana Pendragon, Thomas Smith, Thomas Smith Sr., Bob Taylor, James Darrell Williams, and Kelly Zirbes

For Bertha Merriman

And to Darrell's Mother and Father

"We tell ourselves stories in order to live."
– Joan Didion, The White Album.

FOREWARD

This isn't the way Darrell's story was supposed to unfold. But you could say that just about anybody's life.

At its core, this is the chronicle of the life of James Darrell Williams. This is how he has grown up with Dissociative Identity Disorder (DID), a disorder being by definition "An ailment that affects the function of mind or body." More importantly, this story is of how and why he developed what neither of us particularly considers an "ailment" and how he came to become the man he is today. Initially, Darrell and I were attempting to explain Darrell to himself. We needed to explore how Darrell came to have these multiple personalities, these people inside him that exist and live along with him.

Along the way, the story became something quite different and not at all what we expected. The "why" of it all tended to be buried in layers of psychology, sociology, history, geography and family secrets that no one wanted to tell. Explaining what happened became much more complicated.

History is told by its survivors: Roald Amundsen's South Pole expedition, the Donner Party, Billy Milligan. They leave historians with nothing more than scribbled notes, selective memory and inadvertent admissions. To recreate what really happened requires deductive reasoning, a fair number of educated guesses and the ability to listen between the lines. History is something people only half remember.

We always knew telling Darrell's story was going to be somewhat difficult. To live, survive and ultimately thrive with DID is to live life out of time. Each day is a movie constructed from previews and outtakes with reels all out of order. We wanted to splice the pieces together, fill in the gaps and make sense of it all.

That was my job. Trained as a journalist, I was privy to contacts and resources that Darrell had never heard of. I wanted to tell how his experience was effected by his particular geography, sociology and setting. Darrell and the "kids" – his term for the people who live inside him -- just wanted their story told – and told right. There are big kids and little kids, all of them shadows behind Darrell's hazel eyes. We want to make sure this book allows them to feel safe, understood and accepted.

Balancing my proclivity for research with Darrell's vivid and painful memories was always going to make our account more like two or three books than one. We had no idea how true that would become until we stumbled quite accidentally upon Bertha Merriman.

In doing this work, we also hoped to correct what we saw as dramatizations, colorizations, omissions and, in some cases, oversimplifications in other pieces on the topic of DID. Hollywood focused the eye mostly on the outward manifestations of DID in the years following *The Three Faces of Eve* and, particularly, *Sybil*. Neither of those films comes anywhere near to reflecting Darrell's experience. We both believed there had to be other DID patients out in the rest of the world who could benefit from a more realistic depiction of what they went through from day to day.

We have tried to stay as close to the known science of DID as we have to its history. That is to say, both of its histories; what research has discovered about it and how it is perceived by the public. Complicated concepts have been explained to the best of our research and capabilities. To these ends, we applied each concept as it became pertinent to what Darrell was experiencing at the time. We realize too that science most likely will have advanced by the time this book reaches readers.

We had our experience and others had theirs. We took alternate versions into consideration, but Darrell's experience always remained primary. We learned early on that there is the truth and there are the stories people tell. The most important story we learned was the one kept from Darrell all his life.

Despite numerous warnings to the contrary, we have opted to keep as many real names as Darrell and the kids can remember in this narrative. Certainly we understand the fear of lawsuits inherent in the publishing world, but to make this a "based on a true story" account didn't jive well with the need to tell the true history and psychology that affected Darrell as he was growing up. To be fair, we took a vote. Darrell and I were for telling the absolute truth from the beginning, consequences be damned. The kids inside Darrell couldn't understand for the life of them why we even questioned telling what happened to them.

Though his family has always called him by his first name, a name he always associated with blame and betrayal, Darrell began calling himself by his middle name when he got to California. In order to avoid confusion with the interior person called James, we have opted to call Darrell by his chosen name throughout.

For those whose identities we could not uncover, we left them described by their actions in whatever role they played in Darrell's life at the time. Our hope is that they see themselves and come forward at some time to fill in the pieces of their history Darrell still doesn't know. They deserve to claim their own identities as well as their own places in Darrell's story.

We learned the name of Darrell's birth father and namesake, James Darrell Jackson, from Bertha Merriman. For that alone we would have dedicated this book to her, but without her help and support we might never have gotten so near to discovering Darrell's birthright.

Our undying appreciation goes to Dr. Sharon Higgins. Without her, Darrell might never have known about Dissociative Identify Disorder and certainly would never have learned to live with its challenges.

Thanks go out to those who read early versions and leant both their support and criticism: Mary Barnick, Patrick Campbell-Lyons, Tom Farrell, Dena Foman, Marvin Kanarek, Erin Lale, Karen Michalson, Heidi Nye and Jana Pendragon. We offer deep gratitude for their time and knowledge to my long-time friends and this book's editors, Kathy Jones and Erika Compton.

Our most heart-felt thanks to the aforementioned Mary Barnick and her husband Bo Kirgis. They made the little ones very comfortable, saved us and gave us hope when we needed it most. This book's title was Mary's suggestion.

Great appreciation to Bo Kirgis, our nephew Ian Smith-Grove and my father Thomas Smith Sr. for making the pictures we took for the icons look so perfect.

Also thanks to those who gave us vital information and support: Vincent Astor; Richard Baker; Chip Barnes at Crittenden County Juvenile; Peggy Barnick; Bonnie Bevel; Christopher Bevel; Billie Bowles, assistant to Judge Ralph Wilson, Jr.; Casey Brady; Bright Blue Gorilla (Michael Glover & Robyn Rosenkrantz); Shirley Foote Coy; Calista Doll at the Department of Children's Services in Nashville; Kriss Erickson; the staff of Eye of the Cat, who encouraged us to tell Darrell's story; Kristin Flickinger at AskTheGay.com; Frangela (Frances Callier and Angela V. Shelton) for helping us stay as inoffensive as possible; Ed Frank at the University of Memphis Library for his tireless and thorough assistance with research; Lindsey Fry at KATV Channel 7 Memphis, TN; Hypnotherapist Brian Green; Holmes Hammett; Lisa Koch; Gregory Scott Largent; Stephanie Lee; Lorraine K. Lorne at the Young Law Library, Leflar Law Center at the University of Arkansas; Rena Klock; Michelle Mangione; Gerald Martin; Tom McCormack; Velma Williams McDermott; Debi Hassett Miller; Rick Minnich; Alice Ortiz at the Monroe Journal; Timothy Pack; Sara Petite; Tonya J. Powers at Newsradio600 WREC Memphis, TN for introducing us to the concept of "honor" among Southern men; David M. Reiss, M.D.; Betty Roland; Bill Sayger at the Central Delta Depot and Museum; Grace Slick; Paula Soest; Hal Sparks; Marlene Steinberg, M.D.; Cheryl Sterling at the Woolfolk Library; David Tanenhaus; Bob Taylor; Shellie Ver Meer, CHt, EFT at Inner Vision Hypnotherapy; Samuel L. Waltz Jr., for his Viet Nam era history lesson; Karen Widmer, RN; Judge Ralph Wilson, Jr. and Kelly Zirbes.

Thomas Smith

Long Beach, CA

July 2012

INTRODUCTION
By Mary Barnick

Make no mistake; this book is a love story. Written by someone who loves Darrell Williams for who he is, and accepts the multiple ways Darrell has adapted to live his life, before, up to and including these years together.

Born during the era of the universal "Love Children", who coined the mantra of the decade, "Make love not war", *emphasis on Love*, it is no small wonder this child born of seemingly unstable emotional people, would seek just to be loved.

The author passionately writes about this phenomenon of multiple personalities through medical, historical and personal experiences in an effort to help others understand their relationship. It is one of love.

Whether or not you believe in or accept the "multiple personalities" concept, it would be hard to deny that each one of us experiences an "alternate" moment quite regularly. For example, don't we adjust our "game face" on the job, at school, in the grocery store, at home with family, with the officer writing your speeding ticket, on that first date with the guy or girl of your dreams, listening to the doctor as he gives you bad news regarding a loved one, and the list goes on. Now add to these the anger, joy, sorrow, frustration, fear, insecurities or confidence of any given moment of any given day, and can you see yourself as a "different personality" in each of these scenarios?

Darrell's story gives us insight into a child's, and later a young man's life with trauma, tragedy and family secrets which are nearly impenetrable decades later. And his story reveals how he lived with these. Darrell's "game face" evolved into a personality incarnate, and depending on the event, manifested a boisterous, defensive teen, a sassy, street smart young woman, or a toddler still learning how to communicate with words, or any of a number of others.

Just considering from a distant observation point a lifetime into these 'appearances" of protectors, it would seem that Darrell has been fearful of acknowledging his strengths and weaknesses, in love and life. Rejection can cause the ripple effect of reluctance, doubt, and uncertainty. Not just a lack of, but often the loss of self esteem. Add to this the abuse, neglect, horrifying image of a loved one's suicide, and who would not choose to hide in the protective shadows of an alternate personality?

Thomas Smith brings Darrell's life experience to the reader from the point of helping Darrell understand who he is, and the how and why. If there is medical acknowledgement for these multiples, or not, for Darrell, it has been a lifetime of reality. For Tom, it was not only finding a partner, soul mate, love for life; it was embracing an entire family of individuals who are Darrell.

Meeting them for the first time on Beale Street in Memphis was a memorable moment. I found myself falling in love instantly with, at first, both of them, and then, all of them. One can see the love they share, as well as the joy of having each other. It is a wonderful gift Tom lays before Darrell, this telling the world of his struggles in life, to bring to Darrell the peace of knowing he is truly loved. By many, and most of all by Tom.

PART ONE

BRINKLEY

Brinkley is the most populous city in Monroe County, Arkansas. The population was 3,940 at the time of the 2000 census. It is located exactly half way between Little Rock, Arkansas and Memphis, Tennessee; the city has used the slogan "We'll Meet You Half Way" in some of its advertising campaigns. — From Wikipedia

R.D. and Carolyn with two of their children (Possibly Darrell in their arms and Allen at their feet)
(Photo Credit Unknown)

-- I --

R.D.

It was a shame what Carolyn did to that man. It was bad enough that she went and fooled around on R.D., but then she listened to Bertha Merriman and named that baby of hers after that no good James Darrell Jackson! What would people say? They would think R.D. was less than a man, that's what they'd say. That is, if they ever found out the truth. R.D. wasn't about to let anybody know, not while he was alive and sure not while that boy was still breathing.

As far as anybody knew – as far as he knew – James Darrell Williams was the youngest of five. The Williams family always called him James, a name he came to detest as it was usually followed by an accusation of something he was supposed to have done. After he got big enough and far enough away from his tormentors, he'd always call himself Darrell.

Years would pass before anybody would tell him who his father was. At the time of Darrell's birth, R.D. was making what living he could working odd jobs for his good friend and next door neighbor Gene Merriman. Only a teen himself, R.D. worked in the rice fields until Gene took him under his wing and taught him to drive a bulldozer. Until her accident, Darrell's mother Carolyn worked in one of the small town's factories making shirts.

The Williams were barely adults when they got together. Richard Williams, who always called himself R.D., was just 17. That's him in the photos on Darrell's bookcase, all sinew and swagger. With his father's farm fanning out behind him, the dark-haired youth stares down the camera, daring it to show that he wouldn't be the world's best husband and father if given half the chance. He is every inch the proud young man.

Off his shoulder is Carolyn. She was just 14 when they hooked up, not nearly as self-assured as R.D., but still trying to portray the proper lady in a pleated skirt fashionable for its place if not its time. Change her hair from brown to blond and she'd look just like she did the day she died.

Those who knew the Colemans always said that Carolyn was the prettiest of the girls. She had the looks and figure that could attract a husband or two. A dark-headed Sandra Dee, there was something darkly mysterious hidden behind her innocent appearance.

She has clear, determined, blue eyes that stare straight out from under hair done up for the occasion in a flawless bouffant. It's a picture of someone who doesn't want her picture taken, doesn't want to be frozen in time with these kids and this man. She looks past the camera, focusing on something off in the distance that no one else can see.

She was no Sandra Dee, quite the opposite in fact. Carolyn loved bad boys. R.D. was only the first one she would marry. For the rest of the family's lives, they would tell outsiders that R.D. was a good man, but down inside they all knew better. Even if her parents had seen fit to warn her away from R.D., by the time they knew anything was going on she was already pregnant with Johnny, the first of five children who would bear R.D.'s surname.

Relations don't always add up to family. Just because they were growing up young in the South didn't mean they also matured. There wouldn't be all that many more family portraits because R.D. wasn't generally around that much. Darrell's maternal grandmother explained that Carolyn and R.D. had a difficult marriage, but really it went way past that. Today, one might say that R.D. was violent and abusive. The alcohol didn't make things any easier. Their families just saw them as two argumentative kids.

They would fight pretty often, immediately after which R.D. would just take off to wherever he went when he was mad. Eventually, those two would make up — and make up good. Then who knows what would set them off and the whole pattern would repeat itself just as assuredly as the pattern on the mobile home's wallpaper.

The only thing that would be different each time was the name of the baby Carolyn would be carrying whenever R.D. came back. After Johnny was born, there came Ronnie, giving them two tow-headed little boys. These were the first natural blonds in either family's known history. No one seemed bothered by this turn of events. At least no one ever commented.

R.D. and Carolyn must have been getting along about as well as they ever did at that point because there were a couple of years until Bobbie Lynn, their only daughter, came along. Bobbie Lynn was the first of the dark-headed kids with Alan following about a year later and Darrell not long after that.

There was actually supposed to be a little more time between Alan and Darrell but whether it was from the beating or just because that's how Mother Nature intended, that last child showed up early. Bertha Merriman, who raised all of Carolyn's kids, kept the tiny baby in a shoebox in a dresser drawer by her bed.

It would have taken a strong constitution and a more mature couple to live long with the instability in R.D. and Carolyn's house. By the night R.D. smashed that pale yellow highchair into Carolyn's three-months-pregnant stomach, she was making plans of her own.

No one really knew what ticked off R.D. the night he went after Carolyn. It could have been the frustration any laboring man encounters in a town where there's not much steady work. Maybe it was the idea of his teenage sweetheart with another man. Maybe it was the panic of knowing there was going to be one more mouth to feed, a fifth baby to break the bank.

That night, Carolyn was over at the Merrimans' trailer. There weren't any maternity clothes available, so she was dressed in a pretty little pink nightgown. R.D. hadn't been drinking that night, but the news that Carolyn was pregnant again was more than enough to get his juices pumping.

He'd just come from work with his shirt rolled up to the elbows as always. R.D. was just dropping in like he sometimes did. Given the pattern those two had developed over the years, it's surprising that Carolyn's news came as a surprise at all.

This pregnancy was different. Despite the stories her sisters and mother were already putting together, Carolyn knew the truth. She knew R.D. knew it too. All she wanted was for him to forget what he knew and to go along with the lie. R.D. was too proud for that. From behind the window of her fearful eyes, she watched his face get red.

"What do you mean? That baby can't be mine," he hollered, adding just about every expletive one could imagine. "It's a bastard child! You whore!"

With that, he picked up the nearest heavy object he could find, which just happened to be the same high chair all his babies had been using. He was going to use it to knock this bastard child right out of Carolyn.

It took the whole family to beat him off. Aunt Bertha and Grandma Coleman were both armed with frying pans. Grandma Williams grabbed the next heaviest thing she could find, a heavy plate. Later in his childhood, Darrell would recognize this same plate with its multi-colored circle pattern. He ate dinner off it many times in the years after R.D. came back to take the rest of the kids away.

Right after his attack on his wife, R.D. took off again just as he always did. Unlike all the times before when he'd disappear, this time he didn't come back much. Darrell wouldn't even meet R.D. until 1972 when the boy was five or six; right after Carolyn had the accident. Though R.D. would sometimes come by in later years, he never stayed around long enough to make much of an impression. The man Darrell always knew as his father never would say the boy's name. R.D. would always introduce Darrell as "my youngest."

In rural Arkansas, family secrets seldom see the light of day. There was no reason to talk much about any little family squabble the family could contain within the faux wood paneled walls of the trailer. After all, R.D. was pretty much out of the picture and when he did come around, he just ignored the boy. He didn't stay away completely, though. He always insisted he loved Carolyn in his own way and would continue to love her for the rest of his life.

It came as quite a shock to everyone when the high chair stirred up a memory four-year-old Darrell wasn't supposed to have known. Somehow, the boy knew all about the beating he'd never been told about. He knew what had been said during the attack. He knew every action R.D. had taken to try to keep him from being born.

It was as if Darrell had been watching the action from behind his mother's eyes. Everybody heard the story: Carolyn, Bertha and both his grandmothers. They had been keeping this secret, yet the boy somehow knew every detail.

Maybe he shouldn't have repeated it to them, but then young kids don't know a thing about keeping family secrets. Later Darrell would learn he had apparently experienced what the psychic community calls "blood memory." Shellie Ver Meer, a professional at Inner Vision Hypnotherapy, says a parent or ancestor may pass down memories through DNA. Noted psychic Sylvia Browne calls this process "cell memory" where, as a person moves from lifetime to lifetime, memories that were unresolved in some way, and carried over in the subconscious, may disrupt a person's current life.

Here the repercussions were doled out all around, giving the family something else to not talk about. If they had any doubts there was something odd about that boy, this recitation of facts he'd never learned only widened the distance between Darrell and those who were supposed to protect him.

James Darrell Jackson about the time he met Carolyn
(Courtesy Bertha Merriman)

-- 2 --

EVE

    Brinkley's first education about DID and its place in the world at large would come through Hollywood. Plenty of townspeople would have seen *The Three Faces of Eve* either at the Starlight Drive-In on the edge of town or more likely at the stately Haven Theatre on New Orleans Avenue. Opened prior to 1950 when the town was most populous, the historic haven seats 970. It is part of the regional Imperial Theater chain founded by local businessman L.F. Haven.

To filmgoers, DID and its fraternal twin schizophrenia were just another pair of horrors on the silver screen. These dramas fit squarely with the public's demands for escapism and morality. Hollywood personalized both conditions so that viewers could conceive of a schizophrenic or multiple living next door, but they were exotic enough that viewers could also assure themselves such things only happened somewhere else. A kindly doctor served as hero, vanquishing an unseen villain, mental illness serving as a metaphor for the Atomic threat everyone feared. That's what *The Three Faces of Eve* delivered, right down to its happy ending.

Yet it seemed not even films billed as true stories were necessarily true all the way through.

The main character in *The Three Faces of Eve*, Eve White, was first referred in 1951 by her local physician to psychiatrists Corbert H. Thigpen and Hervery M. Cleckley of The Medical College of Georgia in Augusta. The doctors published a 17-page article about her case in *The Journal of Abnormal and Social Psychology* in 1954.

This was the first documented account of true DID recorded in the 20th Century, so of course Thigpen and Cleckley were persuaded to expand their work into a book. That decision proved both fateful and lucrative. By the time the book was in galley proofs in 1956, it had already been optioned as a screenplay. By the time the book was published in 1957, the film itself was ready for release just in time to steal audience share from its fictional competition, *Lizzie,* released to theaters that same year.

Lizzie proved a line of demarcation between the fantastic themes embodied within the horror genre and the public's growing infatuation with science. In the film, the female lead, played by Eleanor Parker, is hypnotized when it is discovered she has three personalities. These are the shy Elizabeth, the Mr. Hyde-like Lizzie, and the kind, well-adjusted Beth, the woman she always should have been. The film is probably best remembered for giving the world two popular songs, "It's Not for Me to Say" and "Warm and Tender." Both were written specifically for the film. Johnny Mathis performed the songs in *Lizzie* in his role as a piano player and singer.

Based on the novel *The Bird's Cage* by Shirley Jackson, Lizzie was never touted as anything but a fictional drama. Not so with *The Three Faces of Eve.* 20th Century Fox proudly proclaimed it took great pains to tell Eve's true story, but the liberties the producers took are obvious. The doctors who wrote about three personalities in a single body saw their own characters combined on screen into a single doctor played by Lee J. Cobb.

Chris Costner Sizemore, who identified herself as the film and book's subject years later, writes in her 1989 book *A Mind of My Own* that it took her seven psychiatrists and 22 personalities to finally be cured of DID in 1974. That is a story in itself. Complete recovery is the exception, not the rule.

Personalities never really combine into one whole being as they did in *Sybil* and today's experts don't expect them to. Instead, they learn or they are taught to live together in a process called integration. Ideally, they form a big, happy family. For some, that's the only happy family they will ever have.

Darrell's extended family couldn't be blamed for not recognizing, much less believing, what was happening. The Williams family was a pragmatic bunch. They tended to put their money on things they could touch. Psychological forces didn't fit that category. Things like psychic abilities and multiple personalities were only seen in the movies. Such things never happened in small Southern towns and certainly not to Darrell's strong-minded clan.

Alone among his siblings, an outsider to his family, Darrell would grow up different. He was the sibling closest to his mother, for one thing. He looked like her in the same way that at least Ronnie, Bobbie Lynn and Allen looked like their mother. It was strange to them, though, how little he seemed to have in common, physically or otherwise, with R.D.

Darrell stayed with Carolyn longest, making no moves to have a marriage in his early teens like his siblings Johnny, Ronnie, Bobbie Lynn and Allen. Darrell never did act much like he wanted to join R.D. and his other sons in the family tractor-driving business. Even had R.D. acted like he'd wanted his youngest son with him, R.D. had already made no secret that he'd rather see Darrell dead than alive and even R.D.'s father later made an effort to bring that dark vision to pass. The other kids would grow up seeing Darrell as a loner, but he was only alone because he felt he had no place else to go.

Some people learn from example. Others learn from experience. Darrell took both into consideration and then was forced to create himself as somebody new. He had no choice. Darrell's body language wasn't going to deny the feminine streak Bertha Merriman had noticed in him soon after birth. Then there were those blackouts he was always experiencing. He'd find himself in one situation with one group of people and wake up in surroundings that were entirely new.

Darrell always knew something was different about himself. He just didn't know that it had a name. Had the townspeople talked about psychics, most likely by noticing his mother Carolyn's ability to see into the future, the monikers whispered would have been "witch" or "into devil worship." Instead, they never talked about such things at all.

No one in town would have believed in multiple personalities any more than they would have believed in the psychic world. Psychology wasn't a big topic in Brinkley. Most of modern history kept right on rolling through town like cargo trains on their way to somewhere bigger.

It wasn't fashionable during the Sixties and early Seventies to believe in such a thing as multiple personalities. Had Darrell been able as a child to describe what he was experiencing, there would have been no one in Brinkley and few outside it who would have found a proper diagnosis because almost no one would have looked. Even today, not every psychiatrist today believes that multiple personalities are real, though there is an official diagnosis that keeps getting renamed as more is learned about it. What was originally called Multiple Personality Disorder (MPD) is now called, by those doctors who believe it exists at all, Dissociative Identity Disorder (DID).

It may be traditional training that leads to a bias against DID. For many years, it was generally accepted that each person has only one unifying personality. It doesn't take much to figure out, though, that any person has many different personality states in a day. The personality at work may differ from that in the home; the drinking personality may be unrecognizable from the one who is sober. Recognizing these differences challenges the original concept.

Some say alternate personalities are iatrogenic, that is to say they are created by therapists with the cooperation of their patients and the rest of society. That would mean that susceptible patients create whoever or whatever they think people want them to be. That would mean the experts create both the disease and the cure.

In the beginning days of research, the experts were just finding their collective voice and that voice wasn't widely heard. DID isn't the sort of story that would hit even a good local paper like *The Argus Sun* in Brinkley There was nothing local about multiple personalities as far as anybody in town knew.

Even if no one recognized the multiples gathering in their midst, Brinkley was still in no way immune from the stressful conditions that cause them to form. Following World War II, soldiers all over the country returned home suffering from various kinds of psychological distress.

The war changed the way people saw the world. It changed entire families and it hit particularly close to home for the Coleman clan. Carolyn's father, Albert Carl Coleman, had been killed in the Great War and buried with honors in Arlington National Cemetery in Washington D.C.

His friend Richard "Dick" Joshlin had joined the U.S. Navy the same day as the doomed Albert. They remained close friends, fighting side by side in the grand tradition of war buddies through history.

They were so close that Richard, being an honorable man, promised his friend Albert that he would take care of the Coleman family if something ever happened to its patriarch. That's just what he did.

After the war ended, Dick returned to comfort the widow Martha Faye Coleman. Eventually, they married and would stay married for the rest of their lives. Richard helped Martha raise all four of her daughters: Carolyn, Jeanne, Ann and Iris Faye. Martha had two sons by Albert: Larry and Bob. Together, Dick and Martha Faye had the one son who would carry Dick's last name, their youngest son Steve.

By returning to the farm after his service to the country, Dick Joshlin was bucking the trend. Many young men left Arkansas during World War II to serve in the military or to find jobs in defense-related industries. That meant a labor shortage for the farming and timber industries, and that led to the picking of cotton being mechanized. Fewer men working in the fields led to fewer opportunities for returning veterans to support their new families. Even those young men who had returned from the war to start families in town soon left Brinkley for bigger jobs in bigger cities. The businesses that remained, the Wagner Electric Corp. and, particularly, the Van Heusen Plant where Carolyn eventually worked, were often the only places young widows and their neighbors could make a living.

The service provided a way out for young men. Dick's son Steve grew up determined to see at least as much of the world as had his father and maybe even to start a family of his own in the big world just past the Arkansas border.

This was not to be.

Which One Am I?

-- 3 --

DARRELL

We live in a quiet apartment in Southern California where the sun shines through a purple curtain, illuminating mementoes of the past. Our home is peaceful, comfortable and safe. Life was not always so for Darrell.

Robert Dann still lives here. His spirit is everywhere, from the desk in his old office to the bathrobe both Darrell and I use from time to time. It was he who added the sunshine yellow accents to the country-style kitchen Darrell and I now share. Robert Dann was a stern man, but also someone who knew that little kindnesses could always put a smile on someone's face.

This is as it should be. Every person is a product of his or her history. It would be very wrong to ask Darrell to put aside memories of happiness and the lessons he learned from Robert. In many ways, it was Robert who taught Darrell how to be an adult and Darrell will always love him for that. If Darrell loves me only half as much as he loved Robert, I will feel like the luckiest man alive.

There is now a cherry wood bureau that replaced the over-sized kitchen table across from the kitchen sink. The cabinet was one of the first purchases Darrell and I made together. Our intention was to better showcase the blue and white Royal Delph collection that Darrell began with his late husband Robert.

Though Darrell referred to Robert as his husband from the first day they became a couple, theirs was not a marriage in the traditional way. As Darrell says, "God gave us the right to be married, not the state." Regardless, Darrell and Robert had planned to make their union legally official when they heard that the Supreme Court of California, basing its decision on an equal protection argument, would begin granting permission for marriage licenses to be issued in California. Robert died just two weeks shy of the date, June 16, 2008, when the ruling took effect.

One of the goals I had when Darrell and I got together as a couple and eventually became Domestic Partners was to encourage him to be the best person he could be. We got as close to gay marriage as California law currently allows thanks to the contentious passing of Prop. 8 which put an end to the issuance of gay marriage licenses in our home state of California.

Darrell respects me in the same way I do him. There has always been a conscience effort to respect what Darrell had together with Robert especially since Robert had not been gone long before Darrell and I met. Alone in Long Beach, bereft of family connections, Darrell was never truly allowed to grieve his late husband's passing. If you ask Darrell, he still doesn't know how.

More than history and memories, the new cabinet holds Darrell's pills. Lexapro, the commercial name for Escitalopram, is prescribed to Darrell in order to help treat his depression and generalized anxiety disorder. Clonazapam, which Darrell knows as Klonopin, is there to relive his panic attacks. Quetiapine tablets, commonly called Seroquel, are used to treat schizophrenia but in Darrell's case they prevent episodes of mania as well as depression as they do in patients with bipolar disorder. The latest edition to Darrell's daily regimen is Benadryl. The drug is best known for its effect on the common cold or sinus problems, but it is used here to treat Darrell's insomnia and to help prevent his nightmares.

This is Darrell's normal; the drugs helping him daily to live each day as himself. Years of therapy, principally with his psychiatrist Dr. Sharon Higgens, have helped him maintain more control over his mind and body than he had growing up, but the therapy doesn't work alone. His drug regimen helps keep the people inside from taking Darrell over. More than 20 years after first beginning treatment, he still lives in fear even if the emotion's intensity has diminished over time.

It has taken a long time for Dr. Higgens to help Darrell get to know the people inside and to understand what each represents. During their not quite 23 years together, the late Robert Dann got to know eight of the people inside Darrell as each felt comfortable enough to let themselves out into the light. Some four years later, we know a total of 15.

We divide Darrell's "kids" into groups. Two are what Darrell calls "The Whinnies," pre-verbal babies who are drawn to bright colors and spinning toys and are identified when they are out because instead of talking, they stare. A slightly older group calls itself "The Babies": 2-year-old Billy; 2 ½ years old Tommy Tom; 4-year-old Jimmie; and a pair of 10-year-olds, Dot and Robbie. The big kids are J.D. (age 15); James (16); and two 17-year-olds, Steve and Billy Bill. There are currently five girls: Mary Rose (12); Carol (15); Diane (16); Star and Judith Ann, both of whom are age 17.

Darrell sees these people inside him as spirits or souls who, for whatever reason, were born without bodies of their own. They are sons and daughters from the past and future. Their purpose is to be called on in times of trouble. To refuse to share his body with such creatures of God is, to Darrell, contrary to the wishes of the creator.

Which One Am I?

Each person inside has picked out a mask to represent, if not their own faces as they see them, at least a clue to their individual personalities. There are currently more than two dozen masks adorning the walls and display cases here in what was originally a 1920s detached, single-family house but now is rented as a large apartment. Behind each is a person waiting to let him or herself be known. Their true voices they reveal in their own time.

How that time is measured is a question. Why only some choose to reveal themselves is another. When Robert Dann was alive he had a long late night conversation in Italian, a language Darrell has never spoken, with one of the personalities who returned inside without choosing a name. Robert might have pushed the issue, but he was likely either too stunned or too sleepy to think the episode through. There is another now who seems to be speaking French. That one may also go unidentified since no one in the household has any experience with his language.

The identified people are not considered problems. In the house we all share they have found acceptance. Because they have acceptance, they in turn accept the house rules: Darrell is in charge. No one is allowed to take over the body without letting Darrell know first so that he can give or deny permission.

It is not the people inside he knows that cause Darrell to live in a state of constant fear. Patients including Darrell face much of the same stressors as those with Post-Traumatic Stress Disorder (PTSD), a syndrome identified in trauma victims, war veterans, and residents of communities exposed to disaster. The main symptoms of both DID and PTSD are nightmares, flashbacks, hypervigilence and depression. What frightens Darrell the most is what someone inside he doesn't yet know might do.

The unexpected happened before. Not long after his 10th anniversary with Robert, Darrell opened his eyes to find himself at the border between California and Arizona. He was riding in a Greyhound bus that he didn't remember getting on. In fact, as far as he'd known, he'd been sleeping in the bed he shared with Robert Dann back in Long Beach, over 100 miles back. In the days before the older kids were known to Darrell and his psychiatrist, a few of them (James, J.D., Steve and the girls) decided that they wanted to go back to Arkansas to be with the Williams clan. Darrell's older brother Ronnie had been asking him to return, promising to take care of Darrell and help him reestablish himself in ways he never could when he was a teen. The older kids wanted to believe Ronnie.

They also felt guilty that Darrell had long ago promised R.D. that the older man would never see his youngest son again until R.D. was "dead or dying." He was. On a previous and disastrous visit not long before the bus ride, R.D. had come running out of the house just as Darrell was leaving. R.D. yelled the news that he was dying from stomach cancer. The man Darrell still considered his father would spend the last seven years of his life as a resident in a hospital cancer ward. The kids wanted to say their goodbyes to him in a way they never got a chance to do with their mother Carolyn.

Darrell was napping at home in Long Beach when the kids made their move. They packed up all the pictures in the house and put them in a couple of suitcases. They left Darrell's jewelry. They knew Darrell would be upset if he found out they'd taken anything his husband Robert Dann had spent money on. What money Darrell had they put in the front pocket of his jeans. They left his identification at home.

The bus driver shook Darrell awake. The man was asking if Darrell wanted to get off the bus for a bit, maybe get himself something to eat before the big bus followed Interstate 10 across state lines into Arizona.

"Who are you?" Darrell asked him, awaking with a start. "Where am I?"

They were in Blythe, a city of perhaps 20,000 people on the California side of the Arizona border. The bus had pulled into the town's sole McDonald's franchise, an establishment particularly popular with tour buses on their way from California to Phoenix and beyond.

They could have been anywhere for all Darrell knew. The driver became concerned seeing how confused Darrell seemed. He offered to call the paramedics.

Two women who had been sitting across from Darrell told him what they knew. He'd been chatting up a storm their first five hours on the road, mostly making small talk and obviously excited to be "going home" to be with his family, or so he told them. About an hour before the bus stopped in Blythe, Darrell had gotten tired and decided to take a nap. Despite pooling their energy, the older kids weren't able to keep Darrell up for the entire trip. Even decades after assimilation, none of the kids are able to stay out for very long.

Darrell didn't want the paramedics. He didn't want anything to eat. Darrell only wanted to go back home to Long Beach.

He asked the restaurant manager for a pay phone and immediately phoned Robert.

"Where are you?" a panicked Robert Dann wanted to know. Darrell had no idea, so Robert asked him to describe his surroundings. A commercial trucker for many years, Robert was able to figure out Darrell's location with just a few minutes of description. Robert told Darrell to stay where he was. He'd come get him as soon as he could.

Scared, Darrell found a place in the restaurant where he could be alone while he waited for Robert. The local drug dealers kept trying to sell him their wares, but Darrell just brushed them off. His intention was to keep the locals away from him and to keep everybody away from the pay phone in case Robert should call. When Robert didn't call him, Darrell called Robert. Robert's half of each phone conversation was the simple reassurance that he would be there soon.

Robert got to Blythe in record time. He never did say what traffic laws he had to break or what trucker's short cuts he had to take to cut the four hour travel time in half, but it didn't matter. Darrell was just happy to see his husband and to be away from this scary place.

Darrell didn't know what was wrong and he didn't know how to stop whatever was happening from happening again. Waking up in a place he didn't recognize was a new experience for Darrell and not one he cared to repeat. Still unaware of what was happening to him, he only knew that when it did the changes were like a scene changing in a movie: Darrell slowly faded out and someone new faded in. It was all quick, painless and efficient. This was the first time Darrell could remember where he'd slept through the whole thing.

He found himself confused, angry and ashamed. It was a long and silent drive back to Long Beach for Darrell and Robert.

-- 4 --

STEVE

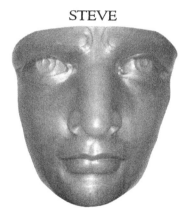

    The youngest of the combined Joshlin/Coleman clan, Steve Joshlin was healthy, strong and ready for life. At 6'6" he stood an inch shorter than his father, but at just 18, the dark-haired youth still had room to grow. By the time Darrell met his uncle, or maybe just by the time he became aware of the man, Steve had already answered the call of the Navy. He had been to Viet Nam on either a six- or 13-month tour of duty.

    Steve came home on leave to find that, while most of the family was still in Brinkley, some members had made the 65 mile trek east to West Memphis on the border between Arkansas and Tennessee. There was more work to be had, something Steve's father Dick Joshlin had already recognized. Steve followed his family to West Memphis, but what he really wanted was the way out of Arkansas itself that he felt only the military could offer.

Dick had brought home stories about his service in World War II. Those tales got taller with every drink the man poured himself, but they all sounded good to a young man like Steve who was thirsting for more out of life.

Steve wasn't all that worried about what his service was going to require. His half-brother Larry Coleman had already been to Vietnam and back. Larry hadn't exactly vanquished Communism while he was there, but President Nixon was assuring the nation that all that was needed to succeed were a few more good men.

Upon his return, Larry had a set of yarns to spin about his adventures in Viet Nam. Like his step-daddy, Larry also came home thirsty. The alcohol made his tales of heroism more striking. Only the drugs made them go away.

Steve was the kind of person who focused on the positive in life. Without waiting for his draft card, Steve had asked his father to sign for him to join the military. Steve wasn't yet 18, but neither were many of the boys he fought beside. During the Viet Nam war, 18 was only the average age of a soldier. Lots of fighting men were younger than that.

Steve saw military service as the key to the rest of his life. He was already in training which would likely have taken place at a US Naval facility adjacent to water such as Great Lakes Naval Station in Chicago or other facilities like it. At these training stations, boats can be docked, and water exercises can easily be taught and run, yet the accommodations and logistics are more easily maneuvered on land. Darrell remembers Steve returning periodically from Missouri, which may well have placed him at Fort Leonard Wood.

As he waited for his real life to begin, Steve was renting a mobile home of his own not many spaces behind the one where his half sister Ann lived with her husband Julian. This rosy future he foresaw was something Steve intended to share. To those ends, he'd found himself a fiancé who was the perfectly marriageable age of 16.

Anyone could have seen by the way Steve doted on his extended family that he'd likely want to rush into one of his one. Steve loved his siblings, half-brothers and half-sisters though they were, and he especially doted on Carolyn. He called her "Sissy Baby." Steve was at once Carolyn's protector and the one man she knew she could count on to help watch her kids. On one family outing, when Darrell took off after a bunch of puppies, Uncle Steve had to explain to the kid that those weren't puppies up on the levee and that coyotes don't much care to be petted.

When he wasn't chasing after the kids, Steve could act like one himself. He used those long, thin fingers of his to build models, taking pride in his ability to create and to give life to the pieces in the box. Once he put together a model plane that could really fly. With the kids standing by, he pumped gas into the fiberglass plane's engine and started it up. Everybody stood there open-mouthed watching it fly, and then stood there open-mouthed as it ran out of gas and exploded into the ground.

Steve picked up the pieces of the airplane and put them away. It was no great loss since he was already busy putting together a scale model of the Navy battleship on which he'd been assigned. After the accident, his mother Martha made sure to keep the ship model as a memento.

Steve put up with a lot from his nieces and nephews and the kids loved him for it. That didn't mean that kids wouldn't be kids, especially the little ones. That's why Steve went along to watch Darrell when Carolyn had to run into the Big Star market, once a fixture of downtown Brinkley. She was only going to be gone for a hot minute and had no intention of letting her child slow her down.

Though Darrell kept complaining and yelling that he wanted to go in too, that wasn't about to change Carolyn's mind. She closed the door and Darrell watched in tears as she walked into the market.

The kid reached for the door, but Steve was too fast for him. "Your momma said 'no.' you've got to wait here," he told Darrell.

If there was a right thing to say, that wasn't it. "I hate you," the child exploded. "I wish you were dead!"

The next weekend, the family was back in West Memphis for a visit. The kids came down with Carolyn and her second husband Danny Poole. Aunt Jeanne was there with her husband Buddy, who as it happened was also her third cousin. The Merrimans, Gene and Bertha, were there as they almost always were at family get-togethers. The grown-ups were spending the day visiting Aunt Ann and Julian Cooper in their trailer near the front of the small mobile home park. It was supposed to be like any other visit.

When he got there, Steve didn't seem his usual self. He was carrying a letter. He didn't pass it around.

Since basic training, Steve had been complaining about a pain in his ankle whenever he ran. This complaint went beyond what a military doctor looked for in a new recruit, but the doctor went the extra length trying to ensure the recruit was combat ready. The results of his examination weren't what Steve wanted to hear.

The doctor wrote the letter telling Steve of his medical discharge. It would have identified the problem causing Steve's running discomfort as Marfan syndrome. This is an inherited disease that, in a mild form, can lead to problems like his father Dick Joshlin's curvature of the spine. In its worst form, faulty connective tissue in the heart and blood vessels can weaken and stretch the wall of the aorta. The aorta can rupture, causing serious heart problems and even sudden death.

A medical discharge is no dishonor, but it wasn't what a young man with plans for his life wanted to happen. With such a severe and sudden diagnosis, Steve needed time to think. He and his fiancé left the family and went back to the trailer they shared. Darrell trailed after them.

Back home, Steve told his young fiancé how his plans for a Navy career were over. Still without a cure, Marfan syndrome allowed for no strenuous activity. The Navy had let him go. If he couldn't do the hard farm work like his brothers and father, he couldn't imagine what he would do. He was counting on his impending marriage to help keep him emotionally afloat.

Would the girl promise to take care of him if the disease crippled him?

The words she didn't say were deafening. "I'm going to take Darrell and go lay down," she answered. "When I get up, we'll talk about it more."

"Make sure he stays in the bedroom with you," Steve responded. "I'm going to clean my guns and I don't want the boy around them."

From the room in back, Darrell could hear his uncle at work.

Click. Click.

There was way too much activity for the boy to fall asleep. Besides, Darrell wanted to be where the excitement was. He wanted to be close to his favorite uncle.

Click. Click.

As Darrell climbed up on the sofa beside his favorite uncle, he could see that Steve was deep in concentration.

CLICK!

Steve stopped what he was doing and smiled down at the little boy. He didn't have to do what he was going to do in front of Darrell, but the young and powerless boy was the only person he could do it in front of.

"I love you," Steve said. "I always have and I always will. But I'm sorry."

He put the gun in his mouth and pulled the trigger.

As he found himself getting covered with blood and brain matter, Darrell wished he could be a baby again so he wouldn't have to see this.

The sound of the gun's retort brought the grown-ups running. Uncle Julian crashed through the trailer's glass door, not bothering with the latch. The first thing Aunt Ann thought of was to take her handkerchief and dip it into her half-brother's blood to keep as one of her mementos. The first thing Bertha Merriman thought of was 4-year-old Darrell. She picked him up and ran. She wanted to keep on running with him until she was far, far away.

In Darrell's mind, there was only darkness. He'd come to the light only momentarily in the hospital. When he came back to himself, the 4-year-old told Carolyn what she wanted to hear. The family used that to piece together the story they would tell themselves; Steve was cleaning his gun and it accidentally went off. After that, Darrell wouldn't be back in his own body until Steve's funeral to see his uncle put to rest in his Navy dress blues.

The family didn't want to take the boy, but Darrell insisted. Darrell needed to know that Steve's death wasn't just one of those nightmares he sometimes had. When he was lowered down to touch Steve in his coffin, that's when the nightmares really began.

For many years, Steve would haunt Darrell. One of the last things Darrell had said to his uncle was to wish him dead and that's exactly what happened not one week later.

Time after the memorial is time lost. The memories are locked away where they are least painful, right there behind the eyes in the mind of somebody else. Not for the first time, Darrell went missing.

Darrell was sure that was Steve in a round light that always seemed to be following him. This is what ghost hunters call an orb, a spherical object that is free-floating and for which there is no discernible cause. This orb stayed with Darrell for as many years as he allowed himself to feel responsible for Steve's suicide. Only when Darrell found himself gazing out over the sea in the California port town of Long Beach did Steve finally find his ship. The orb disappeared.

That little light had been a reminder for decades that Steve's death was all Darrell's fault. The child believed in the power of his own words. Darrell believed that he had brought on Steve's death by wishing it so. No one in the family ever told Darrell differently.

Steve was one of the first family members interred in the Arkansas family plot at Posey Cemetery in Wheatley. His parents would be buried on either side of the grave identifying Steve's rank as Seaman and recognizing his service in Viet Nam. His favorite sister, the one he called Sissy Baby, sleeps eternally to Steve's right, just on the other side of their mother.

BILLY

When a child is young, a short time seems like a lifetime. Ask Billy where he came from and he'll say he's always been there.

One of the chief causes of Dissociative Identity Disorder is persistent trauma. No one can pinpoint exactly when a personality is created or why one child creates multiple personalities while another doesn't. Billy might well have been there even before he made his existence felt in the instant before Steve pulled the trigger.

He wasn't Billy at the time. At first, he was just "Me." That is normally the way each of Darrell's personalities introduce themselves. They won't introduce themselves at all if they don't feel it's safe.

Though he can be any age he chooses to be – all personalities can – Billy feels safest being two. Darrell was comfortable at that age too. He had a father he recognized in Carolyn's second husband Danny Poole and Carolyn was in one of her attentive motherly stages. The subsequent troubles were still a few years away.

Like some of the other younger kids inside Darrell, Billy embodies both Darrell as he was at the same age and Darrell as he wishes he had been: well-mannered, well-cared for and well-loved. The older personalities tend to reflect emotions Darrell either could not or would not allow himself to experience.

Billy's thought processes differ from those of the older personalities. Young children Billy's age use a different process to remember than those who are more grown as shown by Karen Tustin and Harlene Hayne at the University of Otago in a study published in *Developmental Psychology*. Verbal memory is fragmented in those first three years. The infant brain encodes experiences in prelinguistic form. Adults usually cannot retrieve these memories because the adult encoding state is more developed and linguistic in nature.

For most people, amnesia keeps them from remembering much of their lives before age three. The brain provides this cleansing function in order to keep itself from being overwhelmed. For some with DID, those memories are never forgotten. Every day is a replay of incidents the mind would much rather forget.

It would take Darrell more than two decades to get to know the two-year-old. It was Dr. Sharon Higgens asking the right questions that made Billy feel safe enough to make his presence and his memories known to Darrell and his husband Robert Dann. Dr. Higgens had worked extensively with DID patients so she was a believer. She knew how to tell a DID patient from a schizophrenic.

Hollywood and the public still confuse the two, but there's a simple way to tell Schizophrenia from DID. If the patient sees people and objects outside their own bodies -- in front of their eyes -- they are schizophrenics. If patients see people and objects within themselves and behind their eyes, they are multiple personalities.

Personalities may or may not identify themselves with distinct names and personalities. When they split with the host, they generally cause memory and time loss. Darrell describes the split to be like gazing down a tunnel with figures standing in front of the light.

It hadn't been until he was in his 20s that Darrell got a proper diagnosis for the symptoms that had been haunting him his entire life. By the time he met Dr. Higgens, doctors had been watching his health for signs of the heart problems Darrell had been told killed his mother Carolyn and for the cancer that took the life of R.D. In due course, all of Darrell's medical records would have to be changed.

When he was first told about the people inside, Darrell's husband Robert Dann, twenty-six years Darrell's senior, couldn't believe what he was hearing. On the day Dr. Higgens finally diagnosed Darrell, the men had only been a couple for four of the 25 years they would share. Robert was a man's man, serious and tough. He'd been a truck driver when Darrell met him, then went on to work construction. Robert looks very stern in his photos. He believed smiling for the camera was something a real man never did.

While Darrell had tried to explain about the people inside him that concept never did click in the pragmatic Italian's mind. All Robert knew was what he could see and even he could see that something was wrong. Normal people don't have mood swings as extreme as Darrell had. Robert thought the problem was depression or maybe Darrell was just being moody.

"Have you ever heard of multiple personalities?" Dr. Higgens asked Robert at one of her early sessions with Darrell.

Robert was taken aback. "If you're talking about *Sybil*, I've seen the movie but I don't believe in it."

That was all Billy needed to hear. He wasn't about to be denied.

"See?" he trumpeted. "I tried to tell you I'm here. I've always been here and I like you!"

Robert's mouth dropped open while Dr. Higgens laughed. He'd seen a lot of things in his time, but he'd never seen this. That's all it took to convince Robert that Darrell really was what he said he was.

Dr. Higgens asked some more questions.

"What's your name?" she asked.

"I have a name, but I don't know it," said Billy.

"How many 'Me's' are there?" Dr. Higgens pursued.

"There are a lot of 'Me's' the child said.

Billy explained that he hadn't come out because Robert frightened him. Billy perceived Robert as big and mean. Because Robert had always said that he didn't believe in multiple personalities, an offended Billy had kept his distance. On this day, as Billy saw the acceptance come to Robert's face, Billy wasn't going to stay away any longer. Robert cried for what he'd been doing to the little man inside this big man.

Dr. Higgens first made sure that Billy wanted to have a name and he was willing to let Robert and Darrell help him pick one out. She told them to take home a baby book and help the 2-year-old find a name he liked.

Personalities want to be comfortable, so they have to make their own choices about what they want to be called. Some patients have personalities who name themselves after the functions they provide: The Brother or The Baby for instance. Like the personalities of both Eve and Sybil, some pick names seemingly out of thin air. What they all hate most to be called is "personalities." They consider themselves full-fledged people in every sense.

The alternates inside Darrell — his "kids" — mostly choose names associated with people and images important to Darrell's life, though a couple of the big boys based their names on variations of his given name. That's where he first thought Jimmie got his name. It would take years before Darrell figured out that Billy and Jimmie both named themselves after his first childhood playmates.

For the longest time, Billy was the only person inside who would talk to anybody. The first story he ever told was the one about R.D. beating Carolyn. This was the blood memory allowing Billy to remember an incident that it hadn't been possible for him to see. From his perspective, Billy didn't think it was very nice that the man tried to keep him from being born. He thought R.D. should have helped him live.

First dissociations, like the one that birthed Billy, always happen before a child's seventh birthday, though it is possible that Billy split much earlier. After seven, a child's mind is usually mature enough to deal with severe trauma as noted by Dr. Ralph B. Allison, M.D. in his article "Dual Personality, Multiple Personality, Dissociative Identity Disorder - What's in a Name?"

When trauma happens over a long period of time, the affected person may well continue to cope by creating new personalities, repeating a survival pattern the brain establishes in childhood. The damage has already been done, the pattern already set.

Billy is easy to love. He is also the personality most likely to surface or "split" as psychiatrists call the process of a personality taking over its host. His calling card is a cheery and loud greeting, "Hi!" Robert, who loved Billy deeply as he did all Darrell's kids, called Billy his "little man" and let him come out in public as long as they were out together. Billy has been known to plop down in the toy aisle, where he favors playthings remembered from Darrell's childhood. He's prone to Hot Wheels, but mostly those with Redline tires like the original issue came equipped with in 1968.

At home, Billy maintains a huge collection of stuffed animals. He calls these his "babies." Those that weren't gifts from Robert are rescues from thrift stores, trashcans or the side of the road. Billy can't stand to see any baby go unwanted or unloved. He loves the broken ones.

A multiple will always have one person inside who is dominant and in Darrell's case his dominant is Billy. This smart little man makes the decision as to which of his cohorts is best equipped to weather any given emotional storm.

If someone new is needed, personalities can create their own new personalities. It was likely Billy who created Steve, a teenager who isn't allowed out much since he holds Darrell's anger and rage. J.D., James and Steve are relatively similar in voice, though their pitch descends along the triumvirate. J.D., James and Steve are to Darrell what Twelve, one of the 92 "troops" inside the late Truddi Chase, describes in their book *When Rabbit Howls* as The Big Three. They are all angry, but at different levels. J.D. is frustration, James is anger and Steve is rage. The easiest way to distinguish Steve is by the constant ringing in Darrell's left ear. That was the side closest to Uncle Steve's gun when, putting it to his head, Steve pulled the trigger.

At the time Steve was created, Billy needed someone older and more mature in order to protect his own emotions. Like most toddlers, Billy doesn't deal well with anger. That emotion he leaves to the big boys.

Whether a personality is known or as yet unknown, they have to listen to what Billy wants. Nobody likes to make a baby cry.

Which One Am I?

R.D. Williams with three of his sons. (L-R) Darrell, R.D. Ronnie, Johnny
(Photo Credit Unknown)

Billy
(Photo: Robert Dann)

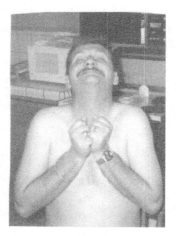

Jimmie
(Photo: Robert Dann)

-- 6 --

MONKEY

Just across the Mississippi in Tennessee, they still call James Darrell Jackson the luckiest man alive. They used to call him Monkey, a nickname bestowed on him by his eldest brother Ray. There's a Girl Monkey too, Betty Roland, the next youngest of the eleven siblings. This seemed like a perfectly appropriate nickname to Ray, since as small children both would climb over any obstacles put in front of them. The nickname didn't stick too well to Betty. The name Girl Monkey wasn't all that appropriate to a young lady growing up.

The nickname stuck to James Darrell Jackson though. He wore it proudly all the way through his life and right into the one after. It's emblazoned for all time on his tombstone, always freshly decorated by his surviving family more than a decade after his death.

Everybody in town knew Monkey. All his friends say the man was full of bull and stories. He was a hard guy to forget and no one has.

The story everybody tells is how Monkey got his truck. On its surface, the Ford F-150 was a lot like any truck a man would drive in rural Tennessee. There was no way this particular truck was going to see much heavy work, not with its interior of crushed fabric and aftermarket everything. It was a beauty for sure and Monkey always did have an eye for pretty things that belonged to someone else.

Monkey wanted that truck but here he was almost 60 with no way to earn the money. He had been working ever since he was a young man, ever since Gene Merriman brought him into his family business to drive a tractor in the fields.

From tractors, Monkey graduated into big rigs. He helped move freight all over the South. Inevitably, he'd pass through West Memphis, which by then had become a primary trucking hub. Whether he ever thought about looking for his namesake son is unclear. It wouldn't have mattered if he did. Ironically, by his late teens Darrell would be trucking himself, riding shotgun beside Robert Dann as they traveled those same Southern trucking routes.

Monkey didn't want to spend his entire life pushing the Mack Cab Overs he favored from one shipping depot to another. He could drive anything but he could also fix them. With the Jacksons being such a tight-knit family, the sedentary life seemed much more appealing to Monkey. In his final years, anybody who wanted anything repaired would go get him from his sister Betty's house. With enough time to sober up, he'd be able to put most anything mechanical back together.

It isn't shameful for a Southern man to take to the bottle. No one was going to say anything against it to Monkey. Not that anyone could identify with the path his life had taken and had led him to drink. There wasn't another soul in town who had exhibited such devastating taste in women.

Coming from a family where the family itself was the most important part of life, Monkey yearned for a family of his own. Everyone could see that he'd gotten off on the wrong foot messing with Carolyn Williams.

He couldn't have been faulted at the time for thinking a woman separated from her husband was fair game. She wasn't, but that isn't anything he was willing to hear even if her closest friend Bertha Merriman had warned him away. R.D. and Carolyn had a history of separation. Getting between those two was just like signing one's own death warrant.

After it all came down, the Merrimans made sure to get Monkey away from Brinkley and out of the state entirely. R.D. had threatened to kill the man for sleeping with Carolyn, and no one had any doubt that's just what he'd do. He'd likely get away with it too.

Even into the 20th Century, Southern society has approved of particular types of violence, especially in response to a perceived insult. As late as the 1930s, it was impossible to convict someone of murder had the killer been insulted and warned the victim of his intent to kill if the insult were not retraced or compensated. Such was noted in a 1996 study by Dov Cohen, a professor in the Department of Psychology, University of Illinois at Urbana Champaign, and his colleagues. The paper first appeared in 1996 as "Insult, Aggression, and the Southern Culture of Honor: An Experimental Ethnography" in the American Psychological Society publication, *Journal of Personality and Social Psychology*.

As long as R.D. lived, there was no safe haven in Arkansas for Monkey. R.D. had promised to kill them all – Monkey, the Merrimans, Carolyn and the kid himself – if the truth ever got out that Monkey had fooled around on R.D.'s wife. With the reputation the Williams clan had for violence and shear meanness, no one doubted R.D. would be good to his word. They'd already seen the violence he'd expressed towards Carolyn.

As much as Monkey wanted to see his son, there was no way he could. It wasn't fear of R.D. that kept him away. It's just that Monkey wasn't the kind of man to intrude on somebody else's life. As far as he was aware, his namesake was doing just fine.

Until she lost track of Darrell after Carolyn's death, Bertha Merriman said she would periodically update Monkey on what his son was up to. Not that she told him everything. At his seventieth wedding anniversary to his wife Almeida, Monkey's brother Ray assured Darrell that, had the family known he was being abused, they would surely have come for him. The secret was never revealed.

Had Darrell known there was a family that wanted him, he never would have headed west after his emancipation from the Williams clan. Only Bertha Merriman would have been willing to tell him the truth but talking to Bertha was out of the question because Darrell thought she was dead. Darrell's second oldest brother Ronnie had assured him that Bertha died of a broken heart after her husband Gene passed away.

Had Monkey known that his first born son was emancipated from the Williams clan, there's no telling what would have happened. R.D. and the dangers he embodied would outlive Monkey by more than a decade. Besides, Ronnie was telling anybody who would listen how his youngest brother had gone to Florida for a sex change and subsequently died on the operating table.

The story of Monkey's other sons comes from his sisters and brothers in bits and pieces. They tell us the only one of Monkey's three sons who knew Monkey at all was Tim Spurgeon. Tim's mother Terri Sue Spurgeon didn't stay around Monkey anymore than had Carolyn Williams. According to the Jackson family, Teri Sue lived in Georgia, though the only record of her existence is in a Kansas marriage license issued to her and a Frank Ray Johnson in 1972. No one knows what caused her to leave or why she gave her son her own maiden name.

Unlike Carolyn, Teri Sue wasn't so good at keeping secrets. When he got to be a man, Tim came looking for his birth father. Tim was already 30 when he finally found Monkey. By then, Tim Spurgeon was a married man with children of his own. He even moved his family near Monkey, in order to get to know him as well as he could.

During a family outing, it is said Tim jumped into a lake to save a small child from drowning. Unable to swim himself, he threw the child to shore before vanishing beneath the water. The lake had to be dredged before they recovered his body. His wife had never been as close to the Jacksons as was her husband. She picked up the children and moved away.

The third son is more of a mystery. The family tells of receiving a call from a woman out in California, in Oakland as far as anyone can recall. She claimed to have had a son by Monkey. No one remembers much more about her.

Alone again after Tim's untimely death, Monkey spent his days with family and friends. He was a regular in town at a café called The Gridiron. Every morning he'd order a dozen eggs, a pound of bacon and a tray of biscuits. If Monkey had money on him, he'd feed everyone in the café. If he didn't, he'd expect everyone there to feed him. Disappointed he was unable to have a family of his own, it seemed to the townsfolk that Monkey was making family out of everyone he met.

According to the surviving Jacksons, Monkey always made his own luck even if he had to travel quite a ways to get it. That's what he did the night he left Covington to get to the nearest Tennessee casino, taking a couple of friends along for support and to keep him company on the drive.

Monkey's friends said later that all they did was look away for a second and Monkey had pulled the lever on the nearest one-armed bandit. Next thing anybody knew, he was being showered in winnings. There's a picture of him taken just after he hit the jackpot. He looks not the least bit surprised. Monkey took home $9,500 that day, all of which he used to buy himself the pick-up truck he coveted.

As the story goes, Monkey still had the Ford when the heart attack took his life as he was waiting to cross the street right outside The Gridiron. His death certificate puts him some 38 miles away on a residential street in Memphis, but his family makes no big deal about the mileage. His funeral, though, was certainly a big deal, what with the family he had and the family he earned. Somebody even brought along a stuffed monkey doll. Afterwards, they gave that to his sister Shirley Ann's youngest granddaughter, Anna Wheeler. Only five at the time, the little girl slept with that stuffed animal until it fell all apart.

The man who sold Monkey the Ford pick-up came around after the funeral telling the family Monkey still owed him money. Nobody believed that, but they let the truck go back anyway. They had their memories. His family would never forget Monkey. In that way, he was the luckiest man alive.

Gene & Bertha Merriman

(Courtesy Bertha Merriman)

-- 7 --

BERTHA

At only 2 pounds and a couple of ounces, the baby wasn't any more ready to meet the world than it was to meet him. It was only half past midnight on January 18, 1966, a day that wouldn't garner much attention. Carolyn Williams named her fifth child James Darrell. She would always tell Darrell that he was named after Brinkley's Dr. James P. Williams Jr., the man who delivered him at Mercy Hospital.

Carolyn also used to tell Darrell that she was expecting him in February. Her count was off. The medical charts show a baby that small, and one born before its lungs fully develop, is more likely 2-3 months early. Less than one percent of all births are that premature. Such children are generally plagued by learning and behavioral problems their entire lives.

A collaborative study between the Stanford, Yale and Brown medical schools found that children born that early had specific areas of the brain that were smaller than in those born full term. These were lingering reductions in the area of the brain responsible for reading, language, emotion and behavior.

Boys are especially affected. Those born prematurely often do poorly in school, have a harder time speaking and are socially less able. The disparity can last for years because it takes boys longer to build up the white matter that facilitates communication between parts of the brain.

Small, weak and helpless, the baby stayed in Mercy Hospital until he could breathe on his own. When the family did get to take him home to the Merriman's house, they carried him in the same shoebox where he'd sleep for the next six months. When Darrell had grown a little bigger, Bertha took him out of the shoebox and let him sleep on the clothes she kept in the top drawer of the dresser beside her bed.

Right from the start, Carolyn wasn't acting like much of a mother and her estranged husband R.D. certainly knew the couple's fifth child wasn't his. Despite the assurances of the entire Coleman clan, he could count backwards. When Carolyn got pregnant, he and she had been on the outs. He hadn't been anywhere near her or her kids for at least a couple of months. People could say all they wanted that the baby had been conceived back in May, but it wasn't just Dr. Williams down at Mercy Hospital who knew better.

Bertha Merriman wasn't fooled either. She'd been a friend and protector to Carolyn for almost their entire lives. Carolyn told her things that she'd never tell anyone else. Once, she even confided in Bertha that she knew for a fact that only three of her four older kids were fathered by R.D. She never did tell which one wasn't. Bertha tried to protect Carolyn and the kids, but there was really very little she could do. Whenever R.D. would start to beat on his wife she'd tell him, "If you're going to beat on her, you're going to have to take her somewhere else. You're not going to beat on her in front of me."

At the time of Darrell's conception, neither parent was in Brinkley. Bertha had been watching all four kids for Carolyn, just like she did every evening or whenever Carolyn got busy. When there were just the four kids, it was Bertha who took pity on the poor children when she saw Carolyn leaving them unclothed and unfed. She knew about the comings and goings in that house. She also knew that Carolyn had taken a shine to James Darrell Jackson — always known as Monkey — who was Bertha's uncle.

During their first month together, the spark between Monkey and Carolyn turned into a raging heat. In his early 30s at the time he met Carolyn, Monkey had come up to Arkansas from Covington, TN to drive a bulldozer out on a job for Gene. He stood 5'9" under a shock of dark brown hair. His eyes turned green when he was happy and bad when he got older. That's the same physical description one might use for his son Darrell once he became an adult.

After the baby's birth, the Merriman's got James out of Arkansas as fast as they could. Since Monkey had been driving bulldozers for Gene at the same time as R.D. was employed, there was no hiding him in town. R.D. was already threatening to kill the man, just like he was promising to kill Carolyn for cheating on him. He promised to kill the Merrimans too if the secret ever got out.

Bertha could see what was coming down the tracks. It was R.D.'s name on the birth certificate, but it was clear he was more concerned in protecting his reputation than he was in protecting the boy. He was already telling anybody who would listen that he wished Darrell had never been born. R.D. also said that he'd kill the child if he could, but getting the police involved might have opened the door to let the secret go public. Nobody wanted that.

Bertha also knew that the marriage between R.D. and Carolyn was over even before Darrell came into the world. R.D. and Carolyn had always had their problems. In fact, some people would say R.D. treated her just like dirt. With his temper, it wasn't too likely he was going to forgive Carolyn her little mistake either, especially when it was staring up at him from the shoebox in Bertha's bedroom.

When Bertha said she wanted to take Darrell and raise him as a Jackson, R.D. was against it. His ego wasn't going to allow anybody to know that Carolyn had been sleeping around on him. To admit to the truth of what happened between Monkey and Carolyn was to bring shame down upon both the name and the legacy of a proud man. R.D. wouldn't have it.

Carolyn was going to let the Jackson and Merrimans have the kid, but her sisters Jeanne and Ann were adamant that she needed to keep Darrell. Her mother Martha Faye was more emphatic. "Hell no!" She had her family's reputation to uphold. For his part, R.D. knocked Carolyn around pretty good and told her to keep her mouth shut. She always would.

Bowing to such pressure, there wasn't much else Bertha could do to protect the baby. Every time she'd see Carolyn after that, it seemed that one of Carolyn's sisters -- Jeanne or Ann or Martha Faye -- was hovering, making sure nothing more was said. Bertha made sure to tell Carolyn not to blame the baby for her own mistakes, though her pleadings fell on deaf ears.

Which One Am I?

The Merrimans stayed in Arkansas until Darrell was three or four. That's when Gene got an offer to work for a bigger company in Houston, Mississippi, a little over two hours south of Memphis. The pay was good, allowing him to buy three more bulldozers and go back into business for himself. Gene needed someone to help drive the new machinery, so he thought of his old friend R.D. Williams. Gene drove back to Brinkley to bring R.D. and the kids down to Mississippi. Darrell was the only one left behind. Bertha lived in Houston with Gene and their three children right up to Gene's death in the late Seventies from a massive heart attack.

Many nights Bertha would lie awake wondering what in the world she could do to make things right. She'd already offered R.D. and Carolyn money for the boy and been turned down flat. What else could she do?

It seemed as if the entire culture was against her, and it was. Losing face was more important to men like R.D., and more socially acceptable, than taking care of any children they may have fathered. In the study *Insult, Aggression, and the Southern Culture of Honor: An "Experimental Ethnography"*, researchers noted that Southern men have had to take action against insults or else lose status before their family and peers. Such culture-of-honor norms are embedded in social roles, expectations, and shared definitions of manhood.

This unspoken code assumes a man like R.D. is manly enough to satisfy his woman enough to keep her from cheating. This code is seen in the equally wild West of Long Beach where Darrell would eventually settle. In California, it particularly manifests in the machismo of the Latin culture and "respect" among young urban males though that is not to say it is entirely absent from the culture at large. The code does not work both ways. There is no dishonor in a man cheating on his wife.

In the Old South, allowing oneself to be pushed around or affronted without retaliation amounted to admitting that one was an easy mark. No one was going to think of R.D. that way. No one was going to know how Carolyn had brought dishonor down upon his good name.

Every time R.D. looked at Darrell, he saw James Darrell Jackson. The boy was looking more and more like his birth father as he grew. Darrell was a constant reminder to R.D. of what Carolyn had done to him. As far as R.D. was concerned, there was no reason for the rest of the world to know. He was going to make sure of it. There was honor at stake.

He didn't want that baby. He didn't claim it, even though R.D. swore to Darrell on his deathbed that he had. After his death, Darrell's brother Ronnie took up the secret. De facto head of the family once

Darrell's eldest brother Johnny walked away from his relatives at Carolyn's funeral, Ronnie would make sure that R.D.'s reputation remained intact.

These are the stories people tell: He may have abandoned the family, but R.D. was a good man; she may have cheated on R.D. but Carolyn was always true to her husband. James Darrell Williams was their son and no one was going to know differently. The family closed ranks. Only Bertha heard the baby crying.

Which One Am I?

50

-- 8 --

DANNY

Danny Poole was from one of the better families in Brinkley, which by then had shrunk in population from its Sixties heyday to barely 4,000 residents. Originally a railroad town, Brinkley was the halfway point between Little Rock and Memphis. According to the town's official history, between 1852 and 1869 the settlement was called "Lick Skillet." When the day's work was completed, the railroad construction crew, mostly immigrants from neighboring towns, cooked their supper over an open fire and returned to their homes when the last "skillet was licked." In short, it wasn't the kind of town where people were meant to put down roots.

The Pooles were different. They had property, careers and reputation. Danny's father George owned a minnow farm, selling bait and tackle to help support the city's recreation industry. His mother Catherine worked for the John Deere Company until the day she retired. After that, she kept busy keeping accounting books and volunteering at the polls whenever civic duty beckoned.

It was Jeanne Coleman, Carolyn's sister, who met Danny Poole first. Those two dated for a while, but Jeanne proved just a little too wild for Danny's taste. Not so much devoted to her men as hooked on them, the pursuit of the male of the species would remain Jeanne's most overpowering addiction right up until the day she became a Jehovah's Witness.

It is hard to say just how Danny ended up with Carolyn. The way Danny remembers it; he didn't marry Carolyn until Darrell was almost six. He might have Darrell mixed up with Allen, who was only a year or two older. Though Darrell always remembers Danny being around, he may be a little mixed up too. Danny wasn't the only man Carolyn was dating after divorcing R.D.

Danny may have found Carolyn just as attractive, though a little more sedate, than her sister. It might have appealed to his better nature to be a savior to Carolyn and her five kids. It might even have been that there just weren't that many marriageable girls in the small town of Brinkley.

Whatever the reasons behind it, Danny and Carolyn got married; Danny did what he needed to do to keep his new family safe. He'd first moved them out of the shotgun house on R.D.'s father's farm, abandoning the house's entire contents to the elements. This was to be a fresh start.

A rental house in town was the next brief stop until the owners sold it out from under them and moved the house in order to expand the farm next door. Danny and his new family then occupied one of the duplexes Danny owned. By the end of the marriage, the family was occupying a big white house about 10 miles outside of Brinkley. The entire brood remained in that house with the black trim right through Carolyn and Danny's dramatic divorce.

Luckily the Poole family didn't care who the kids had for a daddy. They gave Darrell his first Christmas tree and one of the few moments he'd remember from his mother's funeral. "I will always be your Grandma," Catherine assured him.

Catherine Poole was more accepting than most. Almost as soon as he'd outgrown the dresser drawer, it became increasingly obvious that there was something different about Darrell. He had a feminine nature and acted more like a girl than a boy. The family expected him to outgrow that phase, though everyone took notice. Catherine also took a shine to Carolyn who was playing the part of a protective and caring mother.

It was the light that woke him a few nights before the accident. Darrell was sleeping at the end of the bed he shared with two of his big brothers, Johnny and Ronnie. Darrell looked up to see a light that was glowing and growing. Slowly, the light began to turn. Terrified, Darrell ran to his parents' room.

The next night, the light was back and bigger. From deep within it, he could hear voices: two women and a child. He wondered why all the noise didn't wake Johnny and Ronnie but it seemed like only he could hear it. His mother came to his bedroom that night, comforting him and trying to get him to sleep.

The third night, the light turned into a vortex. It opened and he could hear the voices clearly. "Help me!" Carolyn screamed. "I'm trapped under the dashboard. My baby is dead on the back seat." This time when she came to the room, Carolyn knew exactly what it was Darrell was seeing. "You're a soul reader," she told him. Carolyn was a lot more in tune with things her family dismissed than she'd admit to anyone but Darrell.

Psychics say that a soul reader can call on an individual's guides and angels. These angels bring forth images, thoughts and feelings to express the road a person needs to travel. Powerful images for healing and growth often come through. That gift remains with Darrell, but it doesn't fully explain what happened that night.

This was more like what is called an involuntary future viewing. Later in his life, Darrell would experience this type of experience whenever something was going to happen to Robert. Involuntary future viewings are caused by vibration patterns and frequencies that are said to be generated by all events and objects. The largest imprints are caused either by global events that touch many lives or personal events that touch one person deeply. These visions are believed to predict a probable yet malleable future.

The night after the vortex, Grandma Joshlin came in her newly acquired Ford Falcon to pick up Carolyn. They were headed to Memphis to get their hair done and to have new portraits taken. The portrait copy Carolyn brought home that day for Darrell was the first thing her sister Jeanne took from the walls on the day of Carolyn's death.

Adamant that he wanted to go with Grandma Joshlin and his mother, Darrell was screaming. "I want to die with you." He knew deep down inside what those three nights of visions had meant. Darrell was frightened for his mother, and frightened that she would leave him alone in the world.

Carolyn had told Darrell that she believed what he had seen. She believed him enough to not allow him into the car, but she didn't believe him enough to cancel her trip into Memphis. Neither did she believe in herself strongly enough to know she could change what the vision foretold. Nothing was going to make Carolyn and her mother change their plans for the outing.

Danny was surprised when Darrell told him to expect a phone call about 7 p.m. that evening. When the call came on schedule, on the other end was Don Coleman, Carolyn's uncle and Brinkley's deputy sheriff. The Falcon was passing in front of the lot where their rental house had been located when a Buick crossed the center line. The Buick's driver was drunk and he had hit the comparably smaller vehicle head on causing the Falcon containing Darrell and his family to roll 12 times. When the little Ford finally came to rest, what had been the driving position had been pushed by the force of the collision into the back seat. The watermelon riding where Darrell would have been was pierced through to its dark red center by shards of glass from the shattered windows.

Passenger Martha Faye was comparably okay, suffering injuries including a broken jaw, leg, arms and ribs. Not so for the Falcon's driver. Carolyn's skull was fractured on both sides. Her heart was punctured, her liver ripped and pancreas destroyed. On the operating table at Mercy Hospital, the doctors pronounced her dead four times. She'd say later it was her half-brother Steve Joshlin who stopped her from crossing over into the light. "It's not your time," he told her. "You have five kids who depend on you." After her body slowly recovered, Carolyn was allowed to return home. The essence of what made Carolyn Darrell's beloved mother never did.

At the hospital, Darrell remembered watching as Carolyn was quickly wheeled into surgery. He remembered watching as one of her arms fell out from under the blanket that covered her. Closing his eyes for a moment, Darrell must have woken up as someone else because he remembered not a thing after that.

-- 9 --

JIMMIE

Deep down inside, Darrell wished all this drama was happening to someone else. If he could go back in time, he wouldn't have to experience the stress of Carolyn's accident. Darrell's wish took form as Jimmie. Only a couple years younger than Darrell was at the time he came to be, it is he who carries the original memory of the day their mother almost died.

At first it is easy to confuse Jimmie with the 2-year-old person inside Darrell, Billy. When Jimmie talks, which his shyness doesn't allow him to do much, his voice is the first clue. Jimmie's voice is pitched a bit lower and comes out slightly huskier than does Billy's.

Jimmie is the angry child. Hot Wheels miniature cars are a favorite of his just as they are for Billy, but he isn't much allowed playing with them. He will smash two cars together until he destroys them, repeatedly replaying Carolyn's accident, and the incident that brought him to be. When Darrell witnessed Carolyn's arm fall from beneath the sheet while she was being rushed into the hospital following her car accident in the Falcon, Darrell wished he were younger and didn't have to go through the experience. Six year old Darrell blacked out watching the hospital staff wheel his mother into surgery. This may well have been the birth of 4 year old Jimmie.

Studies show that emotionally and physically incapable of saving themselves, those with DID create protective boundaries. The role of personalities like Billy and Jimmie is to withstand the trauma. These personalities take on the memory, filing away the experience so their host cannot be harmed.

The relationship between DID and childhood trauma became known with the publication of *Sybil* in 1973, about the time R.D. had re-entered Darrell's life. Since R.D. never learned to read, if he had heard of this story at all it would have likely been through the 1976 television adaptation starring Sally Field. The tale of a DID patient and what caused her to get that way would have seemed no more real to him than Field did in her role as *The Flying Nun*. A man who could not admit to his own failings would never have recognized the reflection of his own actions towards Darrell as depicted on his flickering TV screen.

After Carolyn's accident, it took a couple of days for R.D. to make it up to the house in Arkansas from his new place in Mississippi. George and Catherine Poole might have taken custody of the children, but Carolyn's care was proving very demanding of their attention. With Danny working to support the family, that left the children to R.D. That was likely a surprise to him. Darrell's surprise was to find out this man was his father. He had never met R.D. until that day and was surprised to have this stranger introduced to him as his father. The only father Darrell had known up to that day was Danny Poole.

The younger Williams children, Bobbie Lynn and Allen, had started back to school just a couple days before at what was then the only elementary school in Brinkley at the time, C.B. Partee Elementary. Since he had never learned reading, writing or arithmetic himself, R.D. didn't much care whether Carolyn's youngest got any fancy book learning. By the time R.D. put Darrell in school, the administration moved the six-year-old child from the first grade back to kindergarten.

There would have been no school at all had Darrell not been as attentive as he was. The kindergarten classrooms were in trailers separated from the school itself. One recess, Darrell noticed a familiar smell. He went over to the propane tank just outside the schoolroom and noticed that when he got close to it, it made him light-headed.

He ran to the principal's office. "Mister, there's a leak in the propane tank," Darrell told him.

The principal was surprised. "How do you know this, son?"

"We have one at home and every time it has a leak it smells just like this," said the child.

Darrell pointed to the tank right outside his classroom. The school was immediately closed, the school buses recalled and students sent home until the problem could be corrected.

Home was no safe haven for the first grader. Darrell's burgeoning homosexuality, a secret by then to no one but Darrell himself, was just another slap in R.D.'s face. After all, the man had only claimed the boy in order to protect his own masculine self-image. Even after claiming the title of Darrell's father for himself, R.D. never did show that he much cared whether the boy lived or died. As he was working, R.D. would take Darrell with him. He'd have the boy perched on the fender of his tractor. This wasn't affection as much as the fact that a fall under the tracks could then be written off as just an unfortunate accident.

Cast into an abusive situation, there was nowhere for the small child to run. Instead, Jimmie did as much as any four-year-old could do to keep Darrell out of R.D.'s sight. In the house next door, Aunt Kitty Vaughn, R.D.'s sister, never knew the true extent of the danger to her nephew, but she did what she could to help. Her husband Arthur suggested they raise Darrell, but R.D. denied the Vaughns just as he had the Merrimans. Invested in the original lie, he was just as afraid of what Darrell would say to others as he was of what others would say to Darrell.

Darrell was over at the Vaughn's place when he asked Kitty if he could meet his grandfather. This introduction, via extreme physical abuse at the man's hands, would remind him of this first meeting for years afterwards. The senior Richard Williams put his hands on the boy's shoulders, pushing down with all his adult weight while working his hands around the boy's neck. This led to degenerative nerve damage and eventually to uneven muscle growth. Never treated, this caused involuntary muscle spasms, driving Darrell to throw back his head unexpectedly. It was this peculiar mannerism that would bring him to the attention of the West Memphis Police as a teen.

No one recognized what was happening to the boy as abuse, or at least no one would call it that. This pattern of non-reportage follows many male DID patients. DID is found more frequently in females than in males, though many organizations and researchers today affirm that between 1 in 4 and 1 in 6 girls are abused and between 1 and 6 and 1 in 10 boys, according to Rob Spring, Director of Positive Outcomes for Dissociative Survivors (PODS) in his article "Denial: A Personal and Societal Journey."

Professionals suppose that these statistics are so skewed not because DID occurs less frequently in men, but because men are less likely to report it. Any abuse towards males, whether it is within their control or not, is seen as a blow to their self-image, masculinity and pride.

Men and women tend to deal with problems in different ways. Men may prefer to cope with situations on their own rather than seeking help. Symptoms are numbed with alcohol or drugs. Violence or compulsive sex may be used to relieve the inner pain. These coping mechanisms can lead to male DID sufferers being jailed rather than hospitalized, meaning they will have a slimmer chance of diagnosis.

In Western cultures men have been taught to limit their expression of emotion. Certain emotions are thought of as feminine while an alternate set is considered masculine. The ideal man as modeled by cartoon superheroes or "proud" men like those Darrell was raised around prioritize "acting" over "feeling." Realizing early on that expressing certain feelings is forbidden within their culture, some boys internalize their emotions. This gives some men ulcers. It gave Darrell people inside. Those emotions that Darrell felt he could not express – confusion, anger and rage for instance – in his case manifested as alternate personalities. If Darrell could not express himself, the boys inside could. If boys weren't meant to feel certain emotions, his brain created females who could.

There are more DID cases reported in the U.S. than anywhere in the world. A 2006 study by Brad Foote, Yvette Smolin, Margaret Kaplan, Michael E. Legatt, and Deborah Lipschitz published as "Prevalence of Dissociative Disorders in Psychiatric Outpatients" by *The American Journal of Psychiatry* reported 6-10% of inpatient and outpatient psychiatric patients suffering some form of DID. Some professionals hypothesize that this seemingly high diagnosis rate is due either to a more aware psychiatric community or to something unique such as the high incidence of child abuse in America. Though the trend has been downward, there are still more than 1.25 million cases of child abuse – one of every 58 children -- reported annually.

Such high reported numbers of DID cases may also be a result of a higher level of DID awareness amongst the American populace. Before the publication of *Sybil*, there had been only about 75 cases of DID reported. Since *Sybil*, there have been more than 40,000 cases diagnosed.

In a 1996 review published in *Transcult Psychiatry*, Joel Paris offered three possible causes for the sudden increase in people diagnosed with DID. The most likely, he thought, was therapist suggestions to suggestible people causing the patient to act in accordance with their therapist's wants and expectations. This assumption has been widely used to discredit diagnoses of DID, most especially that of Shirley Mason.

Paris also notes that new training and knowledge may be leading psychiatrists to more readily recognize dissociation. Lastly, he posits that dissociative phenomena may be actually on the rise, though he posits that this increase would represent only a new form on an old entity: the once popular diagnosis of "hysteria."

Professionals and laymen alike have questioned *Sybil*, whose title character was later identified as Shirley Ardell Mason. The book's author Flora Rheta Schabel had a background in English and Speech which might have led her to embellish in her reporting. There is simply too much detail in *Sybil* for it to read authentically. Blackouts, severe amnesia and loss of time are all symptoms of a personality split. Personalities don't share all their memories with their own host, much less an author like Schabel who would have normally been seen by those inside as someone not to be trusted.

Mason's therapy itself raises questions. She was treated using a combination of sodium pentothal and hypnosis. Nobody would consider using truth serum today and hypnosis is frowned upon because in a hypnotic state the personalities can fuse. Hypnosis can also open the door to a personality who takes control, refusing to leave and return control of the body back to its host.

Historians have questioned whether Mason's 16 reported personalities existed at all. They concede that the patient may have been playing to her psychiatrist's perceived wants and expectations. An argument against this hypothesis is that the therapy portrayed in *Sybil* all occurred in the days before modern tests were developed to prove whether someone is or is not a multiple. The symptoms described in the book are typical of those reported by today's DID patients.

The book concludes with all the personalities folding into one dubbed "The New Sybil," the direct result of the theory of treatment called fusion that was favored by Mason's psychiatrist Dr. Cornelia Wilbur. This new persona may well have been, at worst, the manifestation of a new personality taking over its host. At best, it may have been simply the wishful thinking of a psychiatrist and an author looking for a happy ending.

For true DID patients, there is no storybook ending. Each person inside is the manifestation of a memory. The amnesia that helps someone without DID forget early tragedy and transgressions cannot be counted on by DID patients. In their world, the emotions surrounding the long-ago events make their appearances as flesh and blood.

Jimmie is always going to be angry that Carolyn's auto accident took his mother's love away from him forever. When he needs to be outside Darrell's body, Jimmie is a flesh and blood reminder of what it was like to have lost one the emotional attachment of one of the very few people Darrell thought he could always count on.

It took a good number of years and a series of fortuitous coincidences for Darrell to see Miss Cleo Jackson again. When the house outside Brinkley burned down and R.D. came to take his children down to Mississippi, there had been no reason to keep her on.

Darrell was still living in Arkansas with his mother when the time came for the reunion. Since Carolyn wasn't around much and the still-tiny town of Palestine never did have much to hold the interest of a teenager, Darrell had taken the day to go visiting. There was one woman in town he knew to be a friend of his mother's. He thinks now she may well have been his late Uncle Steve's fiancée, though there is no way to be certain. All Darrell knows is he knew virtually nothing about this woman, though she seemed to know just about everything about him.

Which One Am I?

It was this woman who suggested that Darrell come along on a trip to Brinkley. The teen had no reason to say "no." He relished the chance to once again see the town in which he was born. He even planned to visit the hospital where he took his first breath.

While his ride took care of whatever business she had in Brinkley, Darrell used his downtime to take in the sites. Downtown hadn't changed much. In those days, the Big Star market where he'd cursed his Uncle Steve was still operating. In the days before Wal-Mart came in to under price Big Star and the rest of the local businesses, so were most of the local shops.

That's when he saw Miss Cleo Jackson. She was coming towards him looking both the same and very different from how he remembered her. Darrell had always seen her in the old-fashioned house dress she wore to work, the one that reminded him of what the woman wore in the picture on Aunt Jemima products. On this day she wore a pink suit over a flowered blouse. Her shoes were black. There was a scarf around her neck tied into a bow to close the throat. She hadn't changed her hair at all.

Cleo seemed to recognize something in Darrell as well. He'd obviously grown a bit, but young men will do that over the course of a decade. Their eyes locked.

"Well I'll be damned," said Darrell, happy to see such a reassuring figure. "Miss Cleo Jackson!"

"Who's that?" she asked. Cleo looked hard at the boy, her dark eyes taking him in. There was something very familiar about this stranger, though very different as well. She had a feeling it was one of the Williams boys, though she could not rightfully say which one.

"Darrell?"

"Yes ma'am!"

"How did you recognize me? How did you know who I was?"

Darrell isn't one to forget kindness. His memories of Miss Cleo Jackson would run deeper than even he could predict at the time. Two of the teenage girls inside Darrell, Diane (who is black) and Star (a mulatto), once they let themselves be known to Darrell, would always exhibit traits they associated with their memories of Miss Cleo Jackson's personality.

It is not unheard of for alternates to switch ethnicities, though there is less available documentation of that phenomenon than of alternates making the simpler switch to the opposite gender. Probably the best known example is Truddi Chase, whose story of discovery is chronicled in her memoir *When Rabbit Howls*. Among the 92 troops inside her, her protector calls himself Mean Joe Green. He is a large and powerful black man who has based himself on the former all-pro American football defensive tackle who played for the Pittsburgh Steelers during the early Seventies. People inside can be anything that makes them feel safe and secure. This may be an entity that is bigger and stronger than the abuser or something that can experience no pain at all; anything from animals to vegetables to minerals.

Why something inside Darrell decided to emulate a black woman makes sense according to Kristin Flickinger at AskTheGay.com. Though not a psychologist, Flickinger, like most of the gay community, certainly has seen gay men turn into black women when they are angry or excited. She notes in her column that this may well come from the two groups sharing a style and a certain flare when it comes to dramatic situations. While not all gay men do this, those that do emulate, whether knowingly or not, strong, fierce women. In creating both Diane and Star, Darrell's subconscious was taking its tips from this societal stereotype. But Diane and Star are far from caricatures of strong black women. They are tributes.

Flickinger sees this adaptation as a shared mode of survival. Black women, "have been holding their families and communities together for generations," she writes. And "if you've made it to adulthood as a gay man, you've survived a lot. You've survived expectations to 'be a man,' as well as teasing, taunting and all the rest. Fierce is where you end up as a natural evolution."

As children often do, 5-year-old Darrell formed an immediate attachment with Miss Cleo Jackson when she came to work for the Pooles. The family was living with Danny Poole in the white house with the black shutters, some 20 miles into the fields surrounding Brinkley. In the early days of her second marriage, Carolyn contributed to the household budget by continuing to work at the Van Heusen plant sewing shirts.

While Darrell's parents were both away, someone needed to take care of their young children. Miss Cleo Jackson was the perfect choice. She had children of her own, but her four sons had matured to the point where they neither needed nor wanted constant supervision.

Her role was a cross between that of a nanny and that of a housekeeper. Cleo would arrive early enough to cook breakfast for the family. She would take care of the housekeeping, make sure everyone had lunch and basically run the household until Carolyn got home to fix the family's evening meal.

Cleo had her work cut out for her watching over four and sometimes five rambunctious children. There would be five only when Allen came for a visit from Mississippi where he lived with his father R.D. Allen didn't come over very often, so seldom in fact that Darrell didn't know for many years that Allen was his brother. Darrell thought the boy, only about a year older than himself, was a cousin or a neighbor kid who had been brought over to play.

No matter how many children were present, Cleo remained unfazed. She'd raised her four sons successfully and wasn't about to change her no nonsense manner. If there were a request to be made of the children, Cleo made it perfectly clear she was only going ask them once. Her warning for a transgression was to stare at the offender, her eyes bulging out of the sockets in a manner that reminded Darrell of a scene he'd seen Oscar winner Hattie McDaniel perform in *Gone with the Wind*.

If Cleo's warnings didn't work, she wasn't shy about using a bit of corporal punishment. It mattered not at all that the Williams kids were white. Cleo always treated them just as she'd done her own boys.

Darrell thrived on this type of structure, as most children do. Studies have shown that children from homes which have greater family structure with set rules do better than those without. Lack of structure can cause a high level of stress and resentment in the child particularly at the grade school age if compliance is not recognized or explicitly appreciated.

For her unbending rules, Darrell loved Miss Cleo Jackson. He even begged her to take him home with her one night. His parents agreed thereby demonstrating the trust and esteem in which they held her.

Like the Pooles, Cleo's family lived outside the city of Brinkley itself. Cleo and her family had encased part of the backyard in chicken wire. No one could get in and certainly no one could get out except through the back door, likely a safety maneuver that cut down on neighborhood friction.

Brinkley was still fairly segregated during the time Cleo's boys were growing up. Not unlike West Memphis and Crittenden County which fought the court order as long as they could, Brinkley and Monroe County were at least making strides in the right direction. For a period following the enactment of the Civil Rights Act of 1964, Monroe County schools experimented with "open choice." Brinkley schools, as well as all others in the county, were fully desegregated by the 1970–71 school year. That didn't mean that the populace agreed with this new development. Better safe than sorry, Miss Cleo Jackson's family maintained the chicken wire playground Darrell loved so much until she retired from taking care of children. After that, the enclosed playground was turned into a real chicken coop.

Despite the atypical situation of the era of having a young white child sleep over at a black family's house, the evening went well though not without its drama. After putting Darrell down for the night, Cleo watched in amazement as the little boy, still asleep as far as anyone could tell, pried off the window screen, opened the window and proceeded to walk down the road in the direction of his home. When asked about the incident the next day, Darrell remembered not a thing and today still doesn't know which of the people inside decided they would rather sleep in their own bed that night.

Cleo stayed with the family after Carolyn's car accident and was there through Carolyn's separation from Danny. She was even there after the house with black shutters burned to the ground. The last time Darrell saw Miss Cleo Jackson before meeting her again on the streets of Brinkley 10 or so years later. That was after Carolyn and Danny had broken up and the house where she and the kids lived burned to the ground. R.D. had no choice but to come up from Mississippi to take Darrell and the rest of the kids away.

Darrell asked Cleo for directions to the hospital. He was told that a fire had broken out in the operating room some years before, taking part of the main hospital along with it. As a result, Mercy Hospital had closed. The plans were always to rebuild and reopen the facility, but more than 30 years later, Mercy Hospital and everything inside it still stands untouched by anything more than time and the elements.

Out of all the people Darrell could have run into on his unexpected trip to Brinkley, Miss Cleo Jackson was the most important one to his life. As they parted, he hugged her and gave her a small kiss, partially so she wouldn't see him beginning to cry.

Mrs. Lessie Cleo Morgan, born Lessie Miss Cleo Jackson, passed away in Mt. Ida in November 1997. Darrell would have liked to tell her how much she really meant to him. He would have liked to tell her how he'd always wished his last name was Jackson just like hers. He would like to tell her he's discovered that's what his last name actually is.

Which One Am I?

-- II –

BOB

Carolyn's four other children would come over to Carolyn and Danny's place whenever R.D. wanted to drop them off. That's where they were the day Danny Poole had enough.

Even people down in town probably heard the noises coming out of the big house in the woods. There was Carolyn screaming, the tears rolling down her face. There was Danny with tears in his eyes too, holding his wife down on the floor. Darrell thought Danny was hurting his mother, but it was really the other way around. Young Darrell didn't know that. He was angry that Danny was hurting his mother. Darrell ran and got the sharpest item he could find, a letter opener, and was going to stick it in Danny's back until Darrell's eldest brother Johnny pulled the letter opener from Darrell's hands.

Since her accident, it was hard to tell what kind of mood Carolyn was going to be in from one minute to the next. After coming out of her coma, her convalescence at Mercy Hospital in Brinkley seemed to go on forever. After her release, she'd gotten increasingly addicted to the painkillers the doctors prescribed.

An older Darrell might have recognized his mother's behavior happening as a result of her largely untreated brain injuries, but he couldn't have known that at the time. Neither did Carolyn's husband Danny Poole recognize the cause of her personality changes. To be fair, he was likely spending too much time and energy just dealing with his wife's symptoms. Many a night, Danny would come home to find himself, in his words, staring down the barrel of a gun. Whether that was literal or figurative he was unclear.

It would be hard to fault Danny Poole for leaving when he did. It seemed like everyone else was leaving in one way or another. Darrell never got a chance to say goodbye to any of them.

The oldest boys, Johnny and Ronnie, were now of age to help the Williams family with their work. Johnny and Ronnie would remain in Mississippi, helping R.D. with his work there in Houston. They would never again live with their mother. The young ones, Darrell, Allen and Bobbie Lynn, were growing up quickly. Both Allen and Bobbie Lynn would soon be married. Then there was Carolyn, a woman whom Danny Poole no longer knew.

Carolyn had always exhibited traits that would be easier diagnosed by today's medical practitioners. One she would pass down to at least her youngest son, a tendency towards obsessive/compulsive disorder. Like her sister Jeanne, she was a victim of her own compulsions, in both women's cases using sex to relieve their inner torments. She was likely also to be bipolar, a form of mental disease that shares many of its traits with DID. This fluctuation in personalities is very likely what Danny Poole was experiencing as he returned home each night to whatever woman inhabited his wife's body at the time.

The effects of the two disorders were intensified by Carolyn's physical and emotional trials. Each new medication prescribed to lessen the pains in her body would have had intense and sometimes confusing effects perhaps even exacerbating the undiagnosed problems she suffered. No matter which pills her doctors gave her — and there was a bedside table full of them — no medication could resolve the mental anguish of knowing that her injuries would never again allow Carolyn to be the woman she was before the accident.

In her weakened state, the façade she had been holding up to the world was getting too heavy. Everybody noticed, though nobody made much comment. Mood swings like Carolyn was experiencing were nothing new to the family. It was said that R.D. had them too. He could be nice as pie one minute and the next he'd act like he'd never met a person. As for the woman herself, all of her marriages ended up having their violent episodes. She could always bring out the worst in a man, even mild-mannered Danny Poole.

It is said that symptoms of traumatic brain injury like Carolyn's should, for most, lessen over time as the brain heals. Sometimes the patient doesn't adapt to the brain injury, leading to psychological problems. Brain injuries, especially those not treated, are known for causing extreme stressors in family and interpersonal relationships. That was what was happening here.

Though Carolyn always could see the future, she never recognized it as changeable. Unlike her son, she was always blinded by the visage of beliefs, fears, illusions and patterns to which she subscribed and by which she was raised.

This much she could see. Danny Poole was going to leave and no one could fault her for doing what needed to be done for survival. Since the accident, her injuries had made it impossible for her to resume work at the Van Heusen plant and tiny Brinkley didn't hold many other opportunities for an unskilled woman with children. She'd always had a man to support her in the past and so Carolyn returned to what she knew. Carolyn was looking for a man.

No one is sure how Carolyn met Bob Tackett. She may have already been husband shopping before the accident for all anyone knew. There was a known affair with a military man. That may or may not be him with her in one of the pictures Bobbie Lynn once showed Darrell. The man in uniform and Carolyn have their arms around each other, beaming for a souvenir portrait as they are entering a party. If Danny Poole knew anything about Carolyn's fling, he never let on.

Bob moved in about the same time Danny moved out of the white house out in the country awarded to Carolyn in the divorce. Younger than most of the men Carolyn went after, he stood a muscular 6'1" and wore a thick mustache in the style that was considered masculine during Burt Reynolds' heyday. What he didn't have was a job.

Bob and Carolyn shared a deep need for each other's company that was intense and sometimes violent. The biggest fight during their brief affair was the most dramatic family fight anyone had seen up until then.

The first the children heard was Carolyn screaming that she'd had enough. She and Bob were cussing and hurling accusations back and forth, feeding each other's rage just like wood fuels a fire. When words failed her, Carolyn grabbed a good-sized mirror, the nearest thing she could reach. When she threw it, the glass shattered. The room got as over-heated as if someone had turned a magnifying glass on it.

"I've had enough too," Bob screamed back. He grabbed for the biggest piece of mirror he could reach. He ran for the bathroom and slammed the door shut. He locked himself inside. That's when Bob slit his wrists.

The whole family ended up back in the Emergency Room at Mercy Hospital that night. Darrell doesn't even remember getting in the car. Someone else made the ride.

When faced with continuing torture and neglect, young children may create a fantasy world to which they escape. This is similar to the effects of Post-Traumatic Stress Disorder (PTSD), an affliction first identified in returning Vietnam veterans and one that Carolyn's brother Larry Coleman showed signs of suffering after his return from battle. PTSD wasn't much diagnosed in those days and self-medication may have led to Larry's alcoholism. Some of today's researchers think that DID may be a severe subtype of PTSD.

Once established in childhood, DID can last a lifetime. The damage having been done, new personalities accumulate over time triggered by new situations. Female patients tend to have more identities than men, averaging 15 as opposed to eight for males. This statistic may well change as reporting techniques improve and the stigma keeping men from seeking treatment relaxes.

Bob and Carolyn remained a couple for only a little while after their argument led to Bob's attempted suicide. Carolyn's younger children lived with them in the big white house until the night it burned to the ground.

There was something different about that evening from the beginning. For one the family was going to visit Carolyn's mother later in the evening. The family never went to Grandma Joshlin's after dark, so this was a special treat.

For another, Larry Coleman had brought over his three Chinese Shar Pei dogs. Known for its distinctive features of deep wrinkles and a blue-black tongue, this is the rarest breed of dog today. In Seventies' rural Arkansas, they were as valuable a dog as one could hope to find. He left them behind when they all decided to head to Grandma's.

That's where they were when the phone call came from Danny Poole. Their house had burned to the ground, he told Carolyn. Nothing could be saved. The valuable trio of dogs was assumed to have died in the fire, though no remains were ever found. The only piece of anything remaining was the propane tank. Miraculously, it and its flammable contents were unscathed.

At the news, Carolyn fainted. As she did, Darrell dropped Grandma Joshlin's crystal bowl right through the center of her glass-topped table. Sharp shards of glass flew everywhere.

No one ever knew what caused the fire. Danny Poole wasn't the only one in town who suspected Carolyn had a hand in it somehow, whether it was Bob or Larry or someone else who helped her out. It was always suspicious that no remains of the valuable Shar Peis were ever found.

Carolyn made out okay after the fire. She collected on the insurance and moved on.

Bob's parents let the family live with them for a bit, but it wasn't long until Allen joined his older brothers Johnny and Ronnie in Mississippi at R.D.'s place in Houston. Darrell and Bobbie Lynn were sent to stay with their Grandparents Joshlin in Palestine down the road, a town so small that the entire population couldn't have filled one show at the Haven over in Brinkley. When his mother came to reclaim Darrell and Bobbie Lynn months later, she'd be on the arm of a new man she'd been dating by the name of Don Sinclair.

Darrell liked Grandpa Joshlin well enough. When Dick wasn't drinking, he treated his grandson just fine. It was he who taught Darrell to tie his shoes. He enrolled Darrell in school, but yanked him out again when he figured the teachers weren't teaching him a thing.

School was out the day R.D. turned Darrell's world upside down. It was a warm night in Palestine so Darrell went outside to play in the bed of the truck. R.D. had come over for a visit and so he and Dick decided it was time for a beer. They headed down to the truck themselves which the men in the family always did that when they wanted to hide their drinking from the women and kids.

He heard them coming so Darrell scrunched down and made himself appear as small as he could. He'd already been warned about playing in the truck where sharp farming implements somebody forgot to take out could do real harm to a little boy. He also knew enough to stay out of R.D.'s way, especially when the man had a few drinks in him.

R.D., whose cruel streak ran as deep as the Mississippi River, must have seen Darrell there or else he wouldn't have said what he did. He aimed for the heart. "Did you ever tell Darrell that you aren't his real grandfather," R.D. asked his former father in law.

Dick didn't get a chance to take his first swig before Darrell jumped up screaming. "You're liars! All of you!"

Tears ran down his face and questions ran through his mind. A quick boy, Darrell's mind began to race through all the adults he'd known. If his grandfather wasn't his grandfather, was his father really his father? Was his mother his mother?

Who was he? Who would he become?

-- 12 --

BILL

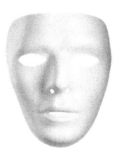

It is mid-afternoon as the black Expedition rolls into the parking lot of the Central Delta Depot and Museum in Brinkley. By the time it does, the truck is covered with a few fruitful excavated resources in the form of uncovered memories and dusty souvenirs collected during a fair number of unexpected turns. During the almost two weeks of our first return to the South, the Arkansas stops have included Palestine, Wheatley and West Memphis. Across the Mississippi River in Tennessee, there has also been a bit of discovery in Memphis. It's taken Darrell a long time to want to get back to his beginnings.

Brinkley is shrinking in population, yet it is more alive than anywhere else we've been in Arkansas. We have come to meet Museum Director Bill Sayger and offer our thanks for all the help he's offered in our research. It is he who oversaw the reconstruction of this historic brick building. The second depot at this location, the current building opened in 1912 and then, after the highways took over much railroad traffic, sat vacant for a good many years. Today it serves as a showcase for the area's history and as a gateway to the National Historic Landmark, an Arkansas Natural Area and Arkansas State Park. This level of rebuilding is an accomplishment to make any man proud.

Darrell remembers this stately depot as an abandoned hulk. It had been slated for destruction until Louise Mitchell, the first president of the Central Delta Historical Society and editor of its journal from 1997 to 2001, initiated a letter writing campaign to save it. Like Brinkley itself, the building is both familiar and strange.

Inside, display cases pay tribute to Brinkley's long history as a railroad town and its association with such storied companies as the Rock Island Line. There are examples of the area's wildlife, most notably the Ivory-billed Woodpecker. Thought extinct since 1944, the elusive bird was reportedly rediscovered in 2004 and is now identified as the nation's largest woodpecker, roughly 20 inches in length and 30 inches in wingspan. Though there were only 20 individuals counted in 1938 and no scientist today can confirm whether the Ivory-billed Woodpecker actually still lives, the search for it is a boon for the area. Arkansas tourism has increased 30% as a result, most of it centered in the areas surrounding Brinkley. Other museum displays pay tribute to local dignitaries. A brass sculpture in what was the Whites waiting room pays tribute to local celebrity Louis Jordan, the late bandleader immortalized in the Broadway hit *Five Guys Named Mo*.

Museum renovations were extensive. The wall between the White and Black women's rooms was torn down to combine them into one, a move Bill says he regrets since it destroyed a part of history, no matter how regrettable in and of itself. Damaged by time and weather, the outside windows are also new. Bill had saved a piece of that time period before anyone cared enough to save and restore the depot. Just to the right as one enters, two of the original windows are on display.

Darrell doesn't see much of the museum's riches. Jimmie and Billy have stopped him in his tracks. It's Billy who sees the windows first. He knows there's something to them, but he's not sure what. Then Jimmie sees them too. He spots three holes in the windows on display. That makes him very nervous. The damage was his doing, him and Billy. When something made them angry, these little boys worked out their frustrations by using their slingshots to break things. From the looks of things, they were pretty good at it.

"They're going to arrest us," Jimmie whispers. He and Billy both have seen enough police shows to know that evidence is kept in order to prosecute wrong-doers. Luckily for the boys, no one recognizes them. They are safe behind Darrell's eyes.

Neither Jimmie nor Billy is aware that there are no police men banging at the door of the museum to come get them. Like most alters, they see only their own reflection in a mirror. They are eternally locked into the place and circumstances that first allowed them to be. Jimmie looks past his own image only when he spies a case in the former Blacks waiting room. It holds a collection of military uniforms and period pictures. In the photos, he recognizes a face. This is a photo of the late Dr. James P. Williams, the man for whom his mother Carolyn had told him he was named and the man she once went so far as to hint could have been his father.

This is the first face Jimmie saw as Darrell was being born. Dr. Williams made him feel safe. At Darrell's birth, Jimmie didn't even cry.

"This is the man who helped us live," Jimmie all but whispers. His face looks to be almost in tears as he continues to stare. Stopping just short of touching the glass, he paws gently at this discovery. He sees nothing else, not Bill Sayger coming over or his beloved friend Mary Barnick telling him it's time for lunch. Jimmie doesn't want to leave. "This is the man who helped us live."

Outside on a picnic table, Mary's husband Bo Kirgis has set out lunch for us. Bill Sayger joins us as well after much prodding from Bo. The museum grounds features an approximately 100-year-old frame depot that at one time was located at Monroe on the Missouri Pacific rail line that connected Brinkley to Helena. There is also a furnished tenant farm house and the Southern Pacific caboose built in the 1980s, one of the last of its kind.

Off to one side is a bandstand which is used for the annual Choo Choo Ch'Boogie Delta Music Festival, named for Louis Jordan's #1 hit from 1946. On today's visit it is vacant, but there is still music. Next door in the parking lot of the Bank of Brinkley, a marching band fills the air with brass and percussion as parents and school supporters cheer them on.

This is homecoming day for the small town teens, but not for Darrell. He has come back to Brinkley to say goodbye.

Bo and Mary have been nice enough to help Darrell fulfill his wish. We've been twice outside Brinkley looking for the house with the black shutters. Danny Poole still thinks it was Carolyn who either set the fire or had someone else do so in order to collect the insurance. Those streets leading the 10 miles out of town are unrecognizable to Darrell and, in fact, may not exist at all. The Expedition may have come near the house's lot, but by now any remnants are long plowed under.

What should have been Danny's father George's minnow farm is also a field. Nothing remains of George and his wife Catherine's brick house either, but what could have happened to such a strong building would just be conjecture.

Darrell slips away during lunch to walk Brinkley's main street. He remembers Dr. Williams storing old medicine in a shed down near a trailer park. When the Southern weather was hot, the shell of the capsules would decompose, releasing the distinct smell of vitamins. There is no medicinal smell today. The trailer park has long been dismantled, the shed disappeared. Blessedly, gone is the downtown Big Star market where as a small child he wished for the death of his favorite uncle.

It is all so familiar yet utterly strange. Darrell felt the spirits around him: his mother, his grandparents, his uncle and one he suspects is the grandfather he never met. They are there in the museum photos, orbs floating above the building and out in the field. They offer neither apologies, nor explanations. They watch him and walk beside him, saying nothing. They only let him know they were there. It has been so the entire visit. It seems to be doing Darrell well.

By the time he returns to the picnic table, everyone's mood has lightened. Darrell and Bill banter secretly, bonding as only two men with similar backgrounds can do. As it turns out, Bill is a bit of a Brinkley expatriate himself. He left town for many years, returning to care for his aging mother.

The other "From Offians" Bo and Mary enjoy the sunshine and promise to return, possibly with their guitars and flutes. No one wants to leave this setting anymore than Jimmie does, but there's a schedule to keep if Bo and Mary are going to get us to our hotel in Memphis and then return home safely.

Waving goodbye to our new friend Bill Sayger, everyone piles back into the black Expedition. The freeway takes us through Wheatley, through Palestine and West Memphis. This time, we don't have time to make any stops. We wouldn't even if we could. Darrell had come to say goodbye, but instead we've made plans to come back. This is the place where the kids inside feel most comfortable. These are the people around whom they feel happiest.

These are the people who help us all live.

PART TWO

WEST MEMPHIS

West Memphis is the largest city in Crittenden County, Arkansas. The population was 27,666 at the 2000 census, with an estimated population of 28,181 in 2005, ranking it as the state's 12th largest city, behind Bentonville. It is considered part of the Memphis metropolitan area, and is located directly across the Mississippi River from Memphis.
– From Wikipedia

Which One Am I?

-- 13 --

JAMES

    The person inside who went out to school in 1972 was the one Billy calls "The Six Year Old." That makes perfect sense to Billy. He knows that's the age when most kids begin their education.

    In his role as The Protector, James sees his primary role as always being on his guard for danger. His conversation comes out more in exclamations than sentences. It would have made sense for him to be at school to protect an apprehensive and frightened Darrell, but it wouldn't have been easy for even him to reach such a taciturn and suspicious student.

    Though the people inside can all change their ages if they want to, only James has done so. Back when Darrell entered Wonder Elementary, he and James were both six. For awhile, they grew up together right there in West Memphis. By the time Darrell reached his teen years, something caused James to stop his age progression when he turned 15.

Having already been in — and rapidly pulled out of — two elementary schools, Darrell was wishing he didn't have to go to school at all. Forming relationships was hard for him back then and it remains so today. Every relationship he'd known in his short life had disappeared. There was no reason to think that new ones would be any different.

It is common for DID patients to see the world as a more dangerous place than it really is. In their continual state of anxiety, they are unable to control the highs and lows of normal emotion. Like James, they are eternally vigilante, always on guard. This over-reaction to stress leads to panic attacks, mood swings and obsessive-compulsive behavior. It is thought today that children who are born prematurely may be especially susceptible to DID. Their under-developed brains may even trigger a split caused by the normal care given such children in the hospital making it not impossible that Billy is right when he claims he's "been here all along."

Resulting from life experience, types and roles of personalities are as varied as humans themselves. James plays the role of Big Brother. Ultimately, it is his job to ensure to the best of his abilities that no one does anything bad to Darrell and he gets even with those who do.

By the time Carolyn and Darrell moved into the mobile home Don Sinclair provided, the already fragile family unit had shattered. The other boys — Johnny, Ronnie and Allen -- were old enough by now to learn to drive bulldozers just like their daddy R.D. did. Carolyn's original plan was for the boys to live in Mississippi helping R.D. in his farming work and for Bobbie Lynn to go live with Carolyn's parents in Palestine.

R.D. always felt that a woman's place was either in the kitchen or the bedroom. Since his female child Bobbie Lynn wasn't much of a cook, he had no need for her to stay with him. However, Bobbie Lynn didn't seem to think living with her grandparents was much of an idea seeing as how she and her grandfather Dick Joshlin never did get along. She found herself shuttling back and forth between Palestine, AR and Houston, MS until she turned up pregnant not many years later, begging Carolyn to sign the papers allowing the 14-year-old to get married.

The separation of the older boys from Carolyn might have had something to do with Johnny throwing the brick through his mother's car window. Right after Bob Tackett left, Carolyn decided it was time for her to move on as well. After they split, something came into Carolyn that caused her to burn every photo she could find and head for her car. It was as if she intended to destroy every memory she had of her family — and they of her.

Carolyn was already driving down the street when Johnny ran right across in front of her. She slammed on the brakes just about the same time her eldest son let go of the makeshift projectile. The brick smashed through the driver's side window, leaving little souvenirs of her faded getaway embedded forever beneath Carolyn's skin.

As the Big Boy and The Protector, it was eldest brother Johnny's role as he saw it to hold the family together. Earlier the day of her would-be escape, he'd watched as the family photos went up in flames and somehow figured out what Carolyn was up to. Johnny wasn't about to let his mother abandon his brothers and sister like they were nothing.

Only Darrell lived with Don and Carolyn full time. For some unexplained reason, the other children never did want to spend much time in the trailer with their mother and her new husband. Nobody said much about it, but Darrell always wondered where the other kids had gone. Darrell particularly missed his oldest brother Johnny. Darrell put their absence down to the tension between Johnny and Carolyn and between Don and everybody else. This loss may well have defined James's role inside Darrell as well as putting a stop to his age progression.

Though he couldn't tell why, for some reason, Darrell was the only one who didn't seem to mind Don, who was older than most men Carolyn brought home. Darrell always thought of him as Archie Bunker from *All in the Family*, a TV hit at the time. Don was also more stable than most. He held down a decent job across the bridge at Wire Rope and Fittings in Memphis. There was an ex-wife and four children as part of the package, but Darrell only saw them once when he was little. He wouldn't meet them again until his teen years when he wandered into a Memphis restaurant to find them all working behind the counter.

Still little, Darrell didn't recognize how different he was but by age seven, the die had already been cast. Researchers say that DID results from a combination of individual vulnerability and environmental stress. Once developed, even a short and seemingly innocent series of events can trigger an onset.

When the family reconfigured, all Darrell's triggers had tripped. Personalities were in full emergence. Until Don finally stopped moving them around and Darrell had the chance to meet young brothers Billy and Jimmy Nelson next door, his only playmates were those still-nameless kids inside himself.

They were nameless because, when they first form, personalities are only vaguely aware of each other. Until integration, they assume it is somebody else's fault that they came to exist at all. For them to integrate, the patient needs to comfort and communicate with each individually, helping them to connect with each other. It is only then that they are able to form a team, a united defense against the outside world.

Integration is a long, sometimes tortuous process requiring the guidance of a trained professional. It is far beyond the intellectual capabilities of most first graders, especially those who don't realize anything is wrong. Kids being kids, each of Darrell's personalities wanted to be the one outside. When this happened, it led to an internal battle for dominance. Switching became frequent, like a small, male version of Sally Field in *Sybil*.

This couldn't have made Darrell an easy kid to teach regardless of which person inside really went to school. He would have been losing consciousness to his separate and distinct personalities, appearing to be in a trance much of the time. His voice might have changed. His mannerisms, body posture and manner of speaking might have seemed a little off.

The problem was compounded by early personalities being unable to share memories. The lesson taught to one on Monday would have seemed like Greek to the one who came to class on Tuesday.

When Billy Milligan's case became known in the mid-Eighties, he said that growing up was a constant battle of making up stories, bending the truth, manipulating explanations to avoid admitting that most of the time he didn't know what happened to him for long periods of time. That is one of the better explanations of life as a child with DID that Darrell has ever heard.

It was impossible for Darrell to concentrate on his school work. External stimuli – colors, sounds, fragrances, and people – set off recognitions of past incidents, both positive and negative in those with DID. Sometimes it is the memory of the incident that causes each personality to be. Sometimes it is just a puppy wandering by the window. The more external stimuli, the more each one reacts. The host is pulled like taffy at the State Fair.

During these early school years, the still-unnamed little ones inside Darrell, Billy and Jimmie, would have been there. They exist today, two little boys astounded by the world around them. Since integration, Darrell has learned to send them to their rooms when he needs to concentrate. If he doesn't, it can take Darrell days to read one page of a book.

Darrell was also having trouble staying awake during school hours. Psychic visitations hadn't ended with Carolyn's accident. If anything, at night they had increased in frequency. Darrell was afraid to close his eyes at night.

Only the day-lit classroom felt like a safe haven. Teachers and administrators did what they could, but whether they were trying to help the student or simply trying to hide the problem and the problem student, the result was the same. By the time early puberty hit, the school administration had skipped Darrell up a grade. In a shadow of events to come, he was exiled to Wonder Junior High next door. He was the Junior High School's problem now.

Somehow that didn't sit right with his mother. Carolyn insisted her still-illiterate child be brought back to the sixth grade. Until he told the administration that the family was moving again which led to his being able to stop attending class permanently, Darrell spent most of his days helping out in the office or the school library.

There is only so much one child can do to protect another. There was very little James could do to keep Darrell safe. Each day Darrell kept hearing his name being called over the school intercom. Every day he found himself needed to help out in the library. James had no real way of keeping Darrell from becoming a favorite of librarian Robert McDeigh.

Which One Am I?

-- 14 --

McDEIGH

No one can rid Darrell of his memories. He can't forget a thing, no matter how hard he tries. He remembers what Robert McDeigh did to him as if it happened yesterday.

To this day, no one in West Memphis will say much about Robert McDeigh. The claim is that someone destroyed all the records from the time — they don't know or won't say who -- after the Wonder Elementary was desegregated. The West Memphis School Board recognizes McDeigh's name, but the story they tell begins and ends with the claim that their former employee has "left the area."

Tall, skinny and insecure by the time he entered sixth grade, Darrell always hid his budding manhood under a loose-fitting long coat. Shorter, thinner with graying blond hair, Robert McDeigh was the first person at the school to show Darrell the slightest interest. The librarian was what the gay community considers a "swish," which is to say he was a demonstrative and effeminate man. This wasn't the brand of manhood readily recognized in West Memphis, yet somehow he failed to stand out. What wasn't discussed did not exist. No one would have thought anything about it that an adult with such a respectable position would ask the young man in his care if he didn't think he'd be a little more comfortable by removing his jacket.

This wasn't the boy's first introduction to the world of the games grown-ups play. It wasn't even the first time intimacy had felt wrong. Darrell was only nine when that happened. He'd been out swimming with the kids when Terry Cummings, Carolyn's sister Ann's 14-year-old son, got right down on his knees in front of him and wouldn't stop until he was done.

Darrell didn't much like his first sexual encounter despite Terry's obvious experience. This was his cousin after all, a kid who would ignore Darrell a few years later during underage adventures in the gay bars of Memphis. No matter how many times they would run into each other, Terry never acknowledged Darrell and what had transpired between them. Terry took the secret with him to the grave when he succumbed to complications due to AIDS at the early age of 21.

In the days when Darrell attended during the Seventies, Wonder Elementary library was situated down the hall from the school's administration office. The school would change that location not long after the Assistant Principal walked in on Darrell and McDeigh, but at that time the library was sufficiently isolated from the school's administrators to suit McDeigh's purposes.

In most ways, Wonder Elementary's library was just like any other elementary school library, packed with the expected rows of bookcases and reading desks. What made this room special was the small storage room behind the librarian's desk. After it was relocated, the new library would be right next door to the school office. It would have no such addendum.

McDeigh made his move right at the holiday. This was Thanksgiving 1978 and Darrell had been excused from class in order to help punch out cardboard turkeys for library decoration. Darrell had already removed his trench coat when he felt McDeigh behind him. The older man's hand went to the top of the boy's shoulder, then it slithered its way down the front of Darrell's shirt.

"Does it feel good?" the librarian asked.

"Not really," Darrell said. McDeigh didn't really want an answer. He ordered Darrell back to the storage room. The older man followed, locking the door behind them.

That's when McDeigh exposed himself.

"Have you ever seen a man?" he asked. "Your father? Your brothers?"

Darrell was in shock and, at any rate; McDeigh didn't wait for an answer. He forced Darrell down on his knees.

Somebody knocked.

In walked the Assistant Principal. The school day was over. It was time to lock up. What was McDeigh doing in the library at this hour?

The Assistant Principal didn't need to be told. He would have heard odd sounds coming from the storage room. He was nobody's fool. Yet there was little he could really do about the situation. Without actually witnessing the molestation and with no other witnesses, he had no real evidence about McDeigh.

There were greater forces at work against the Vice Principal and his young charge. Of all the Southern states, Arkansas had the toughest time coming to grips with the federal order to desegregate. Its eastern border, the Mississippi River, effectively isolated Arkansas from the rest of the South. Overlooked by the Interstate system, West Memphis went its own way, infamously appearing in the pages of LIFE magazine, where it was reported that white residents had a been granted a new school while simultaneously voters had rejected replacing a burned-out school for Blacks.

In this atmosphere, it would have been difficult if not impossible for a black Vice Principal to make accusations against a white librarian. This became an advantage to McDeigh who walked every day between Thanksgiving and Christmas into the school office in order to use the loud speaker to summon Darrell to the library.

Darrell never told. McDeigh had threatened to kill Darrell's mother if the boy ever opened his mouth about it. No one knew so no one could stop the abuse. Even after Darrell had dropped out, McDeigh's actions likely went on for quite awhile. Non-custodial abusers like McDeigh never stop after just one victim.

The only thing the school's black Assistant Principal could do against the school's white librarian was to remove Darrell, the cause of McDeigh's temptation. By Christmas 1978, the struggling student was skipped up a grade and promoted to Wonder Junior High School. In the teacher's lounge at Wonder Elementary, they talked about Darrell's promotion as either the school's greatest success story or its greatest shame. That is, when they would talk about such things at all.

Darrell would complete the rest of 1978 at Wonder Junior High. Like most budding adolescents, he didn't like changing in front of the other boys during gym class. When he discovered the white boy's gym teacher kissing the black girl's gym teacher, that problem was quickly solved. In exchange for keeping his silence, Darrell never attended another gym class. He became as good as anybody else in West Memphis at keeping secrets.

No one at either school in West Memphis seemed to have noticed anything was wrong, but Carolyn was paying attention. In a show of motherly care, she took note of Darrell's test scores and insisted that he repeat the sixth grade. That would bring him right back to Wonder Elementary.

West Memphis has a long history of isolation, all the better to keep its secrets from the outside world. Truckers passing through West Memphis today are too tight on their schedules to veer off into downtown. Truckers like Monkey would have stopped for gas and a bite and then driven straight through. The same went for Robert Dann who, in the early days of his relationship with Darrell, would never have made a side trip down Broadway Avenue to see where Elvis Presley ate breakfast the morning he joined the U.S. Army. Outsiders on a schedule, Darrell's father and Darrell's spouse could easily have taken coffee at the same truck stop and yet never have met.

The Williams clan had more than proximity to The King. Somewhere there is a picture of Darrell as a small child sitting on Elvis's lap, though it might just have likely been destroyed when Carolyn set fire to the family photos. The photo was snapped in Graceland, the Presley family home in Memphis. Elvis's father Vernon Presley was one of the men Darrell's mother Carolyn knew in town.

Even if they had the time to visit Graceland themselves, Monkey, Robert and Darrell were all outsiders and would have been treated as such. They were, in local parlance, "from off." Those "from off" may just be from the next town over or from across the country. Wherever they are from, they are never really welcome and always somewhat suspect. Those three wouldn't have known the local dialect.

When Elvis stopped at The Coffee Cup in 1958, West Memphis was already changing. The national freeway system had bypassed the once-burgeoning nightspots and devastated the downtown economy. Distribution centers like Fed Ex National LTL would turn West Memphis into a trucking hub when both I-55 and I-40 finally reached the Mississippi River just outside of town, but that was far in the future.

The freeways split West Memphis from the rest of the world just as assuredly as Broadway Avenue split the part of town reserved for the White population from the section closer to the Mississippi floodplain where the Blacks could live. The modern world kept right on rolling through town just like the trucks loaded with freight on their way to somewhere more important.

The Civil Rights Act of 1965 mandated desegregation of schools throughout the United States but most towns in Arkansas put off the inevitable as long as they could. West Memphis proved no exception. White supremacy groups in Arkansas never accepted the Supreme Court's ruling in *Brown v. Board of Education of Topeka, Kansas*. They attempted to delay integration through intimidation and boycotts. Wonder Elementary, located in the black part of West Memphis, didn't see its first white student until 1971, the same year Darrell started school there.

Whites fought hardest against desegregation but it was the town's black population that had the most to lose in the short term. Whites still controlled the town's political infrastructure so when Carolyn's sister Jeanne backed over the Black boy who had been tormenting her son, it never made the paper and there was no police investigation. Despite the brazen incident right in front of Wonder Elementary, somehow no one ever claimed to have seen it.

The town was as vested in keeping its reputation as was the Williams clan in keeping theirs. What was never acknowledged never happened at all.

Sex is a big secret in polite society and so Carolyn didn't give Darrell much instruction when she would send him off with one of her other sisters, his Aunt Jeanne. Darrell knew without being told that he was supposed to keep Jeanne happy. The best way to do that was to keep her out of trouble. There she'd be in bed with a man and Darrell would have to stand guard just in case her then-husband Ray came home.

Sometimes, Ray got back from one of his trucking runs unexpectedly. When Darrell was about 12, he was watching for Ray while Jeanne was off on one of her sexual adventures. Darrell was supposed to divert Ray's attention until Jeanne returned home. He was also supposed to warn Jeanne if Ray got home before she did. That's not how things worked out.

Ray returned unexpectedly. The older man walked in and asked Darrell if he knew where Jeanne was, which Darrell of course denied. About that time, Jeanne's car pulled up. Darrell knew he was in for a beating. Ray grabbed him by the collar and threw him across the room, just as angry with Darrell's lie as he was with Jeanne's transgression. He'd tell Jeanne later that he'd just about killed the boy, and it was all because of her.

Not long after that, after she'd driven Ray off and out of the marriage, Jeanne's adventures continued with Darrell as her watchdog. One of Jeanne's boyfriends refused her advances, almost bringing both her adventures and her life to an end. If the man thought she was dying, Jeanne reasoned, he'd come to her side for sure. While Darrell was spreading catsup around the room to set the stage for the false suicide scene Jeanne had planned to solicit the man's pity, Darrell failed to notice that Jeanne had downed an entire bottle of Vicodin. Her son Scotty came downstairs, but his only reaction when he found his mother nodding out on the couch was to call her a "stupid bitch" and return to his room to continue whatever he was doing. It was up to Darrell to run to the neighbors and help get Jeanne to the hospital.

Jeanne never forgot the episode. She made Darrell promise to never tell anyone about it. He never did, though her two best friends found out anyway. They ended their friendship with Jeanne over how much stress she put on the boy. Stressful it was. For Darrell, the episode brought memories of his Uncle Steve's suicide. For years Darrell would wonder why all these people wanted to kill themselves in front of him. He never did forgive his Aunt Jeanne for putting him through such a horrible scene for the second time in his life.

At his young age, Darrell found himself thrust into the role of an adult in order to allow the real adults their fun. The supervising adults violated his psychological boundaries, a role reversal putting him at even further risk for identity confusion. Humans learn either through experiencing the consequences of their actions or by modeling the actions of someone else. People like Carolyn and her sisters, self-centered and immature, are confusing to an adolescent still forging an identity and doubly dangerous to Darrell.

Children whose emotional needs are not met--who are emotionally deprived, or otherwise abused--can also be more vulnerable to sexual abuse. They need attention and some perpetrators exploit that need. That is what Robert McDeigh recognized in his young charge. Unable to read, Darrell is still always eager to learn. He found the best way to learn is by watching others, so being placed with various adults during the long elementary school days always presented a chance for Darrell to learn something new. McDeigh's goal in the situation would have been made all the easier by the school's granting him both easy accesses to the boy and, during school hours, sole responsibility to watch over Darrell while the other students were in class.

Not many years later, a judge would grant Darrell emancipation from both his parents. Another judge, this one in charge of his probation, would send him to school in Amory, Mississippi. Darrell was finally properly tested, the boy the Arkansas school system had passed all the way to Junior High was found to have reading and math skills at the first grade level.

Darrell about age 12 with his mother Carolyn
(Photo: Martha Faye Joshlin)

Diane
(Photo: Robert Dann)

Star
(Photo: James Darrell Williams)

-- 15 --

DON

The boy loved to run. Get Darrell anywhere near the track at Wonder Elementary and he'd just keep going. Sometimes, he would even do things to get himself in trouble so he could be assigned to do laps again.

On the track he could feel the blood pumping through his body. He could feel the pavement passing beneath his feet and a breeze that he could create and control by varying his rate of running. If he ran hard and fast enough, the anger and frustration he kept bottled up inside would come seeping right out through his pores. Hateful droplets fell in rivulets behind him where they waited to be trampled and ground deep into Hell every time he came around the track again.

In athletics he was most alone but alone he was most free. Darrell's life history had made him uncomfortable around others, particularly other men and boys. Alone he set the goals. Alone he created the memories. No one could take those away.

Unable to control his mind, he could master his body. Once, he even tried a cartwheel like he'd seen on the Olympics. Running around the gym as fast as he could, Darrell sent himself tumbling. No one had ever shown him how to do a proper cartwheel before and so no one had ever taught him how to stop. There he went hand to feet until he slammed into the wall. He got up crying but also laughing. Darrell was proud of himself. He had completed something that he set out to do.

Doctors today recognize that exercise releases the pent up energy that the stress response can create. This is important because stress can lead to higher levels of pent up frustration, which in turn can aggravate panic or phobic tendencies. Listening to his body, Darrell had found a way to alleviate the anger and frustration expressed by some of the people inside, most notably James and Steve. It was a lesson he would never forget.

Darrell wanted to keep on running and eventually he did. He knew he couldn't go back to the place where Robert McDeigh did those things to him. Since he was afraid to tell Carolyn about what had happened to him and there was no one else able to protect him, he just didn't go back to the school at all. There was another school, one long-abandoned, nearer the apartment he shared with Carolyn and that became his hiding place during the day.

No one from Wonder Elementary seemed to pay much mind to the missing student. You could say they were used to dropouts, no matter how young. Arkansas has historically been one of the lowest-performing states academically so having a student drop out that early from a West Memphis elementary school was no surprise. Even today, the state has one of the most undereducated populations in the nation, ranking in the bottom five nationally in numbers of adults with college degrees and percentage of high school graduates. To bring back this one missing boy would have hardly helped raise the state's standing.

For all her interest in his disappointing test scores not long before, by the time she discovered her 12-year-old son had effectively dropped out of school, Carolyn said not a word about it. The family had been telling him since he was little how stupid he was and how he'd never amount to anything. Darrell dropping out so young was just a confirmation of what everyone already assumed would happen. For her part, Carolyn had more important things on her mind.

Not for the last time, she had left Don Sinclair. There had been an accident on the job at Wire Rope and Fitting in Memphis. It was Don's job to help spool the high-tension wires used in electrical lines but there was one that didn't want to be spooled. As Don was getting the heavy industrial wire onto its spindle, one of the wires snapped. The end of it hit him in the groin area, debilitating him for years to come. The company let him go. That was more of an excuse than Carolyn needed to hear.

The incident didn't end the marriage right away, though the union of Carolyn and Don likely had already gone past its logical end. She was still going on her adventures, eventually settling on a long-time affair with and eventual marriage to Carrol (pronounced as "Karl") Bevel.

Neither Carolyn's affair with Carroll nor her untreated injuries were making life any easier for anyone. With an arsenal of painkillers, doctors had treated Carolyn's symptoms but never the cause of her mood swings. The prescription drugs she would take during her lifetime included: Dilantin, a drug used to control seizures; Phenobarbital, a drug used both to control seizures and to help patients sleep; and Oxycontin, most commonly used to treat pain lasting more than a few days. Whatever other drugs may have been prescribed for Carolyn may never be known as her medical records were destroyed by law a decade after her death.

All these years after her car accident, Carolyn's behavior had only become all the more unpredictable. One Halloween, on a car trip to West Memphis to take Darrell trick or treating, she began screaming. With the car moving fast, she lunged to open the passenger door and tried to jump out. It took all Don's strength just to keep Carolyn in the car. That incident baffled Don as much as it did anyone.

While Don moved his family around quite a bit in east Arkansas after the tornado upturned that first mobile home he provided, Don did what he could even when Carolyn walked away from one house he'd had built especially for her. There would be temporary Arkansas addresses in Wynne and Forrest City, the former memorable as the first place Darrell saw his mother fall apart. Holding a fireplace poker, Carolyn chased her son through the house until Don was able to stop her. Afterwards, she remembered not a thing about the incident.

The worst part about losing their next home on Church Street was abandoning Darrell's friends the Nelson brothers. Darrell had no one else. His siblings weren't seen much once they moved to Mississippi with R.D. and, besides, they were already striking out on their own. Fourteen year old Bobbie Lynn was first to get married. It took longer to talk Carolyn into signing the permission slip than it did for Bobbie Lynn's marriage to end 12 days later. Darrell's brothers fared better despite each walking the aisle before they were old enough to drink at their receptions.

Darrell lived for awhile with Carolyn and Don in Lakeshore Estates, a trailer park in one of the city's poorest neighborhoods. The once-proud mobile home park got its name because years before some trailers had fallen into sink holes. The result was as attractive as it was ominous; a trailer park spotted with little lakes that were so deep they were dark blue. In 1993, the same Lakeside Estates hit the news as home of Damien Echols, one of the principles in the West Memphis Three murder case.

By the time they got to Lakeshore, Don and Carolyn were already having problems. As she usually did in times of crisis, Carolyn shipped Darrell down to Mississippi so R.D. could watch over him. She needed her son out of the picture so she could either get on with her life or end it. Don returned from a job in Mississippi not five minutes after one of Carolyn's suicide attempts. It was the stress of childrearing that caused her to do something so drastic, she told him.

There were also the affairs that Darrell was now old enough to recognize for what they were. Though he didn't keep count of all of them, he took note of Carrol Bevel. At the time, he and Carolyn were living with Don at the Bilroy Motel on Broadway where Don and Carolyn had hoped to reconcile. After his accident, Don had taken a job there as the motel's live-in manager. From all appearances, that was likely the only income he had after Wire Rope & Fitting let him go and it likely wasn't near enough for Carolyn. Her marriage to Don was doomed from the minute she set eyes on Carrol Bevel.

When Darrell returned that time from his Mississippi exile, he found his mother had secured a job managing an apartment complex. Don stayed there as well when he lost his job at the Bilroy. That was okay since the company eventually gave Don a job at a better complex. It was obvious that Carolyn's affair with Carrol had driven a wedge between them but they were still together. Don and Carolyn would divorce, but always remain friends.

Darrell had seen Carrol Bevel around, but didn't really know who he was. Carolyn first brought Carrol with her when she picked Darrell up from another of his banishments, this time at his Grandparents Joshlin's place. Carolyn moved with Darrell to a hotel apartment at the Star Motel where Carrol was living. Carrol already had a roommate so Darrell slept on the couch as he often did when someone older or just better liked needed a bed. Even after the roommate left, the apartment was crowded. There was never going to be room enough for both Carrol Bevel and James Darrell Williams.

The night Carrol's mother, father, brother and sister-in-law showed up for a visit, it was clear Darrell had to get out of the way. The obvious choice for the preteen to find emergency lodging was the Bilroy Hotel where he could stay with his most recent stepfather Don. Those still-secret sessions with Robert McDeigh had given him a lifelong fear of other men, but he liked Don about as well as he was able to like anybody.

The adult acted quite glad to see him. Don invited his former stepson to come in and sit down on the floor by the bed. In the first of a series of betrayals that night, the older man sat behind him. Slowly, Don inched his hand down the front of Darrell's shirt. Darrell knew exactly what his stepfather had on his mind and he wanted no part of it.

Without a word, Darrell pushed Don's hand away and bolted for the door. Bounding across the threshold, he ran from the apartment as fast as his legs could take him, dodging traffic on busy Broadway to get to a place where he could hide. The first place he came to was a used appliance store across the busy main road. There, among the refrigerators and washing machines stored outside, the preteen, shocked and confused, tried to collect his thoughts.

There was no time for that. Darrell had run in front of a police car which narrowly missed him. As he scrambled to hide amongst the used appliances, the West Memphis Police came out of their patrol car to see what was going on. They shone a light in his direction.

"Sir! Come out with your hands up!" they ordered.

Darrell didn't react, so they repeated the demand.

It was then they saw he was a child. Though he was already practically a teen by this time, Darrell was small in stature and would remain so until he became an adult. People often mistook him for a much younger boy.

The police men asked why he had run through the traffic. Darrell told them what had happened.

As Darrell sat in the squad car's back seat, the police went up to Don's room. Don explained what he had done in a way that made sense to him and, as it turned out, to West Memphis's finest as well. Because of Darrell's girlish mannerisms, he told them, Don's sexual advances to the underage teen were merely to ascertain whether or not the boy was gay.

The policemen took Darrell back to the apartment Carolyn shared with Carrol. Carrol and Carolyn put him to bed on a cot in their room.

It wasn't until months later that Darrell saw Don on the street and it all became crystal clear. He knew then that Carolyn had betrayed her son by declining to press charges against her former husband for the molestation. Darrell couldn't imagine why Carolyn failed to protect him. He never could come up with a good excuse for her actions. Carolyn's failure to protect him made him feel angry and increasingly isolated.

Resentments simmered inside Darrell far beyond what normal adolescence generates. Intense emotions and mood swings were normal for his age, but no one told him that. Had he known what normal was, he would have been better able to identify his differences from other boys his age. His brain's grey matter was not sending information to the part of his brain used for organization and judgment. Instead, as happens to those with DID, it was channeling too much information to the white matter at the base of the brain. In other words, his own brain was forcing him to panic.

Adolescence is typically the time of the first split for those with DID. Though 95 percent its adult size, the brain cells in the grey matter near the frontal cortex begin to develop extra connections at this time. Fear determines whether sensory information is stored there in the thalamus, or sent to the amygdala for emergency processing. In dissociation, the brain splits off not only emotionally charged memories, but also parts of everything that makes someone human.

Darrell wanted to run, but all the avenues were blocked. He could do nothing but turn inward where someone else was better able to express what he felt inside. It was just a matter of time before anger and resentment would send his world up in flames.

-- 16 --

CARROL

When the West Memphis Police came for Carrol Bevel, they found him sitting calmly in his wheelchair. A shotgun was across his lap. The lifeless body of his latest wife, a woman named Carolyn just like Darrell's mother, lay across the sofa. She could have been sleeping -- if anyone ever slept with her head covered up in a blanket.

It was obvious what had happened. Had Carrol been a younger man instead of pushing 60, the police would have taken him right into the station and charged him with his wife's murder. The police could see right away that Carrol was more than the state could handle. It was obvious Carrol would need for round-the-clock-care and that wasn't something they were excited about attempting. And the last thing they needed in or wanted in custody was an angry, elderly prisoner in a wheelchair. As a result, no charges were ever filed. The man would be just as good as locked up anyway. Unable to take care of himself, Carrol entered the first of what were a string of convalescent hospitals. None would keep him long. The first two kicked him out for fighting. The only reason he didn't get kicked out a third time was because he was getting too weak to fight.

It was quite a change. In his prime, Carrol was a specimen. A tall man, he had blue eyes and very white skin when Carolyn first met him. He was what passed for muscular in the days before gyms came into vogue. His black hair was always worn slicked back in the style of a Fifties greaser. In a nod to what was almost modern, during those early Eighties he wore lamb chop sideburns in the style of Elvis Presley. Carrol looked like the kind of man who would be selling used cars, which was exactly what he was doing when he caught Carolyn's eye. Still married to Don, she had been seeing Carrol's best friend, but the friend was a married older man. He was not inclined towards divorce.

In the Southern vernacular, men like Carrol like to call themselves proud men. These are the kind of men who never admit to a mistake. They can do anything and everything better than anybody. To listen to Carrol, he was the best at any job put in front of him. Employers always fell for his spiel. Carrol did everything from driving truck to handling meat to running a little two-hole miniature golf course he had Darrell help him set up. Bravado could always get a job, but it wasn't much use in keeping one. Carrol's boasts always proved to be lies. When the truth came out, his employers let him go.

Carrol's first wife Bonnie Bevel knew just what kind of man her ex-husband was. Though Darrell thought Carrol doted on his son Chris, Carrol was never the kind of man who came to his only son's birthday parties or attended his little league games or paid child support. Those aren't the kinds of things a proud man does.

Carrol would have killed both of them if he knew Carolyn and Bonnie were talking about him. One of the places Carolyn would go when she felt like disappearing for awhile was Bonnie's place, never saying a word to either Carrol or Darrell. Nobody thought anything about it when Carolyn up and left like that. She'd been doing the same thing ever since anyone could remember. When she took off, she'd be gone for hours at a time, leaving Darrell alone in his room and Carrol off doing whatever job he was trying to hold down at the time. If she came back at night Darrell knew enough not to ask any questions and above all to stay out of her way.

The current wife and the former wife had plenty in common. Neither had ever seen a dime from their ex-husbands. Like R.D. before him, Carrol thought only of himself. Carolyn promised Bonnie she'd steal a little money from Carrol's wallet to help out her new friend. That's just what she did whenever Carrol wasn't around to see. It was a help. Bonnie had sworn off marriage after Carrol and was supporting herself and her kids with a job at the Memphis Police Department across the river.

Both were mothers of five, though Bonnie never was told that Carolyn had offspring other than the boy she heard about but seldom saw. Darrell was unaware of other Bevel siblings himself since he only knew about six-year-old Chris. The boys weren't predisposed to be friends even discounting their age difference. Whenever Chris came over to visit, it was understood that Darrell was to let him have his room. The two boys fought over it, though Carrol's wishes always prevailed. To get his way, Carrol wasn't above grabbing Darrell by the throat. What he did after that was subject to his mood. Usually he'd throw the boy against a wall and threaten to throw him down the stairs or over the balcony. Telling Carolyn anything about the threats would only make things worse. The man was going to get his way come Hell or high water.

When she heard years later that Darrell's mother had passed, Bonnie Bevel says her first thought was that Carrol had something to do with it. She was most likely wrong. Carrol wasn't anywhere near the trailer in Palestine that night. The man in bed with Carolyn was Don Sinclair.

Darrell didn't have long to put up with Carrol's abuse. The first time they married, Carolyn didn't stay with Carrol more than a couple of years. This marriage came with a level of physical abuse Carolyn hadn't seen in a long time. Shortly before the end of that marriage, Carrol had picked her up and thrown her down on the coffee table. Darrell came up behind him and hit Carrol with a two by four, but it did no good. The big man simply walked away, returning only when the West Memphis Police showed up to arrest him. Things were a little too heated even for Carolyn. She divorced Carrol and moved herself and her son back into the manager's apartment at the motel with Don Sinclair.

Systems failed the night Don first tried to molest Darrell. Darrell's mother had done nothing to protect him. As a result, the West Memphis Police were unable to protect him. Now that Carolyn had moved the boy back in with his attacker, she was granting tacit approval. The abuse continued. Newly aware of his homosexuality and acutely aware that he was on his own, Darrell didn't resist. He couldn't resist. There was nowhere to run and no one to protect him. He did what he felt he had to do to survive.

Never much of a stay-at-home mom, Carolyn now felt little obligation to act like a wife. She only came home at night. Without ever asking for either his permission or his approval, she changed households frequently. Sometimes she would be with Don and sometimes without him. The only move Darrell remembers is the last one when Carolyn took him to Palestine.

It is not unusual for someone with DID to experience gaps in memory. In Darrell's case, he was doing things he didn't remember doing, seeing people on the street who looked familiar and who seemed to know him but who he didn't know. He was missing vast periods of time and huge amounts of information. These were the beginnings of the fugue states that Darrell would experience for the rest of his life.

Fugue states are a common occurrence in most cases of DID. In these episodes two or more personalities are acting together as if in a musical counterpoint. During the fugue state — which can last several hours or a few months — an individual forgets who they are and takes leave of his or her usual physical surroundings. In Darrell's life, he often found himself waking from a dream only to discover that the dream was real. He knew he was different and realized that other people didn't share this experience. It would be 20 years before Dr. Sharon Higgens would explain to him what was happening. He would spend the rest of his life trying to understand why.

-- 17 --

JOHNNY

Bertha Merriman never did meet Carrol Bevel. She likely wouldn't have liked him even if she did. Nobody liked Carrol. Carolyn's older children were conspicuously absent from her life whenever Carrol was in it. Like everyone else, they just thought of him as mean.

It was a different story with Don Sinclair. Older and more sedate, this was a man who seemed to like having family around. He may have had no choice. After the accident that all but destroyed his manhood and nearly took his life, he never really worked much. Sometimes, Carolyn's family was the only solid source of support he had.

Don was living with Carolyn in West Memphis when the trouble started anew. They were together in one of those places Darrell doesn't remember moving into. This particular apartment was in Don's name, but Carolyn was living there as well.

Which One Am I?

The Bilroy Motel, where Don worked periodically after he was forced to leave Wire Rope & Fitting, had laid him off from his job as manager of the building's attached residential units. In the midst of a lawsuit, the building's owners needed the manager's apartment for themselves. A woman had fallen down the stairs at the apartment building, breaking both arms and a leg. The building's insurance didn't completely cover her injuries, so the business itself was in danger. That's when they closed the attached Coffee Cup diner, where Elvis Presley had that last cup of Joe before entering the military. Eventually they were able to save the place but meanwhile Don was only working part time as maintenance man.

Don was around a little too much for Darrell's taste. So was everyone else. Six months pregnant and abandoned, Bobbie Lynn had come home to Carolyn. She and her unborn daughter shared Darrell's room with him. In the trailer next door were Darrell's brother Johnny, Johnny's wife Susan and Brigitte, Susan's baby. Susan and Johnny had married when Johnny was just 15. Susan was 21 and pregnant by another man. By all accounts, Johnny doted on the baby named for actress Brigitte Bardot, even giving her his last name. When the couple divorced, Brigitte chose to stay with Johnny, the man she always considered to be her real father.

There was never a problem with Johnny. When Darrell was about 12 and Carolyn had sent him off to live with R.D. while she once again got re-situated, he had begun to figure things out. "Why doesn't my daddy love me," he asked his older brother on the first and only full day they would ever spend alone together. As Darrell broke down in tears there in the pickup truck, Johnny held his sobbing younger brother. Johnny never did give him an answer.

The problem wasn't with Johnny. It was with his wife Susan. The woman never seemed to want to be around Darrell. As far as Darrell could tell, Susan didn't like him. That came to a head after Carolyn's death when Darrell went to stay with his oldest brother and his wife. When he overheard Susan tell her husband that she didn't want Darrell around, Darrell bolted for the door. He wouldn't see Johnny again for another 30 years.

Johnny never gave much thought to Darrell's absence. As far as he knew, Darrell was just a loner who didn't like being around family. Darrell thought that the family didn't want to be around him. The fact was that Darrell needed people around him and he loved those who loved him back. This is why the first two of Darrell's interior kids to make themselves known, Billy and Jimmie, named themselves after his first true friends, the brothers Nelson.

Seeing Darrell's loneliness, Jimmie created a sub-personality, the gregarious 10-year-old little boy Dot. Dot assumed the role of playmate and confidant. He is a brother like Darrell never had. Darrell and Dot would spend days running through fields of beans or corn or whatever was growing at the time that was big enough to hide them from the adults.

This instant family with the baggage they brought and the possessions of his they claimed for their own drove Darrell's simmering resentment to a heated rage. His siblings had ignored him his entire life and now they were all under foot. They needed him to give up his room and whatever he held dear. Most importantly, they needed him to give up what little time Carolyn had for him.

It was Don who finally lit the spark. Aunt Jeanne, who hadn't yet discovered Darrell's homosexuality and so hadn't yet disowned him, had come by to treat him to his first airplane flight. It was a small plane and a short trip but it was nevertheless a big thrill for a young man. The afternoon got even better when Jeanne's friend, the man who owned the plane, gave Darrell a set of airplane photos to ensure he would never forget that day.

Darrell rushed home to tack those precious mementos on the walls of his room.

"You shouldn't be doing that," said Don, sticking his nose into Darrell's sanctuary. "You need to ask permission first."

"Who are you to tell me what to do?" Darrell screamed back. "This isn't your house. This is my mom's." Darrell was tired of being told what to do in his own home. He slapped Don across the face. He no longer hated him; he despised the man. That was when everything exploded. Somebody came out of Darrell to fight. That somebody was destructive and full of rage. This somebody didn't yet have a name, though it had to have been one of the big boys. Most likely it was a combination of all three, J.D, James and Steve. When they feel it is needed, the people inside blend together to accomplish common goals.

As Darrell yanked the pictures of planes from the walls, tore the mattress and destroyed the room, Johnny came in to see what all the fuss was about. Darrell almost told Johnny what Don had been doing to him, but he didn't. Darrell didn't know if Johnny would believe him. If Johnny did believe him, Darrell was sure Johnny would kill Don right then and there. If Johnny had known that Carolyn had known about the abuse,

Darrell was afraid that he would kill her as well. After all, Darrell saw his oldest brother as The Protector.

Now that Johnny was busy with a family of his own, Darrell's brain had given him another Protector. This new Protector would put Darrell to sleep when he wanted to come out. He would do things Darrell would never dream of doing. He would set Darrell's world ablaze.

Eventually the police would blame Darrell for the fires, but that first night they didn't seem too concerned. The West Memphis Fire Department was called to investigate the smell of something smoldering in the trailer next door where Carolyn's oldest son Johnny lived with his family. The firemen agreed something was burning but they couldn't pinpoint just what. The only advice these public servants would give was for Johnny and Susan to take the baby and spend the night next door with Carolyn's family. The firemen said it was too hard for them to find the fire at night. They promised to return in the morning to when the fire got big enough to for them to see.

During those first fires, sleep always claimed Darrell right before things started to happen. It was beyond his control, this dream taking him to a place where he could escape from everything that tired him. This night, he recognized himself standing outside the back of Johnny and Susan's trailer, beneath their bedroom window. Next thing Darrell knew he found himself back in the trailer with Carolyn. It wasn't the daylight which woke him; it was the popping and crackling coming from the trailer next door.

A confused young Darrell wondered whether it was him who had set the fire. He wondered how he could have seen in a dream what everyone else experienced only with their eyes open. He had no one to ask and it is doubtful any in his family would have come up with a good explanation anyway.

With no place to go, Johnny moved his family into Darrell's room that very next night. Johnny, Susan and Brigitte had to share that small space with Bobbie Lynn. As had become the pattern, Darrell got the couch in the living room. In addition, Carolyn's brother Larry had come by to spend the night on the living room floor.

The excitement of the night before must have been tiring for the teen because Darrell fell asleep before anyone else. He left the sofa only to use the trailer's bathroom, stepping over his Uncle Larry in the process. He was back asleep on the couch when he heard his mother screaming about a fire and that her son was still inside.

Larry Coleman must have panicked when he smelled the smoke, bolting outside without a thought to the boy. Carolyn's screams woke Darrell just as part of the trailer's ceiling melted and fell to the couch, landing where Darrell's head had been just moments before. Next thing Darrell knew, he had reunited with his family in the safety of the night. He had no idea how he got there.

Though there was no loss of life, the fire was big news in West Memphis. The event even made the papers in neighboring Memphis, which was big news in and of it. It is rare for the bigger city to cover anything that happens in its namesake, Memphis's redheaded stepchild across the Mississippi in Arkansas.

Goodwill fed flames of compassion. People on both sides of the river opened up their hearts and pocketbooks. Donations of food and clothing flowed in. Mary Ann Lopez, who lived with her husband Tony two blocks from the townhouses, offered shelter. Director of Sales for the since-abandoned Quality Inn West in Memphis, she provided the family free rooms in the hotel. The Williams family was only supposed to stay for a short while, filling rooms vacant during of the hotel's off-season, but they ended up staying for two months. Don, Carolyn and Darrell got a room of their own that they didn't have to share with any other family members. Things cooled down.

Donations were still pouring in when the family moved to West Memphis into the River Grove Townhouses where Aunt Jeanne lived with her son Scotty. Johnny had found another place for his family, so Don and Carolyn moved in with only Bobbie Lynn and Darrell.

Since Scotty was quite a bit older than his cousins, 17 at the time, he was in charge the night the adults went out. This would have been a memorable evening even without the fires. Despite telling the papers they were visiting relatives in town when the commotion started, the truth was something else. Don, Carolyn and her sisters Jeanne and Frances had been clubbing. This was the night they met country singer Charlie Rich.

Darrell's sister, 17-year-old Bobbie Lynn Ballard, five and a half months pregnant, was in Jeanne's bed when the excitement started. Darrell had fallen asleep beside her on the floor. He was surprised to find himself waking up on the couch hearing Scotty running through the house screaming "Fire!" Smoke was coming from the closet in Scotty's room. As the teen opened it, flames burst in his face.

Darrell ran into the bedroom to get Bobbie Lynn, but Scotty had already pulled her outside. Once again, Darrell found himself alone in a burning building.

That was the fifth fire at River grove Townhouses in a three-week span. The last four were all on the same weekend within a 24-hour period. According to newspaper reports of the time, preliminary findings by officials on the scene indicated the blaze started in an electric furnace.

Johnny wasn't around for this fire because he had moved his family into a one-bedroom duplex across town. After the fire, Carolyn and Don moved in with Johnny, Susan and Brigitte, bringing along Darrell and Bobbie Lynn. The attached one-bedroom was where Jeanne lived with Scotty. Donations were still coming in strong and money was no object, though apparently still not enough to pay for a separate apartment for Carolyn and her brood. The money was good enough, though, that Frances, Carolyn's brother Larry's ex-wife, came to claim her part of the booty along with her young sons Steven and Colin. They moved right in. The girls took the bedrooms. The boys slept in the living room.

Wherever Bobbie Lynn, Scotty and Darrell went, flames followed. None of the subsequent fires could be called intentional arson. There had already been a fire in a duplex down the block. That one was traced to a lit cigarette thrown in a can of flammable liquid. All the kids, including Darrell, were sneaking smokes so fault was hard to pin. Though this fire would later be added to the charges against him, Darrell was asleep on his hide-a-bed on the night his friend's parents' duplex went up in flames.

Neither could he be held accountable for the two fires on Jeanne's family's side of the duplex. The West Memphis Fire Department said both of them were due to faulty electrical wiring. News reports of the time also note papers stored hear furnaces and trash blocking stairwells. The papers failed to note a series of recent evictions.

That was the point Darrell's attorney would make in court. Common sense showed that the teen could not have been responsible.

In the end, it didn't matter what the evidence proved. Detective Jerry Driver had already extracted a complete confession from Darrell.

-- 18 --

BO

"Are you okay, Billy?"

We are in the backseat of a truck we've never seen, going somewhere we've never been with people we've known for maybe a couple of hours. Billy is more than okay with it.

We have returned to West Memphis, looking for closure and clues. In the 30 years since Billy last saw the house on Church Street someone has cut down the trees and torn out the fences. The house next door where Billy and Jimmy Nelson lived still stands, but its ghosts have gone. Unlike Billy who will always be two, the Nelson brothers grew up long ago. The family has moved away.

Everything looks familiar, but nothing is. Billy remembers the neighborhood as middle class. Now the houses need painting and the yards need work. It's all very different, unkempt and uncared for. The kids are both excited and confused.

The Expedition stops for a moment. Suddenly, so does time.

"My house?" Billy whimpers. "Mama?"

I should have expected an episode like this one. All of the kids inside Darrell live to one extent or another in the moment when they were created. The past and the present are one. To them, what happened before is happening still and will continue to happen forever. Still, this is the most intense and sensitive situation that has ever arisen.

"You have a new house back home, remember?" I tell Billy gently, unsure how he'll react. Billy doesn't usually come out unless it's bedtime or if we're alone together back in Long Beach so him showing up at midday around people he's only just met is an entirely new and somewhat unsettling experience for all of us. I've been frantically searching my mind for a logical and soothing way to tell a 2-year-old that his mother has been dead more than 20 years. Sidestepping DID math, instead I go for the redirect. "We're going there next weekend," I assure the child." Tigger is waiting for us there."

"Tigger?" he whispers. Then, placated by the promise of a reunion with his new puppy, he quietly slips back behind Darrell's eyes.

That's Bo Kirgis driving us back to the home he shares with his wife Mary Barnick in the Ozark foothills. It doesn't say Bo on his driver's license. The nickname was originally bestowed on him by classmates after an unfortunate attempt at a do-it-yourself hairdo during high school. Back then, Bo was short for Bozo after the famous clown. As he grew older, his height, build and affable nature also began to remind people of Baloo, the kind yet funny bear from Walt Disney's animated version of Rudyard Kipling's *The Jungle Book*. "Bo" is short for both nicknames.

Bo and Mary have driven three hours to rescue us when we find ourselves abandoned five days before our scheduled flight back to Long Beach. The kids inside rename them "Aunt Mary" and "Uncle Bo-Bo Bear," instantly enamored of the couple that has come to save us. For the first time since landing in Memphis, we all breathe a sigh of relief.

The Ford Expedition slowly tools through the streets of West Memphis. This is a side trip we'd meant to make with Bertha Merriman. We needed to visit West Memphis and Brinkley and Marion in hopes of locating pieces of the puzzle that is Darrell's life. We needed to revisit the scene of the crime.

Up in the front seat beside her husband sits Mary. She and I have been discussing how Arkansas society has failed Darrell at its most basic levels: family, education, law. She'd been privy to the twists and turns, sharper than any we encounter heading up the Ozarks, which each new revelation has caused in the narrative. The simple explanation of how

Darrell developed multiple personalities long ago turned into an exploration of why he did so. Needing solid reasons, all we've been getting from those who knew Darrell while he was growing up are vague excuses and sever memory gaps.

Call it human nature. Bombarded with conflicting stimuli, the human brain often contracts its narrative as noted by Saul McLeod in a 2008 article in *Simply Psychology*. Humans tend to connect and interpret new experiences through ones with which we are already familiar. We seek meaningful patterns and resist those that are meaningless. Bo points out later that most humans seek to be the heroes in their own tales, or at very least not be the villain.

The pieces come together and the story unfolds. The most popular narrative becomes the truth. The story where we come out best is the one most repeated. R.D. was a good man. Carolyn was a faithful wife. We tell ourselves the stories we need to hear to make our own vision of the truth make sense. We tell ourselves stories in order to live.

Given the propensity towards panic, a DID patient sees things differently. If his story were fictional, Darrell would be called an unreliable narrator. It would not be completely unfair to question his credibility. After all, his story fails to match the narrative spun by his family all these years. Few official papers have survived through the ravages of time, natural disaster and periodic purges by workers for the state of Arkansas itself. His credibility could be questioned, but those who do can never produce an alternate story line that works.

A wrong turn in Memphis brings out the first of Darrell's kids. On our left stands the hospital where Darrell was locked down awaiting his court hearing. Darrell couldn't forget it if he tried, but it's someone else who points out the exact room. There on the top floor, the one in the corner, that's where he tried to break through the window. Someone explains to Bo and Mary that it wasn't that the people inside didn't like the place. James just didn't think it was fair he be locked up for crimes he didn't commit.

It is impossible to say who set the fires that season in West Memphis. It may well have been James who set the first fire in the series but never in the intervening years has he claimed either credit or fault. What he knows as well as Darrell's attorney knew was that someone was setting fires while he was locked up in Memphis. Yet those were the very fires that caused the judge to banish Darrell from Arkansas.

This is the first time any of us meet Billy Bill. He is telling us the story of what happened to James. At the time, we think it is James telling the story. It can't be, though, because James is generally taciturn and abrupt. He operates almost entirely in quick spurts of emotion. It might also have been J.D., though the language used is much too mature for someone who is only in his teens.

It takes months before Billy Bill introduces himself again, this time with an unexpected Welsh accent. He is Keeper of Memories, logical and calm in his recitation of events. Here in Tennessee, we listen to him but do not recognize him as someone new. That's to be expected with the big kids. Because he is using James's voice, for the moment Billy Bill goes unrecognized.

James had already been around. As The Protector, he is always somewhere near the surface. He wants to be available in case a car backfires or someone says something mean. He needs to be ready whenever he is needed. He has been comfortable with Bo and Mary from the start. It was he who kept a lookout for them when they came to pick us up on the legendary Beale Street in Memphis. Once James gives the okay, the others take turns coming out to let themselves meet their new friends. It's Billy, though, who throws his arms around Bo. The kids all love best that Bo and Mary treat them like people rather than afflictions.

In truth, the ones inside are no different from kids in general. They see things or experience events that trigger memories. Their responses can be just as unpredictable as that of any small being.

There's a concern as Bo turns into the housing tract. The lot on the corner doesn't look like much. Weeds have almost overtaken the white posts where mobile homes were once tethered.

Dot isn't as effected as he might have been seeing the place where his Uncle Steve Joshlin took his own life. The 10-year-old notices less that nature has reclaimed this traumatic spot than he does that the fields nearby are newly mown. Dot remembers those spaces filled with corn and bean plants. He remembers running through them. He remembers them as good places to hide from the adults.

He remembers playtime. When Darrell was loneliest, there was always Dot to keep him company. The little boy is so good-tempered and so personable, that it's curious he took so long to let himself be known. In fact, it took Billy and Jimmie quite a few late nights of talking to convince the spot that kept hovering behind Darrell's eyes that it was safe to meet the outside world at all. One of the newest members of the family, he was the first to surface after the death of Darrell's long-time husband, Robert Dann. Dot says he would have come out earlier but Robert's gruff demeanor frightened him. For his first few weeks out, he fails to remember Robert at all. The other kids have since shared their memories. The inquisitive kid is now up to speed.

The abandoned trailer park proves no trauma trigger, no flashback to a time the people inside don't want Darrell to remember. The personable little boy was just glad to be somewhere he recognized and among people he knew.

Traumatic memories in the brain can be triggered by any number of outside stimuli, even one not remotely reminiscent of the trauma or abuse, writes Marlene Steinberg, M.D. in her book *The Stranger in the Mirror*. These stimuli are often difficult or impossible for the survivor to control. The role of the alternates is to protect Darrell from these memories. None of them live in the moment they were created. Instead, they are either younger or older than the event that brought them to life. Dot may not have remembered Robert, but neither does he recall his uncle Steve. It is his personality's job to focus on the good times. That is one way Dot keeps Darrell from re-experiencing pain.

The truck's windows fill with potential triggers as the Arkansas afternoon turns into evening. A stop at the River Grove Townhouses finds the pool filled in and decorative railings removed. The unit closest to the manager's office, part of the wing destroyed in the arson fires for which Darrell was accused, shows signs of a recent blaze. The last place Darrell would live with his family likely hasn't been painted since these tenements were rebuilt while he was under lockdown across the river in Memphis.

We visit just about everywhere we meant to see with the family we'd returned to Arkansas to meet. Just off the freeway in Palestine, there is the mobile home where Darrell's mother Carolyn passed away. It is on a large dirt lot that passes as a mobile home park. Except for the wear and tear caused the time and the region's weather, the trailer looks much as it did the day she died. Across the street, Darrell asks at the diner adjacent to a tire shop about the waitress who knew him. Gruffly, he's informed that she is long gone. The diner itself is closed, its tables still set for the next morning.

Taking the off ramp into Wheatley, fields pass by until Darrell says to stop. Here is the tiny Posey Cemetery where the family plots are found. Though it looks abandoned, recent graves near the entrance reveal the cemetery is still very much in use. Other than the evidence of recent burials, the only change Darrell can see is the service road which cuts across what he remembers as a row of ancient graves. He has no problem finding what he's looking for. Uncle Steve's military headstone is most prominent. Steve's father lies to his right and mother to his left. Darrell's great grandmother is here too. His mother Carolyn's grave is just to the left of that of her own mother.

By the time Brinkley comes into view, the afternoon is beginning to fade. With still a couple of hours to drive we can surmise only that the white house where Danny Poole lived with the family outside of town is likely beneath someone's field. Darrell's grandmother's brick house also fails to materialize. Darrell wants to visit Mercy Hospital where we have been told his mother's medical records are still housed. Because the hospital has been empty for years, abandoned to the elements and local vagrants, no one thinks that is a good idea.

It is said that the first step in helping trauma survivors begin the healing process is to establish a safe environment. This is a place where the survivor does not feel threatened with recurrence of the original trauma and also feels safe from encountering situations that will trigger that memory. Any of these stops could have been a trigger.

"Are you all right, Billy?" asks Bo.

"Yes sir, Uncle Bo," he answers.

"Do you need me to pull over?"

"No sir."

Billy liked Aunt Mary and Uncle Bo-Bo Bear from the first minute he met them. They make him feel safe. They make him feel wanted. They talk to him just like a person. Family isn't always made up of relatives.

This is a day that no one will forget. Upon our return to Long Beach a week later, we'll talk about the kids' reactions with Darrell's psychiatrist Dr. Higgens. She hypothesizes that it is seeing their home again that has made the kids inside comfortable. It is these memories of places that allow them to roam from behind Darrell's eyes.

During the next week in the Ozarks all of the kids except Steve, the keeper of Darrell's rage, will make themselves known. Billy says it is okay for the others to come out and make themselves known.

Billy is happy. He was excited that we'd go looking for his family and he's really thrilled that we've found it.

Darrell Becoming Steve
(Photo Credit Unknown)

Which One Am I?

James
(Photo: Robert Dann)

Billy Bill
(Photo Credit Unknown)

Ann
(Photo: James Darrell Williams)

-- 19 --

MILLIGAN

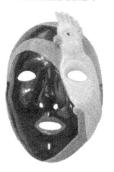

There are a million stories in Hollywood, maybe even more than Darrell's family keeps from him, but only so many ways to tell them. Questing always for the greatest number of consumers and hence the greatest amount of income, popular media is driven to cater to the lowest common denominator. That which is most popular is most profitable. What is most profitable changes with the times.

By the Seventies, the American populace felt disillusioned. The continuing war in Viet Nam, social realignment including the Women's Rights and Civil Rights movements and the presidential impeachment against Richard M. Nixon were very much on the collective mind. Escapist fare patterned after the Fifties style, like the box office flops *Cleopatra* and *Hello Dolly!*, had gone out of vogue.

The baby boomer generation was coming of age. As with every generation before it, this one demanded its own slice of culture. The boomers expected their world to incorporate the once radical ideas of Sixties counter-culture. They wanted it to reflect what they perceived as their own more realistic expectations of the world. They ultimately found themselves in the anti-hero as embodied in box office hits like *Bonnie & Clyde* and *Easy Rider*.

This was an audience that saw itself as sophisticated and worldly. They would have been unsurprised had they been informed that neither *The Three Faces of Eve's* Chris Costner Sizemore nor *Sybil's* Shirley Ardell Mason had actually been cured.

That news was never reported and, even if it had been, it would have taken a long time to make a dent in the new cottage industry growing around Dr. Cornelia Wilbur. Dr. Wilbur had built the theories she used to treat Sybil on Freudian psychology. She promoted the idea that repressed memories were the foundation of alternate personalities. To recover these lost memories was the key to making the patient whole. By 1980, her theory became a formal diagnosis. She soon opened a hospital ward specializing in multiples.

Sybil became the Bible of DID study. All other cases were, and many times still are, measured against it. Its popularity alone would have been enough reason to turn it into a hit TV movie. Its story of a heroic anti-hero's struggle and ultimate triumph over the forces against her made it a shoe-in. Still, its happy ending alone wouldn't satisfy audiences of the day. *Sybil* would undergo one more transformation. Instead of the fairy tale that is the format adopted for *The Three Faces of Eve*, *Sybil* is a darker work. While still yearning for the happy fantasy ending, *Sybil* contains the realism and toughness readers of the time were coming to expect.

Unlike the subjects of *The Three Faces of Eve* and *Sybil*, Billy Milligan never had the luxury of anonymity. Accused of a series of robberies and rapes that occurred at Ohio State University in the late Seventies, his arrest and trial were heavily publicized. His infamy only increased when, preparing for his defense, psychologists diagnosed Milligan with DID. By the time his trial began, 10 of his 23 personalities had made themselves known. By the time his trial was over, Milligan would become the first person in history to be acquitted of his crimes by reason of insanity caused by multiple personalities.

That Milligan's story failed to follow the accepted narrative Dr. Wilbur had first established in *Sybil* and had by now codified makes his tale difficult to digest. That it duplicated the themes of societal breakdown, moral decay and a new awareness of sexuality now making their way to the big screen makes his story seem positively unreal.

By the time of his arrest, Milligan claimed he had not been in control of his body – "on the spot" as the people inside him called being outside – for a good seven years. The dominant personality was rational and emotionless British subject Arthur. The protector was Ragen, the Keeper of Hate with an ominous Slavic accent. Reportedly tormented by years of physical, emotional and sexual abuse, Milligan himself was suicidal and so a threat to the body and everyone it contained. Taking no chances, the people inside him decided to keep Milligan asleep.

Neither Arthur nor Ragen had much control over Adalana, a shy lesbian. As the story was told at trial and in author Daniel Keyes' book *The Minds of Billy Milligan*, it was she who, Milligan claimed, craving physical contact and affection, used Milligan's body to commit the rapes.

Milligan's story was suspicious on a number of levels and his treatment, both medically and legally, easily questioned. Conservative Ohio wanted only that justice be served. A non-guilty verdict based on any reason, never mind one so extraordinary, was seen as justice denied. Some in the Harding Hospital's locked psychiatric cottage, Wakefield House, resented the amount of time and energy Milligan required. They complained that Milligan kept them from helping the other patients. That Milligan was seen to immediately capitalize on his troubles didn't sit well at all.

Riding the success of his first novel, *Flowers for Algernon*, later made into the film *Charly*, Keyes would eventually spend two years getting to know Milligan and his unusually cooperative alters. Keyes wrote two books, *The Minds of Billy Milligan* and a sequel, *The Milligan Wars*. The first book, never a hit in the U.S., ultimately found its audience. The second book found publication in Japan. Publication of the sequel in America was held off in anticipation of a filmed adaptation of that first work. Director James Cameron announced the film project under the title *A Crowded Room* barely two days after his hit *Terminator 2* was released. Milligan and the woman who now co-owns the rights to his story, Sandy Arcara, priced themselves out of the market after Milligan had already helped with research of character with actor Leonardo DiCaprio who had been chosen to play the title role. Milligan and Arcata's monetary demands put an end to the production.

Meanwhile, the medical profession created a circus all its own. Psychiatrist Dr. George Harding had been in touch with the famous Dr.

Wilbur and had invited her to observe and interview his notorious patient. Milligan would be the first multiple personality to be observed around the clock in a mental hospital. Dr. George, as he was called to distinguish him from the famous father whose name he shared, was looking for help getting Milligan to reach a state of what Dr. Wilbur called fusion. Fusion, defined by Dr. Wilbur, is a place where all the personalities became one. Few professionals believe in such a state today, but in the Seventies, fusion was the goal. The first official question about its efficacy wouldn't come until 1977 and the publication of Chris Costner Sizemore's autobiography, *I'm Eve*. This book was the first anyone had learned that, despite what had been written about her and shown in the movie houses, Sizemore was still attempting to heal long after the closing credits rolled.

No one was questioning the proceedings as the room in the basement of Harding's administration building began to fill. The purpose of the meeting was to help Milligan become fused enough to stand trial. The result was a freak show. Only about a dozen hospital employees were directly involved with Milligan's treatment. Nevertheless, the room quickly filled with almost 100 staffers, some bringing wives and cohorts to this historic and unforgettable performance.

Dr. George was ready. His opening act was a series of videotapes showing interviews he and psychologist Dorothy Turner had conducted with Milligan and some of his personalities. The people inside had an unusual amount of trust in Turner, who had worked with them from the beginning of Milligan's incarceration. Without the use of any reported hypnosis, they came one by one to take the stage and speak with Dr. Wilbur.

With the fury of true believers on the clock, doctors pressed on. The people of Ohio wanted justice. Hospital professionals wanted the time back Milligan had stolen from the other patients. Dr. George's reason for wanting Milligan in his hospital in the first place was as an opportunity for his staff to learn, as well as for the hospital to make a contribution to psychiatric knowledge. This was, after all, a precedent-setting case. Failure was not an option for anyone and most certainly not for Dr. George and Dr. Wilbur. There couldn't have been a soul involved who didn't realize Milligan's case was an historical moment. A thorough and proper diagnosis and treatment could have made everyone stars. That wasn't how things played out.

Eventually, the doctors succeeded in "partial fusion" of the personalities. This new personality was dubbed The Teacher. The appearance of this comprehensive personality echoed Dr. Wilbur's creation of The New Sybil. Though he'd fragment again even before his story hit bookshelves, Milligan was deemed competent to stand trial.

The judge described the history of Milligan's life as "mind-boggling." Some thought that also applied to the verdict, which even Thigpen and Cleckley, the doctors who brought the world *The Three Faces of Eve*, described as "a gross miscarriage of justice and denigration of psychiatry." They were not opposed to DID as a diagnosis but they were certainly opposed to what they called its "uncritical application."

For all its historical significance, there remain doubts about Milligan's case. Milligan had worked many odd jobs during his freedom. Sometimes, he worked in hospitals. Some think that is where he learned about DID. That no one in the hospitals where he stayed knew as much about DID as Milligan did, though, makes this accidental education obtained while working as an orderly seem highly unlikely.

More troubling is the story of the personality accused of the crime. When one of the people inside takes control of the body they see the host body and its functions in terms of that personality. A female like Adalana would be unable to commit rape even if she so desired. There are some indications that she was not alone on the spot and that is entirely possible. One victim describes her attacker telling her he was, at one moment, a member of the terrorist organization The Weathermen. At another moment, he identified himself as a businessman. It is not unheard of for two personalities to share the spotlight. The people inside Darrell do that all the time. In Milligan's case, however, it is a subject no one took time to explore.

Billy Milligan was never a sympathetic character. There was the severity of his crimes and the doubts about both his diagnosis and the outcome of his treatment. After his 1988 release after 10 years in treatment, things didn't get better. When Milligan was again arrested in 1996 there was no personality split. This discrepancy added an entirely new layer of doubt to his original story. Following the Japanese success of *The Minds of Billy Milligan*, the State of Ohio took legal steps to recover part of the $453,000 that his hospital stay is said to have cost. To date, Milligan has repaid a small percentage of the debt.

In one way, Milligan's story did fit the narrative. In the public's mind, women with DID are victims. The questionable outcome of Milligan trial made the world see men with DID as villains.

Which One Am I?

West Memphis Apartment Fire Ravages Townhouse Complex

By KEN GARLAND
Press-Scimitar Staff Writer

West Memphis News

Arson investigators from the Arkansas state fire marshal's office and the West Memphis police and fire departments today began sifting through the rubble of a fire which heavily damaged 12 townhouses in a West Memphis apartment complex.

The fire, which officials say they believe may have been deliberately set, raged through the attic of one building in the River Grove Townhouses at 700 S. Avalon in West Memphis.

The Saturday night fire was the fourth blaze reported at the apartment complex in just over 24 hours and the sixth at the complex in the past two weeks, fire officials said.

Capt. Billy Hill of the West Memphis Fire Department said the latest fire was reported to have started around a water heater in one of the occupied townhouses. Firemen were called at 11:21 p.m. Saturday and did not leave the complex until 10:42 a.m. Sunday.

"The first call that came in said the water heater was on fire in Apt. 34," Hill said. "By the time we got there, the whole attic was on fire, and the fire had broken through the roof in one of the apartments. We couldn't tell where it had started, but in Apt. 34 there was fire in the closet where the furnace was located."

Hill, who was supervisor in charge of fire units at the blaze, said evidence uncovered after the blaze was extinguished and the number of fires reported at the complex led firemen to call for an investigation.

"The way the doors in a number of apartments burned and the fact that we got so many calls looks suspicious," he said.

One firefighter, Lt. Bernie Reed, was slightly injured when he fell down some stairs clogged with debris, Hill said. Reed did not, however, require medical treatment, he said.

Three of the four weekend calls were in the same building, Hill said. The first two calls were to the laundry room in the complex.

The last flurry of fires began at 9:48 p.m. Friday when firemen were called to extinguish a fire in Apt. 36, which was vacant at the time. Hill said the fire appeared to have started in the livingroom of the apartment and did approximately $500 worth of damage.

Firemen were called back to the townhouses at 12:12 a.m. Saturday to extinguish a blaze which had started in the stairwell of another vacant apartment. The fire heavily damaged the apartment, located in a separate building.

Both of these fires were believed to have been deliberately set, Hill said.

At 2:54 a.m. Saturday, firemen were called back to Apt. 36 where they had been called two hours earlier. This second fire appeared to have started in an upstairs bedroom and did heavy damage to the apartment, Hill said.

The next call came at 11:21 p.m. Saturday night.

Two earlier fires in December were confined to the laundry room, housed in a separate building in the complex, Hill said. Firemen were first called on Dec. 28, he said, to extinguish a small fire confined to some materials stored near water heaters.

Firemen were called back to the laundry room Dec. 30 to extinguish a fire which "pretty well wiped it out," Hill said.

Saturday night's fire burned through the ceilings of the apartments quickly and raced down the length of the attic, Hill said.

"When we first got the call, we didn't think it would be too bad," Hill said. "But by the time we got down there it had already gotten into the attic and had started coming through the roof. It didn't take us long to get the fire out, but we had to stay there a lot longer putting out small spot fires in mattresses, couches and clothing."

Four companies of West Memphis firemen with five trucks responded to the call, he said. The Marion, Ark., Volunteer Fire Department sent about 16 men to help West Memphis fight the blaze, he said.

The official said the building had no firewalls between the units or between the units of the attic.

"It had a wide open attic from one end to the other," he said.

West Memphis Building Inspector Calvin Avery said he did not know anything about the construction of the building.

"That was built before I came here," Avery said. He said he did not know if the Southern Building Code or the National Fire Code, both of which govern construction of private and public buildings in West Memphis, require fire walls.

"I would have to research it," he said. "I would have to see the plans and to know the length of the buildings. That gets into legal matters. I will not be quoted on this."

West Memphis police officials said they have talked to several residents to see if they saw any suspicious persons around the night of the fire but said they have no suspects.

"Right now we can't determine if we have arson or maybe an electrical short," said police Lt. Jerry Hubbard. "We haven't ruled out arson yet. We're waiting to meet with the state fire marshal to go over the area."

River Grove Townhouse fires in Press-Scimitar
(Courtesy Chris Ratliff, Special Collections, University of Memphis)

JEANNE

Two fires were a tragedy. Six added up to arson.

That's the way Aunt Jeanne saw it. She'd been close to her nephew Darrell for all of his life. He provided a valuable service, keeping her more than once from having to face the aftermath of her own actions.

Jeanne wasn't much scared of consequences in the days since her last divorce. That last man had left her the minute he cleared out her bank account. That was unexpected. He seemed like such a nice man when she met him at the Jehovah's Witness church she'd begun to attend with her mother and sister Ann. At least the farm was still in her name.

What scared her most these days was Darrell. The boy had grown up too fast, two tall, too skinny. Of course, she knew he wasn't a Williams. She had played a big part in creating the fiction of his parentage in the first place. She couldn't be sure just who he was anymore. He always acted nervous and sometimes acted like he wasn't quite part of the world around him. To see him pull back his neck like he was trying to rip his own head right off was pretty scary too. There sure weren't any fires that she could remember until Carolyn moved in with that strange, loner boy.

After she saw him walking down the street with men dressed like women, she figured that he was gay. The Jehovah's Witness religion teaches its membership to believe that homosexuality is detestable, an abomination, abhorrent, and is caused by demon possession. As obsessed with the church as she had been with sex, Jeanne found herself in agreement.

As far as Jeanne, a Jehovah's Witness, was concerned, the boy was just plain crazy. It unnerved her how he was nervous all the time. An older Darrell would know that nervousness gives him less control over the people inside. As a teen, he didn't even know those people were there. When one of them took the spotlight, especially the angry ones like Steve or James, it would be enough to unnerve just about anybody and the adolescent sure seemed to be angry a lot of the time. Jeanne must have seen there was something wrong with Darrell because she would tell anybody who would listen that he needed to be locked up in a mental hospital. If she had her way, he would be institutionalized for the rest of his life.

Accusations against her youngest child didn't sit well with Carolyn. Long after her car accident, her mental state remained untreated and possibly untreatable. The constant pain she must have felt caused her mood swings to be increasingly unpredictable. In her lucid moments, she was the loving and caring mother Darrell always wanted her to be. Jeanne's accusations against her youngest son would cause Carolyn to build a wall between the sisters but it was too late. In the end, it didn't matter what Jeanne said or to whom. Someone else had taken notice of the strange goings-on in the Williams family.

Ever since the first fire broke out, the West Memphis Police Department had been keeping an eye on Darrell. He could feel them watching. He knew it in his bones. He just didn't know what they were looking for.

The first time he was arrested was the day he turned 15. The woman at the neighborhood 7-11 set them on his trail. A boy that young buying lighter fluid looked awfully suspicious.

Darrell wasn't old enough to legally buy lighter fluid. It was the same Zippo lighter that had been issued by the Navy to his late Uncle Steve that made the clerk at the convenience store suspicious. Kids that young didn't have lighters that grand and there had been those fires down the street not long before. It was her civic duty to report him.

That night, the West Memphis Police arrested him. Detective Gerald Martin took Darrell in his charge and brought him to an adult facility in Monroe, AR. The case would be referred to Crittenden County Juvenile Court for a hearing.

Across the Mississippi in neighboring Tennessee, West Memphis had long had a reputation as The Wild West and as Sin City. Anything that couldn't be done in Memphis proper was seen as no problem at all in West Memphis. To those ends, the West Memphis Police Force and Crittenden County Sheriff's Office had a two-pronged mission. They would have to keep an eye on carousing outsiders while making sure anything that happened in Crittenden County stayed in Crittenden County.

They were sure they had this one right. The boy was too nervous, had that tic in his neck and had just attempted to buy lighter fluid in clear violation of state law. Though the evidence was circumstantial, the evidence didn't matter. As far as the plain clothes police officer was concerned, everything about Darrell pegged him as a kid "from off."

There was no way an officer of the court was about to let some misfit teenaged hooligan run over him. The interrogation in the small office in West Memphis was designed for efficiency. Sitting on the edge of the desk, West Memphis Juvenile Officer Jerry Driver told Darrell and Carolyn, "We know you set those fires. You might as well admit it. Even if you didn't do it, tell me that you did it and we'll let you go home right now."

That sounded reasonable. Darrell gave the man what he wanted to hear.

Next thing anybody knew, Detective Martin was coming back in the room with a pair of handcuffs. "My sergeant says I have to arrest you," he told Darrell.

That didn't sit well with Carolyn. "You told me you didn't believe he did it. You told my child that he'd be able to go home with me," she screamed. Then she slapped Driver, who had come in behind Detective Martin, as hard as she could while calling him every name she could think of.

They didn't arrest Carolyn for assault on an officer, but they got even with her anyway. They wouldn't let Carolyn see her son again for a week.

Darrell, who was all of 14 at the time, was having a hard time seeing anything at all. There were no lights in the cell in the adult jail in nearby Marion, AR. In those days, the authorities didn't understand much about juvenile detention. The rules for handling juveniles were yet to be codified. Even today, according to Gerald Martin, the since retired officer who arrested Darrell, the process remains informal. There is no constitutional right to either a transcript or appellate review of a juvenile court decision. Moreover, many judges have denied children and adolescents basic constitutional rights to due process.

There was a jail in West Memphis but it was reserved for misdemeanor offenders. Anyone committing crimes on the level of a felony, as was Darrell's alleged crime, was handled by the adult facility in Marion. The small adult facility was adjacent to the region's juvenile facility. Despite the darkness, it was hard to miss seeing the towers of old food cases stacked in the cell. Some had rotting food still in them and some of it had fallen to the floor. Darrell may have been starving but the roaches were well fed.

For the entire week, the rotting food was pretty much the only thing edible Darrell saw. He was occasionally fed, but never more than once a day. When he got hungry, the jailers told him, he should just eat whatever was on the floor. Taking turns, J.D. and James came out from inside to try to protect Darrell. Their main function was to keep him strong. There just wasn't much else they could do.

Darrell couldn't see well, but the jailers saw well enough to notice something else about the nervous teen they didn't like. The boy had what looked like two ankle bones. All his life, Darrell had been told that was a never-treated break he suffered during birth. Monkey, though, had the identical condition. The protruding bone was where the police aimed their batons each morning in order to wake the prisoner. Even as an adult, the ankle is weak and causes Darrell to take many a tumble. Had they succeeded in shattering it, he wouldn't walk at all.

The week ended abruptly when Chief of Police Dick Ferguson returned from vacation. Though there was no light in the cell, the Chief still didn't like what he saw. He ordered Darrell moved immediately. He ordered the officers reprimanded. In fact, he threatened to fire the lot of them for letting the cell get into such a deplorable condition. Everyone was sorry to hear years later that Chief Ferguson had been killed in the line of duty. Nobody believed his death was an accident.

Released to his mother, Darrell's freedom didn't last. On the evening of the sixth fire Darrell was arrested again. He was pulled right out of Johnny's Malibu in a line of cars that was trying to pull away from the flames that threatened to engulf the River Grove Townhouses. It was strange how the police knew Darrell would be in the Malibu at that exact time. They must have known because they asked for him by name. Once they got him away from his family, they called him every name in the book.

Maybe he shouldn't have done it, but this time Darrell stood up to the men in blue. "You don't need to talk to me like that," he complained. "I'm just a child." That's when the officer slapped him.

With the other children coming home and no man in charge, Carolyn was feeling needed. In one of her increasingly frequent personality shifts, she was now the mother bear protecting a cub. Banging her fists on the police car, she screamed at the officer "You will not treat my child like that!" She kept up her protestations until Police Chief Dick Ferguson came down to the scene. It was he who released Darrell into his mother's custody. He recognized immediately that there was no evidence other than a tip from persons unknown that Darrell would be in the car, though Juvenile Probation Officer Jerry Driver would attempt to remedy that by taping an interview filled with leading questions once he got Darrell down to the station.

Chief Ferguson gave Carolyn a number to call. He knew a good attorney, one who would take the case pro bono. The next day, Darrell, his mother Carolyn, aunt Jeanne, sister Bobbie Lynn, brother Johnny and Johnny's wife Susan came down to the attorney's office for an interview. Only Darrell was asked to remain outside the interview room. Everybody talked but it was only Aunt Jeanne who insisted that Darrell was guilty. Darrell heard her say it because somehow, the door to the room never did get completely closed. The attorney told Carolyn that he thought it best Darrell be put somewhere he would be safe.

The public defender must have known something more than he told. According to news reports of the time, charges against the boy were *nolle pressed* at the request of the prosecution just a day or so after his arrest. *Nolle Presse* is a legal term indicating that the case has been dismissed with the caveat that the prosecution can reopen the case and continue prosecution within 12 months. In short, the prosecutor felt there was not enough evidence to prove the case against Darrell but he left the door open to prosecution just in case.

That left the Sheriff's office with no active case against the boy, yet the authorities still maintained a pending court date. Why a court date was maintained in the absence of a case is one of the most troubling questions about what happened during Darrell's time in West Memphis, though it is a question that is unlikely to be answered. Arkansas adopted legislation in

1989--Act 273 of the 1989 Regular Session--to purge juvenile case files once a child turned 21. The Arkansas State Archives only keeps copies of such crimes for another 10 years after that.

Two officers of the court drove Darrell across the bridge to Memphis. For the next six months, Darrell would be a ward of what is now The University Behavioral Health Center at the University of Memphis. Directly adjacent to the University and VA Hospitals, it is the home of the Department of Psychiatry. Darrell would be housed on the top floor of the training facility then known as Child and Adolescent Service. His room could only be reached with the use of a key and not many people had those. Darrell never did. He could only leave the floor under strict supervision. Other than Don, Carolyn, R.D. and his lawyer, nobody else knew where Darrell was sequestered.

The boy was removed from the facility officially only once. He was taken to a room in order that authorities might administer a lie detector test. Darrell had never seen a lie detector before, but he'd seen an electric chair on TV. Strapped into the chair with electrodes attached to his wrists, the boy came unglued. He was sure he would be killed with no one ever the wiser.

"I'll tell you anything you want," he screamed. "I'll tell you I did it! I'll tell you I'm the one who just shot President Reagan if that's what you want! Just don't kill me!"

Behind the desk, the doctor in charge of the test calmly wrote in his notepad. Then he untied Darrell and had him escorted back to his room.

The officers who escorted Darrell to Memphis had been quite vocal in telling him they couldn't understand what the courts were doing prosecuting him for the fires, or at least not for all of them. They would be just as vocal on the topic when they came to pick him up from the locked down private hospital to bring him to his court date.

The fires hadn't stopped while the accused arsonist was in lockdown and each time, the police came looking for Darrell. Despite numerous threats from the Sheriff's office and District Attorney, Carolyn wouldn't tell them where her son was. His public defender would only tell the court that Darrell's family had spirited him away.

Given the severity of the alleged crimes, the lack of media scrutiny at the old West Memphis courthouse is surprising. The district attorney and judge were themselves surprised to see the accused brought into the courtroom. They claimed they had been searching for him the entire six months or so he had been in Memphis.

The two sheriffs who had first escorted Darrell to Child and Adolescent Service now brought him back to sit beside his mother Carolyn and his court-appointed public defender.

He remembers the judge asking him if he knew about the charges against him. These included the blaze at the River Grove Townhouses and several others that had hit the town in the time Darrell had been away. The district attorney pointed to a witness, the city Fire Marshall who had first filed and then dropped the original charges against Darrell.

That Darrell had actually been in lockdown at the time of the subsequent fires didn't sit well with the judge. There had been property damage, after all. Somebody had to pay.

The scene devolved. This wasn't the story anyone expected. The plot wasn't fitting with the pre-conceived narrative. Yet the moral had to be told. From the bench, the judge sentenced Darrell to five years probation and banished him for life from the state of Arkansas.

"You can't do that," Carolyn screamed. "You can't banish my son from the state where he has family!"

"Mrs. Bevel! Mrs. Bevel!" the public defender said, holding her back while trying to calm her rage.

Threatened with contempt of court, Carolyn would still not be quieted. Trying to take control of the situation, the public defender pointed that there were no charges pending against Darrell. Even if there were, he was underage with no way of supporting himself and there was no legal precedent for banishment.

None of that fancy legal talk mattered. The judge's verdict stood.

Darrell doesn't remember much after that until he woke up in a strange apartment in Mississippi. Sometime during the court proceedings, Darrell had gone missing. Terrified and alone, he found himself waiting for a probation officer named Howard P. Brown.

Which One Am I?

PART THREE

AMORY

Amory was the first planned city in Mississippi. The Kansas City, Memphis & Birmingham Railroad needed a mid-point between Memphis, Tennessee and Birmingham, Alabama for their locomotives, and they laid out the new town of Amory in 1887. People from nearby Cotton Gin Port on the Tombigbee River abandoned their town and moved to Amory. The population is 6,956 as of the 2000 census. – From Wikipedia

J.D.
(Photo Credit Unknown)

-- 21 --

J.D.

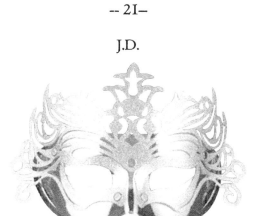

No one knows for certain how long it took Darrell to awake. Judging time is as hard for him as it would be for anyone when a person's chain of events is missing a link or two. Oldest brother Johnny claims no knowledge of what led Carolyn to leave. He was living with his wife Susan in the same Mississippi apartment complex as Carolyn, Darrell and Bobbie Lynn, but he claims no memory of the time. Second eldest brother Ronnie isn't talking at all. He and his wife Lisa lived in the apartment complex as well but physical proximity didn't mean the family had emotional closeness in Mississippi anymore than it had back in Arkansas.

The most dominant of Darrell's teen boys inside, J.D., might know, but he's not the most reliable witness. In his mind, the family was in that apartment for a good year and a half before Carolyn drove away with Carrol Bevel. That doesn't add up but J.D. can't be blamed for his poor accounting. What was happening is still happening in his mind. The past and present meld together yet don't always jell. Anyone who has had the emotional and productive skills of a 15 year old for more than 40 years must have a very different perspective of time.

The clock started ticking the night of Darrell's arrest in West Memphis. News reports peg the date of his arrest as January 18, 1981. Though he was unaware of the date and certainly no one in his family had made plans for a celebration, January 18 was also the day Darrell turned 15. Following the arrest, his public defender immediately sent him to Child and Adolescent Service in Memphis where he would stay under lock down until trial seven months later. That August, the judge banished him from Arkansas and Carolyn moved him to the apartment in Houston near where Bertha Merriman lived. He would turn 16 in Haughton House, the Monroe County Group Home for juveniles in nearby Amory. Whatever happened to make Carolyn now abandon her youngest son had to have transpired during those forgotten four or five months.

Not all the changes in Darrell's young life were so dramatic as his mother walking out on him. If fact, his life during lock up was relatively quiet. It had originally been the angry James down inside Darrell who came out to walk into Child and Adolescent Services. As The Protector, it was his job to keep a confused Darrell safe. It was James who kept Darrell from escaping, not that Darrell had the strength to break his third floor window no matter how hard he tried.

The hospital didn't look like any hospital Darrell had ever seen. Darrell didn't know where he was or why he was there. He thought he was in a hotel lobby until he was escorted upstairs and informed he wouldn't see his family again for the next three months. After that time passed, he was to be allowed visitors. His oldest brother Johnny came with his wife Susan. Carolyn came by to visit her youngest. She brought along R.D.

Darrell wouldn't talk to anyone when he first got there which meant he didn't accumulate the points that the staff required in order to grant privileges such as trips off campus. Breaking this rule cost one therapist his job. During his first week there, a therapist Darrell remembers as being of Native American descent took him outside to the adjacent University of Memphis library. The therapist may have wanted to see if Darrell would attempt to escape. He may have been trying to get the boy to open up. Whatever his reasons, it was the wrong thing to do as the therapist wasn't seen again during the rest of Darrell's seven month stay.

It didn't take long for Darrell to decide the place wasn't so bad. He began to participate, thriving on the structure that had so far been absent from his life. Like many multiples he has a strong attraction to the arts and Child and Adolescent Services offered classes. There were regular therapy sessions. During one of these sessions with a therapist, he watched for the first time as somebody inside pulled him back behind his eyes and took center stage. Darrell still doesn't know who he became.

This was Darrell's first experience with co-consciousness, which according to DID specialist David M. Reiss, M.D. is usually the first step patients must encounter before they can integrate. By definition, this is a dissociated mental state coexisting with a person's consciousness. It is much like watching an actor on a stage with much less control on the outcome of the event. Whether Darrell's therapist witnessed the action is likely buried in the therapist's notes. If these notes still exist, they are in a facility that has changed hands numerous times through the years. According to its current tenants, those notes may or may not be on microfiche that may or may not be in storage.

Darrell did make note of J.D. Like James, J.D. represents Darrell at a certain age, in this case his early teen years. While the more forceful James sees his role as keeping people away from Darrell, J.D. is more affable. It is he who helps Darrell live and operate in the outside world and it was J.D. who walked out of Child and Adolescent Services, back to live with Carolyn in the Pine View Apartments in West Memphis.

What happened during those four or five months in the Pine View Apartments is as difficult for J.D. to remember as they are for any of the family members. At the time, the apartment building catered to low-income tenants and the elderly. Carolyn, Bobbie Lynn and Darrell were the first of the family to move in, taking an apartment in back. They were followed by Johnny and his wife Susan who took the apartment across the hall. Ronnie and Lisa moved in as well, taking an apartment up front.

J.D. knows Bobbie Lynn was living with them at first and Darrell remembers it clearly. When Bobbie Lynn wasn't home, Darrell would watch over her first baby, a daughter she named Christina. He felt a bond with the little girl, though not one that was likely reciprocated. When she turned 18, Christina married a man who took her away from the family and moved her out of state. No one has heard from her since.

Either his mother Carolyn or his probation officer Howard P. Brown must have enrolled Darrell in school because Darrell knows that at least his body went to the facility. He has no memory of a classroom experience, though, so it's likely that one of the people inside attended class on the days when he went. It's also likely that Darrell ditched school entirely, embarrassed by his inability to read and thus to learn. When he was supposed to be in class, the boy would go down Houston's main road to a grove behind the town's WIC office. This was the same office which offered Special Supplemental Nutrition Programs for Women, Infants, and Children including Carolyn, Bobbie Lynn and Bobbie Lynn's infant daughter.

He had discovered an abandoned building. The house was a two story dwelling, though counting the attic would have made it seem taller than that. A thick grove of trees kept the inside of the home dark even during the day time. The old house was peaceful, quiet and virtually invisible from the road.

It wasn't that Darrell was the loner that his family always assumed him to be. The drama inherent in the Williams house made him feel insecure and never particularly loved. There were times when he needed to feel secure in his own person. Darrell only felt peaceful when he was alone.

He never disturbed the ghosts he knew occupied the place, but he explored their home thoroughly. Someone had left in a hurry. A set of dentures waited patiently on a shelf. A set of clothes hung in the closets. There was Victorian-style furniture throughout. No one ever came to ask who disturbed their property. He could as well have lived there forever and sometimes wishes that he had.

The house wasn't far from Howard P. Brown's office in Amory's historic courthouse and that is likely how Darrell or someone inside him noticed it. That someone knew that Howard shared an office with a judge at the Chickasaw County Courthouse, a Classical Revival building erected in 1909 with the designs of architect R. H. Hunt. That someone knew this was the only person in town who would help Darrell.

Darrell would go to the office when he was feeling lonely or when he needed to talk. During one of these drop-in visits, Darrell watched from his probation officer's office on the second floor as a white Chrysler New Yorker drove slowly through the downtown square. At the wheel was Carrol Bevel. Beside him was Darrell's mother Carolyn. Darrell knew no good could come of that.

No one came to Howard's office that day, or at least no one checked it thoroughly enough to find Darrell. Darrell slept under Brown's desk that night. It wasn't until the next morning that Darrell went home.

Seeing Carrol's white New Yorker cruise by, Darrell knew instinctively what was happening. After all, Carrol Bevel had neither family ties nor business anywhere in the state of Mississippi. It was only Carolyn, who he subsequently remarried, who could have brought him to Houston. They drove off once again, leaving 15-year-old Darrell to fend for himself.

When Darrell got back to Pine View, home had left him. The apartment had been stripped to the walls.

Darrell might have anticipated Carolyn's next move. Since before his trial Carolyn had been separated once again from Don Sinclair and it wasn't in Carolyn's makeup to stay single for long. Upon arriving in Houston, Carolyn was no longer the protective mother hen. She seemed never to be in the apartment. It wasn't her children's' place to question where she went or whom she was seeing. Despite their proximity, none of them did: not Johnny, not Ronnie, not Bobbie Lynn and certainly not Darrell.

As it turns out, she was spending quite a bit of time with Bertha Merriman. Since Gene's death, Bertha had stayed in Houston, the next town over from Amory, in order to help into adulthood the children she and Gene had raised together. Carolyn always came alone. The excuses she gave for not bringing Darrell must have been good ones. Bertha hadn't seen Darrell in the flesh since he was eight years old and wouldn't see him again for another 30 years.

Neither James nor J.D. knew where Carolyn escaped to, despite the fact that they had been in control of Darrell's body for most of the time during these difficult months in Mississippi. Traumatic events trigger depersonalization even in people without DID. The book *The Stranger in the Mirror* by Marlene Steinberg M.D. gives a wide range of examples of everyday dissociation. After auto accidents, to note one very common event, some people report feeling as if everything around them moved in slow motion. This happens because in times of trauma, the psyche numbs emotions and puts the body on autopilot as Steinberg notes. Darrell was on autopilot most of the time he lived in Houston. He was splitting constantly, always missing from his own life.

By the day Carolyn and Carrol cleared out the apartment, Bobbie Lynn and her daughter Christina had already moved out. It would be more than a year before anyone in the family knew where Bobbie Lynn and her daughter had gone. The truth was that Bobbie Lynn had taken a job at a strip joint. She didn't want anyone to know out of fear that her aunts and grandmother would try to take her child away. As it turned out, she was right.

Darrell knew there was no sense in staying in the empty apartment, so he went down to the complex's office to ask Pine View's manager for help. The Native American woman was aghast when he told her what had happened. She'd never heard of such a thing as a mother abandoning her child and she told Darrell as much. She repeated her surprise as she tried to phone his brothers. She repeated it as she tried to find his brothers' wives. She repeated it again as she called his probation officer and said as much when Howard P. Brown arrived to pick Darrell up and take him to safety.

Howard P. Brown took Darrell from Houston on the hour's drive to Haughton Place, a big antebellum house a mile out of Amory which functioned as a home for troubled and abandoned teens. Photos show the Mississippi house under renovation and, shortly thereafter, functioning as the comfortable safe haven it was designed to be. Set on nine acres of land donated to the community by Joe and Mary Gertrude Haughton, it reminded Darrell of the abandoned abode he'd discovered back in Houston. Both homes were large, beautiful and peaceful. It was in these settings where Darrell felt most happy and most loved. Just when he was feeling most lost, he found himself at Haughton Place.

The contrast with the places he'd been raised couldn't have been starker. He'd given up on his family by then, or at least he would once he got back to court.

The proceedings were scheduled in the Chickasaw County Courthouse, the same place where Howard P. Brown kept his office and where Darrell had slept the night he saw the white New Yorker.

The first thing Darrell did when he got to the court room was cry. He was on probation. He was scared that he'd committed a violation.

"Why are you crying?" the judge asked him.

"You're going to send me to jail," sobbed the boy.

"On no, son," Darrell was assured. "We're not against you. We're here to help you and to get you help. We want to find the best place for you to be."

In anticipation of the hearing, summonses had been sent to both Carolyn and R.D. The court was not pleased that neither of Darrell's parents had answered the summonses. Darrell quickly explained to the judge that R.D. was illiterate and so would have been unable to read anything sent him. As for Carolyn's failure to show, her son made no excuse.

As is traditional in juvenile cases, the first instinct of the court is to keep a family together. Darrell was asked which of his parents he'd most like to live with.

Darrell didn't have to think long about his answer. "I'd rather be dead before I'd go with either of them, or anybody else in my family," he said.

Howard P. Brown approached quickly and talked to the judge. They made the decision right then and there that Darrell would go back to Haughton Place. He also became an adult that day, emancipated, freed from control by his parents. This legal mechanism also means his parents were freed from any and all responsibility towards Darrell. He was sent back to Haughton Place to live under the guidance of house parents and therapists Warren and Judy Berry because Darrell couldn't live fully on his own until he'd reached the legal age of 18.

The court made one more pronouncement. They issued a warrant for the arrest of Carolyn Bevel. Not only had she abandoned her son, but she had crossed state lines to do it. Carolyn could never again come back to Mississippi without facing arrest. She never again had the chance.

Such is the story that J.D. tells. All Darrell knows is that sometime after the judge pronounced his banishment, he woke to find himself standing in an empty apartment somewhere in Houston, MS.

Which One Am I?

Darrell's 16th Birthday at Haughton Place
(Courtesy Bob Taylor)

Dot
(Photo: James Darrell Williams)

—22—

GERALDINE

Geraldine Myatt was an imposing woman; especially scary to a teen finding he was all alone in a strange place. At least that's how Darrell thought of her when he first met her at Haughton Place. A matronly woman whose weight made her seem older than her years, Geraldine wasn't someone anyone wanted to cross.

The woman couldn't abide a lie. As Darrell would say, if someone lies today, they'll lie again tomorrow. The boys under Geraldine's care knew enough to stick to the truth. There wasn't a boy in the place who wanted to lose Geraldine's trust.

It wasn't that she couldn't smile, but she didn't do it often. The boys in the home saw her as stern. There were plenty of things that made her happy, just not many of them in her private life. She and her husband

C.J. were the relief parents. They took over for house parents and therapists Warren and Judy Berry on weekends and holidays. When they weren't at Haughton Place, the couple was battling financial demons at home. The bills were piling up, with each new addition being the one piece of paper that could bring everything they'd worked for tumbling to the ground. It was the kind of pressure that would make a man want to kill himself.

Geraldine had no stomach for foolishness. Her experience with the teens under her care had made her a hard woman to fool. It would have to be a pretty complicated ruse to get one over on Geraldine.

The boy had tried to reach out. It was Geraldine who had helped him write a letter to his maternal grandmother, Martha Faye Joshlin. All the letter had said was that he was fine and was happy. He also told her where he was. There was never a response, but Grandma Joshlin must have kept that letter. Had he not sent it, there would have been no other way for anyone in the family to know where he was.

Suspicions were raised all around then that holiday season when Darrell's brother Johnny and his wife Susan came rolling up. There had been no phone call, no forewarning. In fact, Darrell hadn't heard from anyone in his family during all the time he'd been living in Amory.

The story Johnny told Darrell and Geraldine was that the family had sent him to come fetch the boy. They were headed over to Houston, about an hour away. That's where their brother Ronnie lived and where the family was convening to celebrate Christmas.

The story struck Darrell as odd. The only family Christmas celebration he could remember was the one Catherine Poole set up for them years back when Carolyn was married to Catherine's son Danny. There had been two husbands and quite a few Christmases since then, all of them seemingly passing without acknowledgement.

The only other holiday of note was the one the year before right there at Haughton Place. It was Geraldine, who Darrell was increasingly seeing as a grandmother figure, who made him happy that year.

Something about Johnny's story didn't seem right to Geraldine either. She grilled him hard. Where were they going? How long would it take them to get there? When were they coming back? She took down the phone numbers for every family member Johnny mentioned.

The car trip across Mississippi wouldn't have taken much more than an hour. That's just about how long Geraldine waited before she started to call around. By the time she reached a very confused Ronnie, Johnny's car was crossing the Tennessee state line heading into Memphis.

The problem with lying is that once started, it is difficult to stop because more lies are needed to cover up the original lie. The problem here was that not every cast member was familiar with the story line. Somebody forgot to tell Ronnie.

Ronnie didn't quite know what to say when Geraldine rang him up asking to speak to Darrell. Nobody else from the family was there, nor were they supposed to be there. Now he had this very angry woman on the other end of the line making threats he had no doubt she would make come true.

Geraldine told him the story as Johnny had laid it out. Now that it had been exposed as the lie it was, Geraldine informed Ronnie that the family had exactly and hour and a half to get Darrell back to Haughton Place. If they failed, she assured him she would alert both the FBI and Federal Police. The family had kidnapped a ward of the government and, to make matters worse had transported him across state lines.

Panicked, Ronnie rang up his brother Johnny at Carolyn's apartment in West Memphis. This is where Carolyn was now living with Carrol Bevel. Darrell recognized the place as soon as they pulled up. The apartment was in the same building and directly downstairs from the one Carolyn and Carrol had occupied when they first got married.

His meeting with his mother was doomed to be a short one. Darrell times it out at about 10 minutes. That was long enough to hit the heart of the matter.

"Why did you leave me?" was the first thing Darrell wanted to know. He knew there was no good answer to the question, but he still wanted to hear an explanation from the one person he thought should have loved him most.

Carolyn, who had been receiving both WIC and welfare during her time in Mississippi, told him that she wasn't happy in Houston. She just didn't feel like she could make it there.

"I still love you," she said.

"No you don't," Darrell shot back. He'd learned a few things about standing up for himself in his time away. As angry as he'd ever been, he wasn't about to let his mother shrug her leaving him off lightly. "If you love me, you wouldn't have abandoned me."

Then the phone call came in from Ronnie. Johnny's face went cold when he heard what his brother had to say. He knew what had to be done, and done quickly. The entire family was going to be arrested if he didn't do something to protect them.

As Johnny hung up the phone, Darrell was assuring Carolyn that he still loved her. "I can't live with you, though," he told her and it wasn't because he didn't want to. He couldn't come back to Arkansas because of the judge's ruling. She couldn't go to Mississippi because the state had issued a warrant for her arrest and Carolyn never did see that state again. The warrant charging her with child abandonment stood for many years.

"I'm sorry," was all she said as Johnny tried to rush Darrell into the car to take him back to Haughton Place. "I hope I'll see you again."

In the few surviving photos taken of Darrell with the Williams family as he was growing up, he isn't there. His eyes focus on something out of range, something outside the frame, something no one else can see. Frozen in this particular moment with this particular group of people, he seems uncomfortable. Over and over again, someone snaps his picture at exactly the instant he has made up his mind to flee.

Darrell's only true smiles are in the pictures Bob Taylor saved. The former director of Haughton Place, Bob was there even before the beginning of Darrell's stay. Gone blue with age, most of the pictures show the big house under renovation, getting ready for its young charges. Volunteers bring life to the home, making it comfortable for the boys who will live there.

It would be quite a long time before Carolyn would see Darrell again. That was fine with Darrell. As far as he could tell, Haughton Place was his home. Geraldine Myatt made him feel loved and protected. The people inside stayed in their rooms.

-- 23 --

HOWARD

Darrell was one of the first residents at Haughton Place. In the same role of film Bob Taylor kept through the years, there is a decorated tree, Santa Claus and paper cups with snow men. It's the kind of fanfare rare in the Williams' home. There's Darrell, front and center. He smiles directly at the person taking the picture. He's happy because the celebration doubled as a party to mark his 16th birthday just a few weeks away. He's happy because he finally feels like he has a family in Howard P. Brown, Geraldine Myatt, Bob Taylor and the rest of the boys who called Haughton Place home. The Williams clan had yet to be told where he was.

It became Haughton Place tradition for each of the staff to draw the name of one of the boys. This first year, Bob Taylor and his wife were responsible for Darrell's gifts.

They asked Darrell what he wanted for Christmas. Darrell told them he'd like a digital watch which was in the early Eighties all the rage. He also requested a pair of Nikes. That brand of sports shoes was new to the market back then and was judged to be fairly expensive. The Taylors had asked him what he wanted, not what he expected to receive.

He was surprised and excited to see both his requests when he opened his presents. This world where people celebrated his birthday and gave him what he asked for was as far from his family as he'd ever been. He couldn't have been happier.

This timeline had an end point. By its charter, Haughton Place could only keep boys until they turned age 18 and became legal adults. For now, Darrell was enjoying the moment.

While living in Amory, Darrell would be under the Haughton Place rules. He enjoyed being one of the two boys assigned to wake up early in order to prepare breakfast for the house. He didn't mind being chosen to clean the bathrooms, or dust the house. Those who completed their chores were allowed to go to town on the weekends. They would generally visit Amory's skating rink or go to the movies. P.C. and Geraldine Myatt let the boys do anything they wanted as long as they stayed out of trouble and were home before dusk.

In addition to their housework, sometimes the boys would do odd jobs. The cemetery next door which Bob Taylor's family owned would hire the boys to help with grave digging. When the townspeople needed help, Darrell and the rest would help them with their gardening. They were always paid for this extra labor, allowing them to earn spending money. No matter what was needed, Darrell always looked forward to work days. The idea of having something to wake up for appealed to him.

Though Haughton Place was technically a Monroe County facility, most of its funding came directly from the community. Howard P. Brown sat on the facility's board of directors. He was as instrumental in its fundraising as he had been in directing Haughton Place's construction.

All Darrell knew was that Howard P. Brown was his probation officer, the man he had to report to. When they met, Howard was recently divorced, the father of a five-year-old daughter. Howard must have been older than Darrell acknowledged because he began preparing for his retirement from the probation office soon after Darrell met him. Howard began the process by closing out every file except Darrell's and that one he closed soon after. In fact, Darrell's file closed long before the end of his five-year probation. As Darrell's probation officer, it was Howard's call whether or not to do so.

After closing his active records, Howard P. Brown kept in contact with Darrell. He was the only one of Howard's court-appointed wards with whom the older man maintained a relationship. This made Darrell feel more like an adopted son than a ward of the court.

Howard may have taken an early retirement to allow himself to follow his dream. Howard went to Nashville after he closed out all those files. He wanted to be a country singer, but throat cancer put an end to that. Shortly after his cancer diagnosis, he returned to Amory to write songs and raise Irish Setters. The last time Darrell saw Howard, the man had promised him he could have one of the dogs just as soon as Darrell found a stable place to stay. That never did happen.

Howard did his best to help Darrell get settled. After the teen's emancipation, Howard placed Darrell up for adoption. There was an older couple who wanted Darrell, but his first full weekend with them at their pig farm outside Starkville put an end to that plan. Attempting to drive the man's tractor through what Darrell thought was a puddle; the teenager upended the machine. That wasn't the reason the couple gave for ending the adoption proceedings. The woman told Howard that her husband was jealous of the attention she'd been giving the younger man. "My husband is a bigger child than any kid," was all she said in parting.

Everyone hoped that the second attempt would stick. From what Don McCracken told Howard P. Brown, there was no reason to believe it wouldn't. Sure he was single, but his background in the clergy left him with a calling to help the less fortunate. No longer working for the church, he'd found a place for himself in education. Don McCracken held a decent job working in the admissions office of the University of Memphis about an hour south of Amory in the town of Starkville.

During the two months Darrell lived with Don McCracken, it seemed at first like this adoption was going to work out. When his potential adoptive father worked, McCracken would bring Darrell along to the University. Still illiterate, Darrell nevertheless enjoyed sitting in on the lectures. He liked listening. He loved learning. He found out he could figure out how to do just about anything simply by watching what others did and then trying to replicate the results. During this time, Darrell felt his world was expanding, both inside and out. Darrell had no complaints to make when Howard P. Brown came to check up on him except that he needed Howard to leave him a pack of cigarettes.

Living conditions Don McCracken provided for Darrell were cramped by any measure. The apartment's main room served as both the living room and kitchen. The bedroom was separate, but really the place was no bigger than what would be considered a studio or bachelor apartment rather than a traditional one bedroom. That didn't bother Darrell much. The living arrangement with Don wasn't all that different than how things had been when he lived with his mother, except at first he slept in Don's king sized bed instead of on the couch.

In all the wrong ways, Don McCracken began to remind him of Don Sinclair. At first, he didn't think anything of sharing a bed since that one was all there was. It was when McCracken began to get too friendly in ways Darrell didn't like that he moved to the couch. His would-be father tried to talk him back. He said men and boys did these kinds of things with each other all the time.

When Howard came to check up on him the next month, Darrell asked him again to leave his cigarettes. Smoking was a habit Darrell had picked up at age 9 when his older siblings would bribe him with cigarettes as treats when one or another of them had done something they didn't want their parents to discover. Still, something seemed a little off to Howard P. Brown. "What did you do with all your money?" he asked Darrell.

"What money?" Darrell responded. Howard had signed Darrell up with the Department of Social Services. He should have been receiving Welfare checks at McCracken's address. The checks were being sent, but Darrell never received a cent.

If there was one thing Darrell learned from Howard P. Brown, it was to stand up for himself. If there was one thing he learned from Geraldine Myatt, it was to always tell the truth. That's what he did. He never did hear what Howard said to Don after Darrell told him what Don had been doing, but he could tell from McCracken's face that it was far from a pleasant conversation.

"You shouldn't have touched me," was the last thing Darrell said to Don McCracken.

Darrell was already 17 and would soon be too old to live at Haughton Place. There was a vocational school 300 miles away in Gulfport. Bob Taylor, who was also one of Howard's partners in Haughton Place, had made the initial contact. The men were looking for the best way to get vocational training for Darrell as the young man had settled on a desire for a photography career. Bob had no reason to doubt the facility's promise that the boy would be trained as promised. But when the bus finally arrived in Gulfport after its long trek through the state, Darrell was told the school offered no photography classes at all. He only stayed overnight. After the first class, Darrell and two other boys, both of whom felt they had also been lied to, walked away.

By the time he arrived back in Amory, all the wind had been knocked out of him. "Just send me home," he begged Howard.

"But you don't have a home," said Howard P. Brown.

"Just send me back," an angry and frustrated Darrell snapped, and Howard knew what he meant. Though the boy was scared to return to Arkansas in violation of the judge's lifetime banishment, both he and Howard had run out of options. Within days, Darrell was on a plane taking off from tiny Starkville airport on the half hour flight to Memphis. His brother Johnny was waiting for him at Memphis International. Johnny drove Darrell straight to their mother's place.

Her brief second marriage to Carrol Bevel was over. Carolyn was living alone in a mobile home not far from her parents' place in Palestine. The mobile home park just off the 40 Freeway was nice enough back then, but Darrell wouldn't stay there for long.

Carolyn was single as far as Darrell could tell during the brief moments he saw her but he also knew she was making plans. He knew she was chasing some man who drove an ambulance. He knew she was still seeing Carrol Bevel. He didn't know about Don Sinclair.

Darrell never did get to accept Howard P. Brown's gift of the Irish Setter. After he returned to Arkansas, Howard went on to get his Ph.D., continuing to work as a professional counselor and going on to work as assistant professor of behavioral studies at the University of Missouri at St. Louis until his death in October 1995.

Darrell wishes he'd had a chance to thank him for helping him grow up. Darrell wishes he'd had a chance to tell Howard P. Brown that he was right.

-- 24 --

ROBBIE

It is Mary Barnick who notices him first. "Someone's here with the most beautiful brown eyes," she says. "Who are you?"

He doesn't answer. Ten year olds can be quiet like that and of the two inside Darrell, only Dot is gregarious. The little boy just sits there enjoying the music. All the while he beams the angelic smile that will soon become one of his most identifiable features.

It's music that Robbie likes. We are here visiting Bo Kirgis and Mary Barnick and have been for the better part of a week. After dinner each night we retire to Bo's recording studio, trading songs, trading licks and enjoying the company and the music.

Somewhere inside, Mary Rose is listening to. She is a recent addition to the interior family, a 12-year-old who we discover loves to sing. Unlike Billy and Jimmie who represent Darrell as he once was, both she and Robbie represent Darrell as he wanted to be.

The only one not holding a musical instrument is Darrell. Had he been raised by Monkey as part of the Jackson clan, he most likely would have learned to sing as many members of the Jackson family do. However, for the Williams family, music was never a big part of their lives. There was never a musical instrument around, or at least never one that Darrell was allowed to touch. He was never taught to play a lick. Somehow though Robbie knows.

Mary Barnick watches those beautiful brown eyes as they focus on her fingers and those of her husband Bo Kirgis on their respective fret boards. Robbie is watching their every move, anticipating what comes next. Mary says she thinks he probably already knows how to work an instrument. It seems that Robbie has been watching people play, silent but attentive, for a very long time.

Robbie would have made himself known earlier, but he wasn't sure that his choice of name would be okay with the rest of the family. He's named himself after the late Robert Dann and Robbie doesn't want anyone to be upset. Its okay, we tell him. He can call himself anything he wants.

Robbie would have been recognized sooner had the lights been up in the Mirage Coffee House back home in Long Beach. Someone might have seen Darrell's hazel eyes getting darker and changing color. Someone might have seen Robbie start to smile.

There is always that smile of his when our friend Michelle Mangione is on stage. Darrell likes her music too. He feels as though she's singing about his life. He likes that she sings about trust, honor and forgiveness; about doing the right thing even when it hurts. A favorite song is Michelle's "America the Blue." Michelle wrote it after meeting a homeless Vietnam veteran on Venice Beach, though really it could have had its genesis anywhere. "Do you believe in what you say? Is it the same as what you do?" she asks in the opening verse. "Better hold on to yourself and hold on tight." The song isn't about Darrell, but it could about anybody. It's the chorus's opening plea that brings the tears: "Take me back to where I belong."

Darrell's kids like to go see Michelle because she hands out small percussion instruments and they "get to play in Michelle's band" as they like to call the experience. That's how Dot came to break Darrell's favorite ring. Dot was a little rambunctious that evening. Using the table as a drum, he banged down on it just a little too hard. As far as the little ones know, they still have the bodies of kids their own ages. At 45, Darrell is a little older and a little stronger. Sometimes the kids forget that.

All the kids love music but it is Robbie who wants to play. It becomes evident during his first lesson that Robbie knows quite a bit about the violin. What finer points he doesn't already know have to be demonstrated only once. He picks music right up just as Mary foretold.

The only recurring problem is in holding the bow. Since Robbie sees his body as that of a 10-year-old, he has trouble convincing the arthritis in Darrell's middle-aged fingers to do what he wants. This is an internal struggle the two will have to work out between them. This is a conflict no one feels is fair to foist upon the young lady who is just being paid to teach Robbie to play the violin.

The hardest part was finding a teacher for Robbie in the first place. In any new situation, Darrell's psychiatrist insists that people be told about his DID up front. Like disclosing his sexuality, this serves two purposes. The first is to let those who don't feel up to working with someone with this rather unusual condition bow out gracefully as did the first potential violin teacher. If someone is going to have a problem, it is best not to get too attached.

The other purpose is to let the person know to be ready for whatever may happen. Billy is usually curious about any new situation so the 2-year-old can be expected to pop out. Had Robbie felt frustrated or had his teacher been too tough, the older boys, J.D. and James, were ready to defend him.

By borrowing energy from some of the others and from Darrell himself, Robbie is able to sustain the entire half hour. He decides he'd really like to try to teach himself. That's fine with everyone else, especially when it is discovered that, despite being forewarned, her employers have not told the girl about Darrell's DID. No one feels it fair to put her into a bargain she didn't make willingly.

Many DID patients exhibit artistic tendencies. Until her death in 1998, *Sybil* subject Shirley Ardell Mason lived quietly in Lexington, Kentucky for more than 20 years, painting and running an arts business out of her home. At least 50 finished paintings were found on display in her Kentucky home, all sold later at auction after her death. Those signed by Mason were said to notably differ in style from those signed by her interior personalities.

These paintings were valued more for their signature than for their contribution to the art world. The psychological community was still split on DID's validity. Few studies have explored the correlation between art and mental illness. None have centered on DID. Not one is recognized as definitive of the existence of even a mildly tortured artist.

Skeptics criticize most of existing studies because of low test samples, usually under 40-50 test subjects. Another argument is that interviewers may have biased their subjects. It is also possible that the artists misrepresented themselves and their mental states.

The closest a study has come to quieting disbelievers was the one by Arnold M. Ludwig, published in 1995, in a book called *The Price of Greatness: Resolving the Creativity and Madness Controversy*. Ludwig studied the lives of 1,004 artists by reading 2,200 biographies.

Ludwig found that, as teen-agers, between 29% and 34% of future artists and musicians suffered from symptoms of mental illness. Only 3% to 9% of future scientists, athletes and businesspeople suffered similar symptoms. As adults, between 59% and 77% of artists, writers and musicians suffered mental illness, while only 18% to 29% of the other professionals did. The artistic achievements of about 16% of the artists studied improved during times of mental upset.

What causes such results is unclear. Mood disorders may allow people to think more creatively. It may also be that mood disorders bring a range of deep emotions and these symptoms together might lead to artistic creativity. Because they tend to be less able to filter out interference, some have said that those with mood disorders are simply drawn to solitary pursuits.

Interestingly, a 2005 paper by Dr. Alice Flaherty of Harvard Medical School makes the point that creative thinking, like manic depression, schizophrenia and DID, also involves unusual frontal lobe activity. Her paper makes the point that the traits of creativity are similar to some of the side-effects of mental illness. It also notes that the neurological brain states are the same.

The Flaherty study also indicated that unusual activity in the frontal lobe, and in particular the prefrontal cortex, may cause a person to draw unusual connections between seemingly unrelated items or ideas. Some cultures call this insanity. Others call it genius.

There's a fine line of demarcation. Call it Ego. As defined by Sigmund Freud, the ego separates out what is real. Many with mood disorders struggle to fit in and to find a way to be part of society's reality. Some artists have no such struggle. They maintain it is everyone else who is out of step. These are artists ahead of their time such as Vincent van Gogh or Johann Sebastian Bach, two artists whose works are valued far more today than they were during their creator's lifetimes.

It isn't Robbie's goal to be a violin virtuoso. It isn't even his goal to be good enough to join Michelle Mangione on stage someday. He'd have to be a lot more mature than he is to get over stage fright. For the moment, he's perfectly content to grab a box of Red Hots and use it as a maraca to play along when Michelle sings. He also likes to whistle along over the music at the end of Michelle's song "I Know What It Feels." Robbie feels very proud that Michelle said once from the stage that she wished she had thought of whistling when she was recording the song.

All Robbie wants to do is to know enough so that he can sit on the back porch or in the studio back there in Arkansas and play violin along with his Aunt Mary and Uncle Bo. He looks forward to evenings when Bo can show him all he knows about the instrument. He might even want to learn the guitar as well. Mary has one that she's holding for him, as eager to see him and the rest of the kids as they are to see her and Bo.

Until then, they listen attentively to a CD Bo and Mary recorded under the name Jubal and made sure to pack with us before our return home to California. What Darrell likes best is how Bo and Mary's music reminds him of himself as a kid. Every chance he'd get, he'd sit on the swing out in the yard and, at the top of his voice, sing songs for God. He never cared if anyone heard him. Darrell always knew that God did.

The kids inside really like the beautiful mesh of concertina and guitar in the version Bo and Mary play for us. When she sings, Mary's voice tells of the wonders of nature, of God and family and of fables the kids wish were theirs. The music speaks of acceptance and of peace. This is music that is universal. This is what makes it most personal. Every last one of the kids inside knows that each song is for them.

"Take me back to where I belong," sings Michelle Mangione as the kids try to keep up with their boxes of Red Hots and rice-filled plastic Easter eggs. Until meeting Bo and Mary, no one knew where that was.

--25--

BIANCHI

The unusual acquittal of controversial DID patient Billy Milligan might have opened the flood gates. That he was guilty, or that someone inside of him was, added another layer of responsibility to courts nationwide. It wasn't enough to deduce whether an accused individual was guilty. The question would now be which of the people inside the accused was guilty. If the finger could be pointed at any one as the culprit, the next question would be how then to fairly punish a host who might have been unaware of those actions? The topper, of course, was that there was still controversy in the psychiatric community as to whether DID existed at all.

The first test came soon enough. On October 22, 1979, Kevin Bianchi was arrested in Washington State for raping and murdering two university students. The night before he was to be interviewed by a psychiatrist in order to determine mental competency to stand trial, Bianchi was watching television. The movie being aired happened to be the award-winning Sally Field version of *Sybil*.

Bianchi knew that there would be multiple opportunities to stall the court proceedings if he claimed to be unaware of the acts. A claim of DID would also allow him to possibly circumvent Washington's death penalty. There is no indication he had heard of the landmark Billy Milligan case, but he knew that, if deemed legally insane, he would most likely be sentenced to a mental hospital rather than being put to death.

The next day, Bianchi announced to his lawyer, Dean Brett, that there were large gaps in his memory. The attorney brought in Dr. John Watkins, a memory expert, to interview his client. In the video of the session, a hypnotized Kevin Bianchi introduced himself as Steve Walker. This "evil personality" admitted to the Bellingham murders. He also admitted to a then-unsolved series of murders in the Los Angeles suburb of Glendale that the press had dubbed the Hillside Strangler murders. In a coup de grace, Steve implicated Bianchi's cousin, Glendale auto upholster Anthony Buono as an accomplice in the California crimes. Eventually both Bianchi and Buono would be found guilty of the 10 murders that terrified Southern California over those two months in 1977.

It was Detective Frank Salerno rather than the doctor who sounded the first alarm that something was amiss. Bianchi's performance had not convinced Salerno of the existence of other personalities. The detective noticed that Steve referred to himself as "he" instead of "I." Watkins, however, remained convinced of the diagnosis. So too was the second expert called to examine Bianchi, Dr. Ralph Allison, who reportedly appeared afraid of Steve. It took a third psychologist, Dr. Martin Orne, to determine Bianchi was a fake. He informed Bianchi that most multiples have more than two personas. Bianchi dutifully brought forth a third, Billy, and two more to boot.

The people inside do not appear on cue, particularly around people whom they neither know nor trust. Bianchi also pretended to touch someone who was not there. For Orne, this was the giveaway since hallucinating is not a symptom of DID. Under pressure, Bianchi admitted the lie.

The reactions of the three professionals mirrors how DID was seen in the late Seventies. It also reflects how DID is seen today: Some understand, some are afraid and some don't believe it at all: Acceptance, fear, denial.

It was a time of strange confluence. The original filmed adaptation of *Sybil* starring Sally Field had only come to television the year before it had found its way to Bianchi's prison TV screen. Billy Milligan's groundbreaking acquittal had been the year before that. This was the year that what was formerly called Multiple Personality Disorder (MPD) and had been treated as a hysterical dissociative condition with no coded diagnosis, was added to the American Psychiatric Association's *Diagnostic and Statistical Manual of Mental Disorders, 3rd Edition*. It would officially become Dissociative Identity Disorder (DID) in the 4th Edition published in 1994.

Following the pattern set by Sybil's psychiatrist Dr. Cornelia Wilbur, new cases were being discovered, if not treated, through hypnotherapy. Many of these cases were tied to a new hysteria sweeping the nation: Repressed Memory Syndrome (RMS). Though not included in *DSM-IV* nor used by mainstream psychotherapists, recovered memory therapy (RMT) became quite popular in the early Eighties. Like DID, it looks to childhood abuse to find the causes of psychological trauma. Echoing Wilbur's methodology, RMT practitioners make use of hypnotherapy.

Dissociative Identity Disorder had entered the mainstream, yet its notoriety threatened its downfall. Anyone who doubted the veracity of Billy Milligan's acquittal or failed to see hypnotherapy as anything but a parlor trick had their opinions validated by Kevin Bianchi. That the professionals offered three clashing opinions as to his claimed DID failed to sooth suspicions. The public remained as confused by the difference between DID and RMS as they had traditionally been by that between DID and schizophrenia.

The use of hypnosis only deepened the public's confusion. It was already known professionally that hypnosis and DID were a bad mix. While many hypnotherapists today report encountering patients with DID, this is usually a discovery made during treatment for more common afflictions such as substance addiction or smoking.

Unlike the two opposing views held by the public, hypnosis is neither a magical truth serum nor a parlor game sleight of hand. Hypnosis is a willful act. Like quitting an addition, the subject has to want it to receive it. Another truth is that it is entirely possible to tell lies under hypnosis. In such a trance state, the altered state of consciousness will reveal emotional truth, but not literal truth. Testimony gathered in this way is not admissible in court.

Yet some psychiatrists continue to follow procedures set by Dr. Cornelia Wilbur's work with Sybil. Wilbur's technique is known as abreaction, which is to intentionally induce flashbacks via hypnosis or drugs. It is interesting to note that, before Wilbur used it, abreaction had already been dropped by The United States Navy at the end of World War Two as they found it made post traumatic stress victims worse, with no observable benefits.

With or without abreaction, the standard treatment for DID necessarily involved memory recovery. By 1983, accusations leading to the McMartin Preschool trial would thrust the treatment of DID and particularly memory recovery onto an entirely new level of controversy.

The death of memory recovery as an accepted form of treatment was caused by the theory's most infamous application. Members of the McMartin family, who operated a California preschool, were charged with numerous acts of sexual abuse of children in their care. The first accusations were made by Judy Johnson, one of the children's mothers. She told police that her son had been sodomized by both her estranged husband and by McMartin teacher Ray Buckey. Ray Buckey was the grandson of school founder Virginia McMartin and son of administrator Peggy McMartin Buckey. Further accusations claimed that people at the daycare had sexual encounters with animals and that "Ray flew in the air."

Local police sent an unusually specific and alarming letter to some 200 parents of children at the daycare center. Several hundred children were then interviewed by Children's Institute International, an abuse therapy clinic in Los Angeles. The interviewing techniques were highly suggestive. Children were invited to pretend or speculate about supposed events. Day care sex abuse hysteria began to sweep the country, adding to a general panic about satanic ritual abuse that, fueled by unquestioning media coverage, would continue until the early 1990s.

Dr. Michael Maloney, a British clinical psychologist and professor of psychiatry, reviewed the tapes of the children's testimonies as an expert witness. He referred to the interview techniques as improper and coercive, finding that "many of the kids' statements in the interviews were generated by the examiner."

During these years of magical thinking, DID was still considered as a common and very serious psychological disorder by many psychiatrists, psychologists, and other mental health specialists. In 1984, Thigpen and Cleckley reported that in the 25 years since their case was reported, they had hundreds of patients sent to them by therapists or self-diagnosed. Of these, they found only one case other than Eve who they thought "to be undeniably a genuine multiple personality."

As recovered memory therapy fell into disrepute, so did the number of DID cases reported fall. This was not because people disbelieved the diagnosis. Health insurance and malpractice insurance companies began to balk at the costs involved in DID therapy. As Cameron West, Ph.D. reports in his memoir *First Person Plural*, his insurance company "didn't understand why a person with DID would need special psychiatric care."

Some skeptics attacked the therapy because most patients' mental health degenerated during treatment but improved after therapy. Neither did basic research into human memory reveal any mechanism for repressions and recovery of traumatic memories during childhood. These issues, plus the fact that there were no confirmed cases of Satanic Ritual Abuse (SRA) confirmed despite a decade of searching, made much of the public skeptical of the psychiatric community as a whole.

Some studies state the rate of Dissociative Identity Disorder cases in the United States today at .01% to 1% of the general population. Other studies indicate that dissociation occurs in approximately 2-3 percent of the general population. Still others have estimated a prevalence rate of 10% for all dissociative disorders in the general population, as George Lowenstein wrote in his 1994 paper, "The Psychology of curiosity: A review and reinterpretation" for the *Psychological Bulletin*. By contrast, according to the World Health Organization's mental health publications, schizophrenia affects .5 to 1% of the population worldwide.

The numbers may not tell the entire story due to the nature of the physical, mental and sexual abuse that are widely recognized as the triggers leading to dissociation. The Diagnostic and Statistical Manual of Mental Disorders, Fourth Edition, Text Revision (*DSM-IV-TR*) recognizes four main categories of dissociative disorders used by mental health professionals in North America: Dissociative Amnesia, Dissociative Fugue, Dissociative Identity Disorder, and Depersonalization Disorder. Each has a different rate of occurrence.

Also causing confusion in the calculations of numbers of DID cases is the strong prejudice, especially in the United States, against reporting the childhood sexual abuse that is widely recognized as one of the chief indicators of DID. Males who have suffered sexual abuse are particularly loath to report it. Taking this bias into account, some experts say that 7% percent of the population may have undiagnosed dissociative disorder.

Despite that it could neither be satisfactorily proven nor unproven in the eyes of the public nor of the legal profession, DID never did catch on as a defense tactic. In the years since Billy Milligan was acquitted of his crimes, criminal defenses based on DID have remained relatively rare.

Part Four

Palestine

Palestine is a city in St. Francis County, Arkansas, United States, along the L'Anguille River. According to the United States Census Bureau, the city has a total area of 3.2 square miles, of which, 3.16 square miles of it is land and 0.04 square miles of it is water. The population was 741 at the 2000 census. — From Wikipedia

Which One Am I?

-- 26 --

BOBBIE LYNN

      The farming community of Palestine, AR, barely 20 miles from Brinkley, was in as much of a heyday as it ever would be on Darrell's return. Like most of the surrounding communities, Palestine's barely 800 souls make their living from the fields of rice, soybeans and corn surrounding the tiny town.

      The biggest business in town at the time Darrell lived there with his mother was the truck stop run by the Union 76 company. It was pretty much the only business in town after it drove the smaller independent gas stations out of business. The truck stop was a full service establishment, with a diner attached. Darrell would help out doing odd jobs when he wasn't doing anything else. He would clear tables, fill in for a sick waitress or help clean the place after closing time. There was no money involved. Darrell took his pay in free coffee and tea.

The truck stop long ago moved to Forrest City, which locals pronounce as "Far City." The town is only 10 miles east on State Highway 70. It was its population of almost 20 times that of Palestine that made the move attractive to Union 76. The gas pumps in Palestine are gone now, the building torn down. The business operating out of the trailer that replaced the building sells tires, something readily evident by the piles of used rubber that have replaced the grove once sheltering the truck stop. Only the diner still stands. For the last few years it has been reopened and renamed Heads Café.

Now about 16, Darrell was spending as much time as he could with the people who populated the truck stop because there was never anybody at home. He was technically living with his mother Carolyn in the mobile home park just across Main St. Carolyn was living in the first trailer to the right, taking care of the residents of some 50 trailers that were there at the time. She was also in charge of renting out empty spaces to the travel trailers coming down Route 70. The management position must have kept Carolyn very busy because for the six months Darrell was with her, he only saw her three times counting the day he showed up on her doorstep.

His homecoming was at first uneventful. Palestine was familiar enough, since Darrell had lived with his maternal grandparents, Dick and Martha Faye Joshlin when he was very young. There was also that portrait; the one Carolyn had posed for the morning of her automobile accident. She had promised the portrait to Darrell, but now it hung on the trailer wall.

For her part, Caroline acted like Darrell had never been gone. She certainly didn't let the boy put a dent in her schedule. Carolyn would be gone most all day, as she always had been, returning at night to rent out spaces to weary travelers who pulled off the highway. His long absence hadn't made Carolyn any fonder of her youngest.

Carolyn tried to kill Darrell one night when they were in the trailer with Carolyn's mother Martha Faye. They'd gotten into an argument, as mothers and sons sometimes do. They both held such simmering resentments against one another that the argument in the mobile home turned into a cage fight.

"You're nothing but a fake mother," the 17-year-old accused Carolyn. "I wish I'd never come back."

"I wish you'd never been born," his mother spate back. "I hate you. You've ruined my life." With that she turned to the small kitchen and grabbed the biggest knife she could get her hands on.

Darrell ran to his room, but since it had no door to slam, in his furry he began to destroy everything he could find. He was tearing things, throwing things and that's when his grandmother Martha Faye Joshlin decided she had had enough.

In Martha Faye's hand was the pearl-handled derringer she always carried in her bra. This wasn't the first time Darrell had seen the gun. His grandmother had pointed it right in the face of his grandfather Dick Joshlin once when her husband was drunk. Dick had been out of control, as he sometimes got when he was drinking, and had grabbed Darrell's sister Bobbie Lynn hard by the hair. Martha Faye wasn't going to see her husband harm her granddaughter. She warned him, "I'll kill you, you son of a bitch, if you even think of hurting that little girl." Dick knew she meant it, too. Martha Faye had done the same thing to her son Larry Coleman when he got drunk and, in Martha Faye's opinion, out of control. Now, Carolyn's mother was pointing the derringer right at her own daughter.

"I'm sorry Carolyn," Martha Faye said, "but I can't let you kill this boy."

Darrell ran for it. He found safety under a freeway underpass. That's where he stayed for the day.

The next time the two saw each other, Darrell was sitting inside the diner. He was having his usual coffee as his mother walked in with Carrol Bevel and his son Chris in tow. She might have asked how Darrell was. She might have asked if he needed anything. There was nothing but silence.

Darrell was really regretting his return to Arkansas. There would have been another year he could have stayed in the welcoming environs of Haughton Place. He was coming to understand that, if he were to make his way in life, it would not be with his mother's help or her support. Carolyn was collecting Welfare money on him, as Don McCracken had back in Amory. As with that failed adoption, Darrell never once saw a dime of it.

For all its bucolic charm, tiny Palestine offered little to a youth on the edge of manhood. Darrell headed over to the highway, stuck out his thumb and hitched a ride the 54 miles to Memphis.

The biggest city in Tennessee offered opportunity. It also offered a degree of perceived safety. Memphis was where Darrell's sister Bobbie Lynn was living with her second husband, Ronnie Bowlon.

Bobbie Lynn and Ronnie had met at Babe's, an adult club near Memphis International Airport. Bobbie Lynn was working there. Ronnie was a bouncer. Babe's owners were known for having run-ins with the law. During the time frame when Bobbie Lynn and Ronnie had worked there, the club had been temporarily closed while its owner faced charges of unlawful drug sales and prostitution. In the Eighties such charges no more effected the club than would a speed bump on the five miles between them and Memphis International. Operations might slow down a bit but the charges weren't going to stop anybody. It would take another 30 years and a flurry of identical charges for authorities in Memphis to close the club for good.

The Bowlons were working to support Bobbie Lynn's eldest daughter Christina and Candace, the girl they had together. Bobbie Lynn never did marry Christina's father who, at any rate, never believed Bobbie Lynn when she told him the girl was his. To his credit, Ronnie Bowlon stepped up to the plate, giving Christina his last name and raising her alongside Candace, the daughter the two had together.

Darrell saw as little of Bobbie Lynn and Ronnie in Memphis as he had of Carolyn back in Palestine. When they were home from the club, they would close the door to their room and stay there. Beside the two girls, the Bowlons were also supporting a hefty drug and alcohol addiction.

He'd never had any experience with either drugs or alcohol himself, so when Bobbie Lynn and Ronnie took Darrell to one of their friend's house and offered him his first marijuana cigarette, he accepted. This was his sister and her husband. They were family. They would never do anything to hurt him.

They didn't tell him the joint was laced with PCP and Darrell wouldn't have known what that was even had they told him. More commonly known at the time as angel dust, PCP is a dissociative drug originally used as an anesthetic according to Richard Rudley in *The Encyclopedia of Psychoactive Substances*. This category of drug reduces and potentially blocks signals to the conscious mind from other parts of the brain. It induces hallucinogenic effects and typically blocks access to one's senses; certainly not the recreational drug of choice for someone with DID.

In Darrell's case, the drug made him feel as if he was about to burst into flames. Tearing off his shirt, he apparently flung himself outside because as he awoke the next morning he found himself shirtless, lost and alone, partially buried in a snow bank. Bobbie Lynn had gone home without him and he was alone among strangers. He felt confused and abandoned. This was the first and last time Darrell ever smoked marijuana of any type.

His time in Memphis wasn't all bad. With almost a million inhabitants, Memphis offered choices. With so much time on his hands and no one to watch over him, Darrell began to explore. Encountering the city's well-established gay subculture, Darrell began to do as he'd been taught back in Haughton Place. He learned to stand up for himself. He resolved to always tell the truth. He vowed to make himself the opposite of everything he'd seen in his family.

Yet it was family he craved. In the most heated moments of their last time together, he'd never denied loving his mother. Over the years since, Darrell has amassed quite a collection of mother and child figurines. In these pieces, a loving mother gazes down upon the happy child in her arms. These belong to Billy. This is how he wants to remember his mother. These are little souvenirs. Some represent who Billy is and others who what he wants to be. They are all small reminders of a childhood that never was.

Darrell never could stay away from Carolyn entirely. Sometimes he would return to Palestine, though it always seemed that his mother was somewhere else. They would only have one more conversation in life. That was when he asked to be driven to Brinkley, where Danny Poole owned a heating and air conditioning company.

As she often did, Martha Faye Joshlin came along on that trip, though whether it was to serve as company or referee between her feuding daughter and grandson is impossible to say. With Carolyn at the wheel and Martha Faye up front in the passenger seat, Darrell sat in back where he could see Carolyn occasionally glancing back at him in the car's rear view mirror. It seemed to Darrell that Carolyn was looking back at him quite often.

"Mom," Carolyn asked her mother, "do you have our burial plots paid up by now?"

"Yes, of course," Martha Faye answered. "But why do you want to know?"

Up in the driver's seat, Carolyn locked eyes with the young man riding in the back seat behind her. "I just thought I'd ask."

Which One Am I?

When Carolyn looked him dead in the eyes, Darrell knew exactly why she was asking. He overheard her telling Martha Faye about a life insurance policy she had taken out that was to pay $50,000 to each of her children upon her death. Darrell couldn't have known it at the time, but this one-sided conversation would be the last he'd ever have with his mother.

Arriving at Danny Poole's place, Carolyn's second husband was visibly surprised to see them. He recognized Carolyn and her mother, of course, but not the tall, skinny kid who climbed out of the back seat.

All Darrell wanted was to take a walk with the man he still thought was his father. Danny's mother had loved him; that he knew. She had shown him as much, giving him the only family birthday party he could remember until Robert Dann threw a surprise party with all his friends when Darrell turned 30. Catherine Poole had also given him his only Christmas as a child.

Darrell had come to Danny for acceptance, love and a sense of family. Darrell was looking for a saint, but that wasn't going to be a word he would be able to use when describing Danny Poole.

Once he was told who Darrell was, Danny knew exactly why Darrell was there. His admission, "you know I'm not your father," came unbidden yet not entirely unexpected. The disappointment hit Darrell deeply. He always thought that, if anyone cared, it would be Danny. This was the last conversation Darrell would have with Danny Poole for three decades.

Upon their arrival back in Palestine, Darrell and Carolyn did their best to avoid each other. Darrell still spent as much time as he could in Memphis with Bobbie Lynn and Ronnie, yet he'd always invariably return to Carolyn's trailer. He wasn't getting much attention at either locale, at least not the kind of attention he craved.

This was the kind of life he was used to. Carolyn had never been around much as he was growing up and he didn't expect her to be around now. There were always the people inside to keep him company, though they hadn't yet learned how to fully protect him.

Knowing already that Carolyn was not the kind of woman who could live by herself for long, Darrell might have anticipated her next move. Still, it was a surprise to him when Carolyn reconciled, one last time, with Don Sinclair.

There was only one more week after this surprise that Darrell would live in Palestine. Don started up with his advances, expecting Darrell to be the same pliable, scared little boy he once was. Remembering what he'd learned from Howard P. Brown, Darrell advanced right out of the trailer, out of Palestine and out of Arkansas.

Sticking his thumb out on State Highway 70, he returned back to Memphis intending to live with the Bowlons. It wasn't family the way Darrell wanted it to be, but at least he didn't perceive any immediate danger.

Which One Am I?

—27—

DIANE

It seemed like Diane was always there, waiting behind his hazel eyes to be with him whenever she felt Darrell needed her. She was with Darrell when things got too rough at home with Carolyn and he'd retire to his secret place below the overpass where State Highway 70 crossed Main Street. They would spend the day together trying on dresses and the high heels Diane still loves to wear when Darrell lets her.

Like many girls at 15, Diane wasn't particularly concerned with modesty. It wasn't until years later when Robert Dann expressed his discomfort with the provocative way both she and Darrell were dressing did she turn her attention to gowns more befitting a ballroom than a backwoods bar. Diane takes her inspiration from styles that actress Diahann Carroll might have worn on *Dynasty*, the nighttime drama that had become a hit during those years. Even though Diane is of African American descent, she also modeled her dresses on the styles worn by Diana, Princess of Wales, from whom she ultimately drew her name.

Darrell was aware of two other female personalities as well: Carol, a white 16 year old who eventually would name herself for Darrell's mother and assume the traits Darrell wished Carolyn had possessed; and Star, a 16 year old mulato with a hellish temper who nevertheless took her name directly from the heavens. They too would be under the overpass when Darrell needed them. It's just that at the start only Diane had the gumption to go out in public dressed up.

There are many published accounts of DID patients who switch genders or even species. Sybil had at least two male personalities, Sid and Mike. In his book *First Person Plural,* Dr. Cameron West, Ph.D. tells of his 12-year-old alter Sandy developing a crush on a 15-year-old alter of a female patient while in therapy. Author Erin Lale tells in her autobiography *Greater Than the Sum of my Parts* of her alter Lynx, a personality she ties to the tradition of animal spirits in her native Cherokee culture. There are reports that some therapists have even uncovered alternate personalities who are inanimate objects.

There is no way to completely pinpoint the genesis of Diane, Carol and Star. The most logical starting point would have been during Darrell's episodes of sexual abuse. While an over-simplification, it is not entirely incorrect to say the DID patient thinks to him or herself, "This wouldn't be happening to me if I were...." Whatever the wish, the brain makes it so.

Together, Diane and Darrell would spend time with the biological girls in town. At least a few of those young ladies had fruitless crushes on Darrell. Neither did anything happen with the boys in Palestine, though it wasn't for lack of effort. In particular, Diane liked to go with Darrell over to the Union 76 station. There was this one boy she always liked to flirt with. At 18, he was an older man, who seemed worldly to 15-year-old Diane. The boy was tall, muscular and had the color of dirty blond hair that Diane thought attractive but Darrell never would.

Mostly Darrell and Diane would just sit under the underpass and talk. Their secret place allowed them to be anything they wanted to be, but mostly they just wanted to be safe. In order to be safe they usually had to make sure they were alone.

Palestine wasn't the easiest place in the world for a feminine teen to express himself. Memphis, though, was something else. There were worse Southern towns in which to be gay, especially for underage boys who liked to dress as girls. Through the luck of geography, an almost 17-year-old Darrell brought all three of the girls he knew of at the time into a drag scene that by 1983 was extremely well-established.

What was happening in Memphis echoed the gay rights movement that had taken hold in New York in 1969 with the Stonewall riots. In Tennessee, the rebellion against discrimination that began as police loaded the first group of drag queens into their paddy wagons was nowhere near as angry and violent as the scene surrounding the Stonewall Inn in New York's Greenwich Village. There was a certain Southern gentility at work. Local drag queens nevertheless played just as influential a role as they had during the uprising a thousand miles away in New York. In Memphis the queens sought acceptance by modeling their scene on a well-established and accepted Southern institution known as the cotillion.

As practiced in Southern society, the cotillion, a word that means "petticoat" in French, has only a few elements in common with the dance that swept Europe during the 19th century. Like the dance established in 1850, the cotillion is still part of a dance program for a social event. Today it is most associated with debutantes' "coming out" balls where it employs a dance program of couples performing sets of figures to a classical piece of music. Substitute country for classical and the dance bears striking similarities to the American square dance.

The purpose of a cotillion in Southern culture is to present eligible young ladies to society. The higher the stature of guests, the higher the level of elegance in the program.

In a scene in *Midnight in the Garden of Good and Evil*, the cotillion is presented as the key to establishing society's pecking order. Writing of himself as John Kelso, *Esquire* columnist John Berendt travels to Georgia to cover a murder trial. While in Savannah, he meets drag queen The Lady Chablis who surprises Kelso by crashing a black cotillion. The scene in the filmed adaptation is played for anachronistic laughs, but Chablis' description of the cotillion as presented in the original book presents a set of emotions that real Southern belles would be loath to admit.

"The girls with the light skin are the ones the successful black men are gonna marry," she tells the author. "It gives them status."

Stonewall is frequently cited as the first instance in American history when people in the gay and lesbian community fought back against a government-sponsored system that persecuted sexual minorities, but Memphis wasn't far behind. The Stonewall riots had happened in June 1969. In Memphis, the first public Miss Gay Memphis pageant was held at the Guild Theatre on Halloween of 1969 with no arrests. In both instances, it was drag queens who led the fight.

Following the incident at the Guild, the Memphis drag scene found its home at The Door, a bar which had been serving the local gay community under a string of different names ever since it opened in 1960 as The Twilight Lounge. A newcomer to Memphis, antique dealer George Wilson had purchased the bar in late 1969. It became so popular a hangout that by 1971 it was renamed George's Theater Lounge. Everyone knew it simply as George's. The area surrounding the club was called Georgetown.

According to scene historian Vincent Astor who continues to work the Memphis clubs as both himself and his drag persona, Lady Astor, in 1971 George's was raided by the police department for cross-dressing (a strange ordinance on the city books) and lewd behavior (a performer kissing another man who had just tipped her). Testing the ordinance, the club threw a drag show. They were not raided again. John T. "Buddy" Dwyer represented the men in court and on October 9, all charges were dismissed by Judge Ray Churchill. Memphis drag queens became heroines just as those at Stonewall had become. They had successfully turned the cotillion on its head, using tradition to celebrate society's outcasts. The city's drag queens had sparked gay pride in Memphis.

All of this was anathema to young Darrell. He'd never heard the term "gay pride." In fact, he'd never heard the term "gay" used in this context. He was most familiar with words like "queer" and "faggot" and the other epithets thrown his way during his short life.

Darrell didn't know that gay bars existed, much less how to find one. He only found J-Wag's by accident. J-Wag's was a tiny bar with a dance floor that could sometimes serve as a stage. It was a neighborhood hangout that didn't even look like a bar from the outside. Darrell thought it was just a place where he might buy something to drink.

Darrell had stumbled upon one of the oldest gay establishments in Memphis and one of the few open 24 hours. J-Wag's would become known for its drag shows in its later years before it was razed to expand the UT Medical Campus in Midtown Memphis as well as a Trolley Line.

As Darrell entered, it seemed to him that everyone inside turned his way. The 17-year-old bolted outside.

The bartender followed right behind him. "Honey, what's wrong with you?" he asked. "Why did you run out like you're scared?"

"Because I am," he answered truthfully.

"But you're gay aren't you?" the bartender asked.

"Yeah," Darrell answered with some uncertainty.

"Well, honey, you're home!" Darrell's new friend assured him. "We'll take care of you."

They did take care of Darrell, especially after he learned how to drink. J-Wag's was the first place Darrell would touch alcohol. He felt comfortable, safe and at home in the tiny bar in ways he hadn't felt since leaving Haughton Place. J-Wag's would also be the place where Darrell would swear off drinking hard liquor for the rest of his life.

Like most young men, Darrell didn't know his limit. This led to one evening when he became so drunk on his usual cocktail of coke and bourbon that it was all he could do to stagger out of J-Wag's. In the alley beside the club, he came across an industrial-sized wire winding spool someone had left leaning against the building. This was the type of spool that some people have used as coffee tables. It was also the type of spool that Don Sinclair worked with when he was employed at Wire Rope & Fitting. Somehow Darrell found an old rug which he wrapped around himself and promptly passed out under the wire spool.

Becoming so drunk is unusual for Darrell. Usually, the effects of alcohol, drugs or even illness can be spread amongst the people inside. One or some of them may feel under the weather, but others will be completely normal. For whatever reason, this time that wasn't the case. Darrell was out cold.

The comatose teen didn't go unnoticed. Patrons entering J-Wag's thought someone had died, so still did he lie. They brought this to the attention of the bartender. He brought the news to the attention of the owner. The owner came out to see what everyone was talking about.

It took awhile to bring Darrell to his senses, but when the owner finally got him to his feet he made Darrell promise to never again drink in J-Wag's. Darrell kept that promise. For good measure, he'd never drink hard liquor anywhere else.

That didn't mean he'd stay out of the bars. The gay scene and particularly the drag scene were freeing experiences, particularly for the girls inside. Darrell still went to J-Wag's, but, he'd also get to know the crowd at George's, Memphis's premiere drag scene. They'd get to know Darrell as well, or at least to know Diane and Star. Carol, being the most conservative of the women inside Darrell, refused to participate. She was too classy for such a scene. The idea of men throwing dollars bills at a woman on a stage seemed to her decidedly whorish.

Darrell ended up making his presence known at most all of the Memphis clubs. The only bar in town where the owners both knew and cared that he was underage also provided a pivotal meeting. In the days when the bar that still operates as a gay bar was called The Other Side, Darrell would have to sneak in through its backdoor. One night, a tall blond teen opened the door for Darrell and waved him in. He'd come to know the boy later as Wayne Chisholm.

-- 28 --

WAYNE

Ever since they'd had their fight and Carolyn moved Don Sinclair into her trailer, Darrell was spending less time in Palestine and more time in Memphis. Effectively, he was living with Bobbie Lynn and Ronnie Bowlon but since those two were spending so many hours either working or imbibing, Darrell was effectively as alone in Memphis as he ever had been anywhere else.

Still, Memphis had two major advantages over Palestine. Darrell wasn't living with anyone who was trying to take sexual advantage and Memphis was a big town with a thriving downtown area that offered opportunities. The only difficulty as far as he could see was that Bobbie Lynn and Ronnie lived on Memphis's outskirts. Downtown was a good eight miles away.

With little money in his pockets and no other way to get there, Darrell would walk to the city center near the Mississippi River. Trying to find the shortest way there, he would try different routes and on one such exploration he came upon a park. The park had an odd set-up in that it was surrounded by thick trees that made it difficult to see what was happening within. Still, Darrell had been alone in stranger places.

Once he made his way through the foliage, Darrell was surprised to see many young men he recognized as about his own age. One of them Darrell came to know as Wayne Chisholm.

They'd met before when Wayne had waved him through the backdoor of The Other Side. Darrell didn't recognize him though, seeing Wayne for the first time in the daylight.

In this park, where some of the gay men of Memphis met surreptitiously, Wayne was a stand-out. He was a couple years older than Darrell and at 6'1" quite a bit taller. With his blond hair, blues eyes and pale skin he could have been mistaken for any boy on the beaches of Long Beach back in California had he not had those buck teeth. Even if his dental work didn't give him a pronounced lisp, it would still have been easy to tell he was gay.

Actually, Wayne was as unsure of himself and his sexuality as was Darrell. Wayne knew the local gay scene that Darrell hadn't even known existed. While waiting to meet Mr. Right, Wayne was earning spending money from Mr. Right Now. He was a hustler who only wanted to settle down. During all the time Darrell and he were friends, though, the only men attracted to him were the ones he didn't want.

The two boys were both survivors and the need to depend on each other helped make Darrell and Wayne fast friends. They would hang in the parks together and sometimes sit on the swings. They would visit the museums of Memphis and, of course, they made their presence known in the local bar scene.

As it happened, Darrell soon found out he wasn't the only family member visiting the gay bars of Memphis. He'd run into his cousin Terry Cummings once in awhile, but Terry never would speak to Darrell. Terry never did acknowledge Darrell's presence in the bars, much less what had transpired sexually between them years before, one of the first dents in Darrell's trust in his family. .

Terry's rejection was bad enough, but then Darrell ran into his uncle. R.D.'s brother was known by the other bar patrons as Bruce when he was in his street clothes and as Loretta when he was in drag. The family always called him Bruce Larry. By the time Darrell entered the scene, Bruce Larry was a well-established presence in the gay community who would go on to own a gay bar of his own in Memphis for a time.

Darrell was sitting with some friends when he saw Bruce Larry come up. "That's my uncle," Darrell pointed out. "I'm not your uncle," Bruce Larry retorted. Then he kept on walking.

Despite Bruce Larry's denial, news of the familial connection spread through the scene. In fact, had it not been for that connection to Bruce Larry, Darrell may never have attempted drag in the first place. The star of the show at The Other Side, a drag queen who always looked just like the late country singer Dottie West, took a particular shine to Darrell after the story reached her. Unlike regular patrons, she allowed him into the dressing room in the back while she got ready to perform.

"Have you ever done drag?" she asked.

"No," answered Darrell shyly.

"I think you'd be good at it because you have the face for it," she said. Before Darrell realized what was happening, she had him made up and was picking out a gown for him.

Pushing Darrell to the stage, his new mentor told him, "Just tell the man what songs you want." Darrell was scared, but he got out on the stage and performed.

Following his debut, Darrell would continue to perform for some time. He'd perform as Diane or Star usually, though sometimes he'd call himself by some other name. Down inside him, Carol took a backseat to the excitement, not approving of what she considered slutty behavior on the part of her two cohorts. Carol didn't like Diane and Star having to sit on the laps of strange men. She really hated how they had to rub men's faces in their cleavage. Carol didn't think any of this was ladylike. Still, it all served a greater purpose. Like most performers, Darrell worked for tips. These were the only income he had.

It wasn't that Carol was entirely absent. As the dominant over the girls inside, she was always keeping an eye on the situation. One night, a straight man came into the bar to hassle the performers. He kept trying to lift Darrell's skirt to get a peak underneath. Darrell asked him to stop, but that only caused the man to continue his antics. After a few more warnings, Carol had enough. She ripped off one of her heels, putting it right through the customer's raised hand as he reached for the edge of her skirt. Once the shoe was removed from the man's appendage and after security escorted him from the club, she calmly wiped the blood off her stiletto, put the shoe back on and continued the show as Star.

This type of violence was out of character for Carol, though all of the people inside have their violent sides. For the most parts, Carol's concern is being classy, mirroring the way Darrell would like to create the myth that allows him to lovingly remember his own mother. Like Diane and Star, though, she learned from watching the family's former housekeeper Miss Cleo Jackson how a woman sets her boundaries and how a woman demands respect. That Carol would take this boundary setting to such a level as to defend the girls and Darrell when mishandled reflects the role she plays in Darrell's life. Carol is part of a triumvirate of emotions reflecting that of the older boys. Carol is frustration, Diane is anger and Star is rage. This pattern of threes is a repetitive theme in Darrell's life.

Someone else made his appearance known in the clubs of Memphis. Darrell didn't know him at the time anymore than he knew any of the other people inside him, but Billy Bill had made it his job to watch over Darrell and everyone inside. Normally acting as the Memory Keeper like Sybil's Vicky or Eve's Jane, on these nights Billy Bill is the bouncer of the bunch. He stands apart from the others, watching.

Studies show that in any DID case, there always seem to be one personality who remembers everything that happened to the first born. In Darrell's world, that role is taken up by Billy Bill. Though he's not yet up to speed on current events, Billy Bill will use his Welsh accent to tell anything anyone wants to know about what happened to Darrell during his life.

Billy Bill is not alone in being from outside the country. Darrell's late husband Robert Dann once had a midnight conversation with a personality who spoke only German. There is another who speaks only French. Since no one in the household, including Darrell, speaks either language and a stunned Robert neglected to ask, these two mysterious Europeans remain unnamed.

As Darrell spent more time with Wayne Chisholm and the drag family of Memphis, Darrell felt himself becoming distant from his birth family. Given his history, that was not a particularly difficult or unwanted evolution. Darrell and Wayne would find different places to call temporary homes. Once, they walked the five miles to Wayne's mother's house located in a housing development far out of town. She was welcoming and they stayed with her for about a week. Other times they'd make friends with other men who they would stay with as long as the situation was good.

Darrell didn't abandon the family entirely as he would sometimes return to the second floor apartment Bobbie Lynn and Ronnie Bowlon shared with their kids. The pair was friendly with the family downstairs from them, a husband and wife with two children, a boy and a girl.

One night, as Darrell was preparing his drag, the husband from downstairs walked in on him. The man didn't seem offended by seeing a teenager putting on women's makeup. In fact, for a long time after that he would make a point of driving Darrell into town to the clubs. The man would also make a point of being back at the club by 3 a.m. to bring Darrell home. He'd drop Darrell off then the man would catch an hour or two of sleep before he had to get up again to begin his own 6 a.m. work shift.

Darrell felt the acceptance he hadn't experienced since leaving Haughton Place. He put the Williams clan out of his mind and, for awhile there, almost forgot about them. As things worked out, that's exactly when circumstances brought his family back to once again turn his world upside down.

Bo Kirgis & Mary Barnick with Darrell & Tom
(Photo: Mary Barnick)

Carol
(Photo: Gregory Scott Largent)

-- 29 --

MARY

    Whenever we have a phone conversation with our friends Bo and Mary, the call follows the same pattern. The conversation inevitably begins with updates: "How are you?" "How is the family?" "How is your weather?" "What's the latest news?" Then the phone gets handed to Darrell.

    The kids always want to talk and they do it all at once.

"Hi Aunt Mary! Hi Uncle Bo-Bo Bear!" Billy explains. "Love you!"

"Hi!" says shy Jimmie.

"Hi Aunt Mary! Dot! Dot! Dot!" comes Dot's trademark greeting.

"Hi!" Robbie jumps in. "Love you Aunt Mary! Love you too Uncle Bo!"

"Hi," says Darrell, pushing the little ones aside for the moment. "It's me. How are you?" He stays on the line with Bo and Mary a good long time.

"Who was that?" Mary asks when Darrell hands the phone back. "He's intelligent and thoughtful. I really like him."

The thoughtfully intelligent one is Darrell and until this moment, we hadn't realized how few people get to meet him. It always takes Darrell a long time to warm to new people. It takes him even longer to develop a sense of trust. With some people, he never does.

When Darrell first meets a stranger, that person generally encounters some mix of J.D., who tries to fit in, and James, who is on guard for protection, and perhaps a little bit of Darrell himself if the people inside feel he's up to it. Because thoughtfulness is not theatrical, it's the boys from behind Darrell's eyes who make the biggest impression. Like many teenagers, they are a confusing mix, at once inquisitive and wary.

No one is afraid of charismatic Mary Barnick. A California beach girl who has moved to the mountains of Arkansas, Mary is a modern Earth Mother, a giver of life. She conveys a warm combination of motherliness and sensuality. She loves. She cares. Darrell responds the same way as everyone inside. They all find Mary Barnick beautiful both inside and out.

The Expedition was still about 28 miles away from the home that would be ours for the next week when Mary first met the girls. At the big Ford's wheel, Mary's husband Bo Kirgis suggests a stop at the Super Wal-Mart in Batesville. This is, he explains, the closest store to the house where one can purchase fresh produce.

We didn't want to believe that fresh produce and Arkansans didn't mix until the first evening we cooked for our hosts. At the nearest of the two markets in town, anything green was on its way to becoming seed. The plump sweet potatoes displayed under a hand-lettered sign proclaiming them "Locally Grown" looked good, but there was already a starch on the table. Finally picking out one of the three pre-wrapped heads of cauliflower, it looked like we'd finally found something fresh. Unwrapping the plastic-wrapped vegetable back at Bo and Mary's house, the leaves around the head — brown, limp and well past their prime -- told a quite different story.

The Wal-Mart store looked like any other we'd ever been in, except it was much bigger. "Oh look! They have groceries," Star exclaimed as Bo and I each grabbed a shopping cart. While our local outlet that replaced the mall in downtown carries packaged goods and milk, Star had never seen a Wal-Mart quite so extensive in its variety.

This embarrassment of riches isn't lost on any of the teenagers inside Darrell.

"They got women's shoes here?" Diane wonders aloud.

"Yes," answers Mary, "but don't you mean men's shoes?"

"Doesn't matter to me if they're men's or women's," Diane answers.

"Come on girl!" says Star, slapping Mary good naturedly on the shoulder. ."Let's go do some shopping!" With that, the women in our little family disappear into the racks of merchandise.

Mary found herself surprised that Darrell would want to go off with her. After all, he was a stranger in a strange land. So was she. Though we had introduced her to the idea of DID, to experience it is another thing entirely. Mary says she heard a bit of a sassy attitude come up in Darrell's voice. There was obviously something going on inside Darrell. Mary decided just to go with the flow.

Like any teen-aged girls, Carol, Diane and Star think shopping is fun. That is a good thing because, like some men, Darrell has never cared for shopping. He never did it much growing up and doesn't care to do it now.

The girls like looking for new things and especially clothes. In years past they had their own wardrobes, as all the kids inside did. That ended when Darrell found himself homeless in the years before he met Robert Dann. The girls didn't get to dress up much even after Darrell moved in with Robert. Robert wasn't comfortable seeing Darrell dressed as a woman when they went out together in public so Darrell always tried to maintain a more masculine persona when they were together. The girls settled for dressing up only on Halloween, Robert and Darrell's anniversary.

Though all Darrell's kids have been uncharacteristically quiet on this trip back to Darrell's homeland, Diane and Star have been particularly so. As women of color, they have both been acutely aware that the South hasn't been historically welcoming to non-whites. They overheard comments made while we were in Tennessee. In the relatively cosmopolitan retailing giant, there is a sense of liberation.

They want new shoes and head directly to the pair they want. Star tells Mary that she needs a comfortable pair of slip-ons, but with heels. They pick a pair of black Earth Spirit loafers with a 2-inch heel that is conservative by the girls' standards. They had to have them.

A teen-aged girl and a middle-aged man have different definitions of comfort. Ever since Darrell fell down the stairs of the second floor apartment he shared with Robert before moving downstairs to our current abode, heels of any height are a problem. The girls, when they are excited about finding something they like, tend to forget this. When they look in a mirror, they see their own bodies, not Darrell's. Never worn, the shoes still sit in the back of the closet. They have company in several pairs of boots with even higher heels that Darrell may have let the girls wear once if at all.

From Mary's perspective, she thought those shoes looked a bit small but figured choosing them was a matter of vanity. Darrell wishes she'd said something because they shoes are, in fact, the size the girls wear. Attractive though they may be, they are not anything Darrell can wear comfortably for any amount of time.

Darrell doesn't mind sharing his body with the others. He sees the people inside as spirits or souls who, for whatever reason, were born without bodies of their own. Providing time outside to the people inside is just what psychiatrists tell DID patients to do. As Cameron West, Ph. D. notes in his autobiography *First Person Plural*, "I turned away from my guys, and the more I ignored them, the worse things got." No matter the patient, people inside them will not be denied. In Dr. West's case, it is self-destructive Switch who demands attention by slitting West's arm.

As Dr. Sharon Higgens instructed Darrell, each interior person needs his or her time outside. Each needs to feel acceptance and it's not enough just to verbally proclaim that they are. Each needs to spend time with people who acknowledge them as individuals.

These people are rare. Darrell is normally loath to let strangers know of his condition because many times he feels that person is treating him as they would a young child. Not even the children inside like being treated that way and it is particularly galling to the adult man that Darrell is. Long term therapy has allowed Darrell to function like any man his age. Those DID patients with the constantly violent personalities that Darrell thankfully lacks may also need medication in order to function normally.

Mary Barnick accepts Darrell and each interior person just as they are. Riding shotgun in the Expedition, Mary sees a truck bearing the logo of Dot Industries, a Michigan-based trucking firm.

"Oh look!" Mary exclaims. "That truck says 'Dot.' Dot! Dot! Dot!"

"Where?" answers Dot, popping up for a moment to take in the passing big rig.

Mary treats the kids inside the same way she treated her own children when they were growing up. She goes with the flow just as she does when faced with any new, traumatic or tragic circumstance. In Mary's mind, Darrell's switching is what it is. The kids appreciate that. They love Mary for accepting them just as they are.

Which One Am I?

—30—

CAROLYN

Still just 17, Darrell was a good 250 miles away when he got the vision telling him to return to Palestine. He'd been staying with a man he'd met who lived on the far side of Nashville. The man had promised to train Darrell for a position in management, but that all changed when the vision came. Something was seriously wrong with Carolyn and Darrell needed to get back to her side.

At first, Darrell tried to deny what he was seeing. He told himself it was all a dream when, in the vision, Darrell felt his mother touching him. It wasn't a touch one felt from a living person; it was a cold touch as if she were in a tub of ice. For three days he felt depressed. His heart felt as if it were being popped out of him piece by piece. He couldn't think straight. All his thoughts kept going back to Carolyn.

Which One Am I?

After having thought nonstop about his mother for three days straight he knew he had to return to Palestine. The man he was staying with asked for a clearer explanation of why Darrell had to leave so suddenly, but the best Darrell could tell him was, "I just know." Two days before Halloween 1983, this man who had promised to get Darrell a good-paying job drove with him more than four hours across Tennessee and half of Arkansas. He dropped Darrell off at Carolyn's trailer. After that day, Darrell never heard from him again.

The trailer was as it had been. It was what the trades call a single wide, meaning it was a mobile home made up of only one trailer. The master bedroom was in back, with a second bedroom that was hardly big enough for a twin bed carved out of the space between the bathroom and living room. This guest room was where Darrell stayed when he chose to and where Carolyn's mother Martha Faye Coleman would stay when she was needed.

The living area held a sofa, coffee tables, end tables and two extra chairs. The kitchen was up in front. This was one of two standard kitchen placements in the mobile home industry during the Seventies.

The only distinction between Carolyn's rented trailer and the others in the park were the multitude of medicine bottles that crowded the top of the refrigerator. The importance of all these medicines to Carolyn was reflected in the quantities she kept on hand in the large, white bottles usually only seen in medical dispensaries.

Johnny and Bobbie Lynn met Darrell outside the trailer on Darrell's arrival. In his taciturn way, Johnny broke the news that their mother was dead. Darrell was incredulous, not so much that Carolyn had died but that she had been dead three days without anyone letting him know. Bobbie Lynn had the number where he was staying. In a pattern that would repeat through most of their interactions, first Bobbie Lynn claimed that she didn't know where Darrell was. Then she changed her story and claimed to have lost his number.

It was then it hit him. What Darrell had seen in his heart and soul had really come true. For the next two days, Darrell went missing and somebody else took charge of his body. The next time he'd be himself was when he found himself staring down at Carolyn in her coffin. There was a bandage on her left breast that was not quite hidden by the dress she would be buried in.

During an autopsy, a forensic pathologist makes a y-shaped incision in the body's chest and opens the rib cage with a Stryker saw, a specialized saw which will cut through bone, but not soft tissue. A bandage might have been used to cover the upper end of such an incision had an autopsy been performed. Carolyn's sisters Jeanne and Ann both insisted that Carolyn had told them she didn't want an autopsy, but this is a message that failed to reach any of Carolyn's children. Even if one had been performed, no records of the procedure are known to exist.

Darrell heard the official story people would tell about his mother's passing. About a week before her death, Carolyn had been admitted to Forrest City Medical Center, about 15 minutes from Palestine and the small town's closest medical facility. Her regular physician had scheduled a much-delayed family vacation beginning after her admittance, so he prescribed her medications and left Carolyn in the hands of one of his junior physicians.

From the second doctor's reports, Carolyn's stay was anything but a vacation for the medical center staff. Carolyn would run up and down the hospital halls screaming "He's trying to kill me! He's trying to kill me!" Even though her regular physician had left orders not to release Carolyn until his return, handling a patient in this condition proved too much for both doctor on duty and the hospital staff. The doctor had increased the dosages of some of Carolyn's medications, switched the prescription on some of the others and finally, in direct violation of her own doctor's orders, had sent Carolyn home.

Forrest City Medical Center doesn't keep paper records for more than 10 years. They do, however, keep an historical log on microfiche in the facility's archives. Hospital officials acknowledge, however, that a case of this age is difficult for them to research.

According to Don Sinclair, who was still living with Carolyn in Palestine, on the morning of her death he had come out to the kitchen about Noon. Carolyn, he thought, was asleep on the sofa in the living room. This was out of character for a farm girl who was used to waking with the chickens. She might have slept through the morning, but only when her pain made it necessary to take a fair dose of drugs. As her former husband and on again/off again paramour, Don would have been very much aware of Carolyn's habits.

The landlord had just been over to collect the rent. Once that was taken care of, Don decided to make them both some breakfast. "Carolyn! Do you want some coffee?" he called. Then, when there was no response, he called her again. Finally, he went over to check on her. Carolyn had no pulse.

When the paramedics arrived, Don says they told him Carolyn had died of a massive heart attack due to a cholesterol clot passing into her system. This team of paramedics would have had to be trained as vascular surgeons to make such a diagnosis which would have been far out of their job description. Paramedics are trained to treat ailments rather than diagnose. It would have been up to Carolyn's doctor to run the tests to determine the cause of death.

It seems more likely that Don Sinclair himself provided the reason Carolyn died. It is also likely that, for reasons of his own, he pulled his answer from the air. In fact, Carolyn's death certificate gives her cause of death as acute myocardial infarction; a heart attack in simple terms. The secondary cause is given as natural causes due to a history of heart condition, a story that likely also came from Don. If Carolyn did have a history of heart problems that was something she had kept secret from everyone.

The circumstances of Carolyn's death didn't make much sense to Darrell. Neither did they add up to Bertha Merriman. Don had told Bertha that he had woken up late that morning to find Carolyn in bed dead beside him.

There were too many unanswered questions about his mother's death as far as Darrell was concerned. Even though the rest of the family seemed to take Don Sinclair's explanation at face value, Darrell took it upon himself to ask the questions no one else would. He was waiting for Carolyn's primary physician to return from his vacation and then he told him what had been said.

The doctor was extremely surprised and displeased that his subordinate had released Carolyn to her family's care. To do so was in direct contradiction to his instructions.

He was also surprised by what Darrell had been told was the cause of Carolyn's death. Not long before his vacation, the doctor had tested Carolyn's cholesterol levels. There was no evidence of high cholesterol in her body at all. Don Sinclair's version of Carolyn's death was, Carolyn's doctor told her son, an impossible scenario. Given her physical health, no pinprick-sized blog of cholesterol could have shaken loose from somewhere in her body, made it up to her heart and caused her death.

It might have been that the doctor in charge at the hospital didn't clearly explain to Carolyn the changes he was making to her medication. In her frenzied state of mind, it might also have been that, even had the doctor explained the changes, Carolyn failed to grasp his words and what they meant. On the night before her death, she may well have taken the same number of pills she usually took before bedtime without realizing that the dosages of each pill had been increased.

There was Carolyn's cryptic question to her mother the last time Darrell was in a car with her on their ride to visit Danny Poole. Carolyn's questioning Martha Faye about whether the family burial plots were paid in full may have also been her misinterpreting what psychics like her call a death dream. The wisest among the psychic community say to dream of death means that one should start connecting with others before they are lost for good. That she was suddenly concerned about her final resting place also point, in Darrell's mind, to an intentional overdose. Yet that is the scenario he would most like to dismiss.

There is a clue that she did understand a death dream's implications. Carolyn had begun calling around, asking for Darrell to return to Palestine. A renewed physical closeness may have allowed them to mend the bridges between them, but that's something that would never be even if Carolyn had lived. Darrell could not forgive Carolyn's betrayal. She had chosen Darrell's molester Don Sinclair over her own son. While Don was living with Carolyn, there was no way Darrell was going to go back.

It wasn't until two days after Carolyn's burial, on the day after Darrell returned to Palestine, that there came a knock at the trailer's door. Carrol Bevel and his Elvis Presley sideburns had stopped by.

"Is your mother at home?" he asked.

"She'd dead, you bastard," Darrell fairly spate at the man. Carrol Bevel had quite a reputation for meanness and so Darrell assumed the worst. He figured if anyone was mean enough to have taken his mother's life, it would have been Carrol Bevel. For many years Carrol's first wife Bonnie believed the exact same thing. "I know it was you who killed her." Then he slammed the door in Carrol's face.

The true cause of Carolyn's death may never be known. Though no one ever admitted to removing them, the big white bottles of pills Carolyn kept all disappeared from the top of her refrigerator the day of her funeral. As for getting the truth through her medical records, Forrest City Medical Center's records were destroyed per hospital policy some long after Carolyn was sent home. Had they been kept just a little longer, they might have been there when we began our search.

Which One Am I?

-- 31 --

CATHERINE

Danny Poole was a coward for leaving Carolyn. That's what his mother Catherine always said about the situation and she said it often enough right to her son Danny's face. Catherine Poole loved Carolyn Williams and had ever since Danny announced that he and Carolyn were going to be wed. It was still love, though an emotion perhaps dotted with a touch of pity, Catherine felt for her daughter-in-law after Carolyn's near fatal car accident.

The doctors sure weren't doing much to help Carolyn keep from being plagued by pain. What Carolyn needed was a strong man to help out at home. How could that fool son of Catherine's go and abandon Carolyn and those kids just when they needed him most?

Catherine set out to make sure Carolyn's family knew that there was at least one Poole who still cared about them. When she ran into Carolyn's youngest son at the funeral home out on Brinkley's Main St. where Carolyn's body lay in state for two days, Catherine made sure Darrell knew she hadn't forgotten him. She and Danny's father George acted just like they were still members of the Williams family. They even followed the hearse carrying Carolyn's casket out to Wheatley for the burial.

Catherine felt sorry for Darrell, who seemed so lost and out of sorts. She would have taken him home with her if she could, but she figured the family would pull together around the tragedy. Her son Danny Poole, however, didn't seem to think a thing about Carolyn's death. His parents were there to show their respect. Danny didn't show up at all.

The young man wanted Danny to say he was his father, but Danny had abruptly put an end to that. Despite his disappointment, Darrell always held a place in his heart for Danny's parents. The only Christmas presents he can remember receiving came from the older Pooles. Catherine knew he had a special fondness for Volkswagen vans and that's the toy car she would bring him each year. To this day, several metal models of Sixties-era VW vans remain on display at the house we share in Long Beach.

Neither did Carrol Bevel attend the funeral. Divorced from Carolyn for a second time, he'd been busy starting a new family and in all the excitement, no one had let him know about Carolyn's death. Whether the slight was accidental or intentional, nobody admits to remembering. Of Carolyn's four husbands only R.D. Williams and Don Sinclair came to say their goodbyes.

Not one of Carolyn's former husbands helped her to her final resting place. Carolyn's oldest son Johnny was one of her pallbearers, and so was her brother Larry Coleman. Another pallbearer was Chief of Police Dick Ferguson, the same man who had helped Darrell get released from jail and who later that day had both of his legs broken during a routine traffic stop. R.D. might have helped carry the casket, but he stood much shorter than the other volunteers and R.D. also felt he didn't have the strength to carry Carolyn's casket.

R.D.'s sister Kitty and her husband Arthur gave Darrell his ride out to Posey Cemetery. The burial itself is a blur. Someone was there watching as the pallbearers brought Carolyn to her final resting place. That someone wanted to protect Darrell from this emotional deluge, one which his relatives were hell bent on keeping him from expressing. Each time the tears for his mother would well in his eyes, Aunt Jeanne would poke him in the ribs. That was the only time anyone touched him at all during the ceremony. "Don't upset your grandmother Joshlin," Jeanne kept admonishing him. "Don't you make your grandmother cry."

Darrell only regained full control of his consciousness at the moment when he noticed he was in an abandoned cemetery, standing alone over his mother's grave. He was supposed to ride back to Wheatley with R.D. but had Aunt Kitty and Uncle Arthur not lagged behind the rest of the family and noticed Darrell standing there, he would have had to walk the three miles back down to Highway 17 where everyone convened for dinner at Gene's BBQ and Family Restaurant. R.D. didn't say a word to Darrell when he saw him walk in. Nobody did.

The family was building its energy for what they knew laid before them at the trailer in Palestine. This would be the first time all five Williams' children – Johnny, Ronnie, Bobbie Lynn, Allen and Darrell – would find themselves together at the same time under the same roof since Darrell was age six. This would be no warm reunion.

By the time Aunt Kitty and Uncle George delivered Darrell to the trailer, mayhem had broken out. Each family member was there to claim a little something or even a lot of something for themselves. Bobbie Lynn was arguing with Johnny's wife Susan and Ronnie's wife Lisa over which got to keep Carolyn's clothes. Susan wanted the furniture too but Grandpa Dick Joshlin put a stop to that. According to him, the furniture had been on loan. He and Grandma Martha Faye intended to take it back. The only furniture Susan ended up taking that day was the bed Darrell had been sleeping on.

Martha Faye and Aunt Jeanne had already taken down the portraits Carolyn had taken the day of her fateful car trip to Memphis and had long ago promised to Darrell. Grandma Joshlin told Darrell later that they took them because "We didn't want Don to end up with them."

Don didn't end up with much of anything, but neither did Darrell. While Bobbie Lynn, Susan and Lisa tore through the trailer, including his room, Darrell sat apart from everything, silent and powerless.

One conversation from the family's time together in the Palestine trailer still sticks with him. Not more than a day or so after Carolyn's death, two letters in her handwriting had arrived. Both were addressed to Darrell. One came to Johnny's house in West Memphis to be delivered to Darrell in care of Johnny's wife Susan. The other had made its way to Ronnie's house in Houston, to Darrell in care of Ronnie's wife Lisa.

Both Susan and Lisa told Darrell they had received letters for him. Both told him they had left his letters back at their homes. Darrell continued to ask for the letters. The next time he mentioned them, both women told him the letters had been lost. The time after that, he was informed the letters had been destroyed. Today both women refuse to admit they received any letters at all. But they did.

Within a couple of days, the trailer was empty. Everything Carolyn had ever cared about had new homes. Only her youngest son was left unclaimed.

Carolyn wasn't the only one Darrell never said goodbye to. He never would see Catherine Poole again. As with virtually every passing in his life, Darrell always resented and regretted not having been given a chance to say goodbye. Neither would Darrell's brother Johnny be around much. For his own reasons, Johnny chose that day to walk away from his birth family and sever virtually all ties.

After the funeral and burial, Darrell eventually found himself with nowhere to sleep and no reason to stay in the South. Eventually, he would meet a man in the bars, John McGee, who promised to take him somewhere, anywhere else. Darrell was unaware of Carolyn's effort to reach out to him until about a year after Carolyn's death when the new couple stopped at Darrell's grandparents' house in Palestine on their way out of Memphis.

Martha Faye Joshlin pretended surprise that her youngest grandson had spent so much time homeless. Had she known, Darrell could have come live with her, she assured him. She loved him, she said, and he could have stayed there in Palestine with her just as long as he didn't bring any boyfriends home. Boyfriends just like John McGee.

Nothing Martha Faye Joshlin said that day mattered at all to Darrell. Whatever comfort she might be offering came too late. He knew his Aunt Jeanne had made sure his grandmother knew he was living on the streets. Martha Faye had been at Carolyn's funeral. She had watched as, one by one, every person Darrell thought cared for him turned their backs and walked away. Darrell loved his grandmother but at the same time hated her for what she failed to do to protect him. Darrell saw his only option to be getting as far away from the South and his family as he could. John McGee was, in Darrell's desperate condition, his savior and best hope.

Grandma Joshlin wasn't going to let Darrell leave without asking about the letters she knew her daughter Carolyn had sent him. Had he seen them? Had he read them? The answer was "no."

Though Carolyn hadn't shared with her mother the contents of either letter, Martha Faye thought it was all pretty obvious. One was very likely Carolyn's suicide note, she told Darrell. The other she thought most likely contained a story she didn't feel was hers to tell. She could hint at it, though. Out of respect for his elderly grandmother, Darrell didn't think it was right to badger her even though he sure wanted to do just that.

Darrell drove away with John that day with questions that would bother him for the rest of his adult life. What had his mother wanted him to know? Why had she written those two letters so close to her death? Did she know she was going to die? Why did his sisters-in-law destroy the letters, if in fact they actually did? Carolyn had told Bertha Merriman that she was only sure that three of her children belonged to R.D. Did the letters say that too?

Just who were Susan and Lisa really trying to protect?

Which One Am I?

-- 32 --

FRANKIE MAE

It isn't much of a drive from Wheatley over to West Memphis on Arkansas's eastern border. Cruising at the speed limit, the journey takes just under an hour for a vehicle heading northeast up AR-78. Carolyn's funeral had been a trying day for everyone so R.D. decided to stop at his mother Frankie Mae's trailer home in West Memphis. He'd continue the return trip through that little bit of Tennessee and back home to Mississippi the next morning.

Frankie Mae Williams had been living in her West Memphis trailer for decades by the time Darrell, R.D. and Frankie Mae got back to it from Carolyn's funeral. She was living alone as she had been every since her long-ago divorce from her last husband, the senior Richard Daniel Williams. The divorce came at the urging of her children, all 10 of them. They'd been telling Frankie Mae for years that she deserved better than the abuse Richard Williams served up. Even the two children Richard had actually fathered with Frankie Mae, Kitty and the senior Williams' namesake R.D., agreed that separating their parents was the right thing to do.

R.D. also needed a break from the angry young man he had been charged with bringing to live with him in Houston. Darrell's relationship with his father had always been contentious. By the time he'd turned 12, Darrell had become more verbal in expressing his feelings of frustration when he thought he wasn't being treated right. About to turn 18, he was already long emancipated from the family. He didn't feel much connection to them after all his time living in foster care and neither did the family express much of a connection to him. Darrell still didn't know where he belonged, but he was pretty sure it wasn't down in Houston with R.D.

Despite his rebellious state, Darrell held nothing against his paternal grandmother. He loved her for being one of the few constants in his life. She was always there for him. Truth be told, she rarely ranged much further afield than her front porch unless someone came to pick her up. When Darrell lived with his family in West Memphis before the infamous fires, he would visit Frankie Mae whenever he could. The day of the funeral, though, was the first time he had seen his grandmother since his court-ordered banishment from Arkansas.

Funerals are always of more value to the living than they are to the dead. These are times when families remember what brought them together and reaffirm themselves as a unit. Whatever united front the Williams clan hoped to present to the world had cracked long before Carolyn was laid to rest in bucolic Posey Cemetery. Her second husband had not come to pay his respect, no one had thought to invite Carrol Bevel, and her eldest son Johnny chose that day to turn his back on the entire family.

Neither was Darrell feeling much a part of anything larger than him. He'd heard others asked how they were feeling after Carolyn's death. He'd heard them asking their loved ones if there was anything they needed or could be done for them in their time of need. None of these kindnesses were addressed to him.

By the time R.D.'s truck pulled up beside Frankie Mae's trailer, Darrell was furious. He felt slighted at the funeral of the only person he truly felt loved him. His mind reeled with the family's other slights, how they had told him all his life that he would always be homeless, nothing more than a beggar on the streets. Darrell had always been the one who was different and treated like a stranger "from off." He'd been falsely accused of arson, had always been called a liar and many times called a thief. And still R.D. refused to introduce him as "my son."

Darrell was tired of being ignored and weary of having his feelings discounted. These days, already his resentment ran deep. Darrell always wondered why the next oldest brother, Terrance Allen, got to be called by his middle name from the minute he made that choice. For James Darrell, though, the family never called him by anything but his given first name. He hated the way it sounded. It seemed that whenever his family called him "James" it was in connection with something he may or may not have been aware of doing but was being blamed for anyway.

Failing to acknowledge Darrell's emotions, his family made the teen feel more invisible than any of the people inside him. Darrell realized he had to do something to get someone's — anyone's — attention. He would become the person they had accused him of being all along.

Frankie Mae had a case, the type women her age and of her time period would use to store their hair rollers and make-up. Frankie Mae was using hers to hold her jewelry. There was nothing fancy or expensive about any of the costume pieces Frankie Mae had squirreled away in the old green case and Darrell knew that. Still, he also knew that it would be one of the first things a woman of such limited means might find missing. This was especially true since she'd had her grandson staying overnight and, never mind the lack of evidence, everyone in the family said Darrell already was a thief.

It took no longer than 48 hours for the jewels to be missed. When the call came in to Mississippi from his uncle Bruce Larry asking if anyone knew what happened to the jewelry, Darrell and R.D. were in Houston, some 150 miles south of Frankie Mae's trailer in West Memphis.

When R.D. confronted him, Darrell didn't deny a thing. The accused teen practically threw Frankie Mae's jewelry at R.D. Then Darrell threw out some of the words he'd been saving for the man people had always hinted was not his father.

What Darrell wanted to say was, "I'm here. I'm alive. I'm hurting too." He only had time to blurt out a question.

"Don't you want to know why I took it?"

Before he finished his sentence he could see R.D. wasn't hearing any more of what his youngest was saying now than he ever had. The relationship between the two had always been contentious but had taken a particularly hard turn since the Mississippi court had awarded Darrell his emancipation from his family.

Since then, every time that the two got together, there would be loud and angry arguments. At that time, R.D. was remarried. His new wife was Francine, a woman R.D. had scooped up after her husband abandoned her for a younger woman. When R.D. was living with Francine in the house that she got in the divorce, an argument between R.D. and Darrell had escalated to the point where R.D. ordered the teen out of his house. That wasn't technically R.D.'s house, Darrell pointed out. Only Francine had the legal right to order him away. Once he calmed down, R.D. agreed and apologized to Darrell.

This time, however, R.D. left himself no time for a cooling off period. He had Darrell pack up what few clothes he owned and drove him down to the bus station. Buying Darrell a one-way ticket to West Memphis, R.D. told him to go live with Johnny.

Darrell wasn't going to let their parting be any easier than the relationship had been itself.

"If you do this," Darrell cursed R.D., "you won't see me again until you're either dead or dying." R.D. couldn't have imagined how good Darrell would be to his word.

When the bus stopped in Memphis before crossing the Mississippi into Arkansas, Darrell put his extra clothes into a locker at the bus station and never went back. It would be a very long time before he returned to West Memphis again.

Part Five

Las Vegas

A growing retirement and family city, Las Vegas is the 28th-most populous city in the United States. The 2010 population estimate of the Las Vegas metropolitan area was 583,756 out of a state population of 2,700,551. The name Las Vegas is often applied to unincorporated areas that surround the city, especially the resort areas on and near the Las Vegas Strip. The 4.2 mi (6.8 km) stretch of Las Vegas Boulevard known as the Strip is mainly in the unincorporated communities of Paradise, Winchester and Enterprise. – From Wikipedia

Which One Am I?

-- 33 --

ALLEN

All his physical possessions gone, stolen and awarded like spoils of war between the warring factions of his family, Darrell began to rid himself of his emotional attachments. If the family didn't care about him when he was alive, he reasoned, they sure weren't going to care about him when he was dead.

Darrell was already dead to his relations, of that he was sure. Each slight he'd felt from his family took form as dark figures arriving unbidden to stake their claims in the spaces once filled with hope and love. Human nature abhors an empty soul.

Peeping out from their rooms behind Darrell's eyes, the people he still didn't know all knew something was wrong. They didn't know what needed fixing, but instinctively they knew it was the job of one of them to help. They didn't yet recognize each other's existence only that their very survival was at stake. Each responded in their own way to Darrell's internal trauma. One by one they surfaced, accessed the situation and were replaced by someone new.

Darrell was experiencing Revolving-Door Syndrome and not every professional believed in a patient using that avenue. Had Darrell been able to or even thought about going to a psychiatrist, it would have been hard to find one who recognized what he was experiencing. The world of psychiatry normally defines Revolving-Door Syndrome as a pattern that applies to patients who join mental health programs seeking treatment, leave the program for a time and then return to treatment at a later date.

In the world of DID, Revolving-Door Syndrome may still apply in the traditional sense but it can also take on a more specialized meaning. A pattern emerges in times of great trauma as recognized by Robert A. Phillips, Jr., Ph.D. who The Troops for Truddi Chase identify as Stanley in their memoir *When Rabbit Howls*. Unsure of a situation's requirements, in Revolving-Door Syndrome the people inside emerge fully-formed, one after another in rapid succession.

When Darrell felt he was most alone on the streets of Memphis, the truth was there were always others with him. This period of homelessness was as stressful as any Darrell had previously experienced. Those inside him knew this and waited. To keep the people he met in the world from knowing he had no place to stay, Darrell availed himself of local churches which, for nothing but goodwill in return, would feed him and allow him to bathe. Darrell would not allow himself to become either a beggar or a bother. It was his goal to ask no one on the streets for help.

It was his history with the always-supportive Memphis gay scene that first came in handy. Darrell's buddy Wayne Chisholm was still there and able to offer whatever support one teen can offer another. And then there were the men.

There was one man in particular who needed a favor from Darrell. The man had come out as gay relatively late in life, but in his younger days he had married a woman and fathered a child. His former wife had left the area soon after his revelation led to their divorce. The man had never seen his son again.

More than anything else, the man wanted his elderly parents to meet the grandson they knew about but had never met. He wanted them to meet and get to know the child they dreamed would carry on the family legacy. Darrell was the proper age to pose as the missing boy and Darrell didn't have a problem with the request. Darrell welcomed the chance to make two old people happy and to be, no matter how fleetingly, part of a loving family. Darrell moved in with the man.

Everything was fine until Darrell's buddy Wayne Chisholm came to stay. While Darrell's relationship with the man was strictly platonic, Wayne didn't work like that. Wayne's way was to tease the men who showed interest, always promising more than he would ever deliver. The man fell for the ruse and for Wayne, leaving Darrell inbetween two alliances: one with the man who gave him shelter and the other with his only friend. Forced into picking sides, he thought about the game Wayne was playing and decided he wanted no part of it. In Darrell's mind, sexual teases are liars and Darrell never could abide a liar.

It was becoming increasingly clear that honesty was not a trait that could be found in Wayne Chisholm, so when the television set came up missing from the apartment where they were living, Darrell was disappointed yet hardly surprised. It wasn't even surprising to Darrell when Wayne blamed him for the theft.

There were arguments Darrell could have made as the man chose to drive the two teens just over the Mississippi border that night instead of calling the authorities as the man was well in his rights to do. Darrell might have pointed out that he had been soundly asleep on the couch when the man returned home to find his television missing. Though he didn't see Wayne Chisholm take the television, Darrell might have pointed out that no one other than the man besides Wayne and he had access to the apartment so the television couldn't have been taken by anybody but Wayne. Besides, if Darrell had really taken the TV, why would he stay in the house?

Those arguments never got made. At that time, Darrell didn't have any more faith that the man would believe him than he had in humanity as a whole. The man delivered Wayne and Darrell to a part of Mississippi that Darrell recognized as vaguely familiar. From there, the two teens began to walk. They headed south, aiming at Houston. After walking all that night and almost all of the next day, they finally arrived at Darrell's brother Allen's house.

The only thing close between brothers Terrence Allen Williams and James Darrell Williams were their ages. After all, Allen was still in diapers when Darrell was born and still learning to feed himself when R.D. brought him to Houston as R.D. followed the job the Merrimans offered down in Mississippi.

The two boys didn't see each other much growing up. For many years, Darrell didn't even recognize Allen as family. Those times R.D. would bring Allen with him to Brinkley or West Memphis for a visit, Darrell always assumed Allen was just a neighbor kid come by for a play date.

Raised by Bertha Merriman and schooled by R.D., Allen was expected from an early age to follow his father into the family business. Everyone save Darrell was raised by Bertha, but Allen was the only sibling to grow up with minimal input from his mother Carolyn. Allen grew up rougher and became the kind of man who would never back down from a bar fight. He is the only one of Carolyn's five children to have spent time in prison.

Wayne didn't stick around more than three days after he and Darrell got to Houston. Allen hadn't proven all that welcoming to this person he didn't know and Allen's house, situated in the woods outside town, Wayne found absolutely scary. Wayne found himself missing Memphis. Here in Mississippi, Wayne knew no one except Darrell. Wayne particularly missed his mother but he also missed his life on the streets. There were no men here who would give him money for allowing them to believe that someday he might have sex with them.

From Darrell's perspective, the episode with the television set theft had shown him what kind of person Wayne really was. Darrell could extrapolate from that what kind of man Wayne was becoming and he didn't like what he saw. They had been tight back in the day, best friends and supportive buddies. Now that he knew what he knew, Darrell couldn't say he was sorry to see Wayne go.

It wasn't long after Wayne disappeared from his life that things went south between Darrell and Allen. Allen had been working in a woodworking factory at the time and he got Darrell a job there as well. Two weeks later, someone on the factory floor said something to Allen that offended him. Allen said something back to the owner. Both Allen and the uninvolved Darrell were fired that day. Darrell couldn't understand why he was penalized for something Allen did and a huge argument erupted between the two brothers. Darrell decided it was time to go.

Over the next two months, Darrell returned to the streets of Memphis. He went back to the churches that had helped him before. He went back to the bars where they made him feel accepted. Darrell never would see Wayne Chisholm again.

He did try to reconnect with his family. Bobbie Lynn had given him a place to stay, but these days she was one step ahead of him. Every time Darrell would track down an address for his sister, he would find that she and her family had recently moved.

Darrell made one last attempt at being part of the Williams family. He did what R.D. had told him to do when the man put Darrell on the bus and sent him to live with his eldest brother Johnny. That situation came to an early head while, when Johnny was at work, Darrell overheard his sister-in-law Susan talking on the phone. "He scares me," she was telling one of her sisters. "I don't like him here. I don't want him here."

It didn't take Darrell long to figure out who the "him" was whom Susan didn't want around. Darrell knew it was time to leave.

Out of options and devoid of hope, Darrell returned to the bars. He knew there was one man there who had shown interest in him. Word around town was that the man was no great catch, but Darrell knew he didn't have it in him to wait until he could catch the next golden ring. All he needed was a lifeline and John McGee was the only man who seemed willing to toss one Darrell's way.

Which One Am I?

James Darrell (Monkey Jackson with his winning slot machine.
(Courtesy: Betty Roland)

Bertha Merriman
(Courtesy Bertha Merriman)

Ray & Almeter Jackson
on their 70th Anniversary
(Photo: James Darrell Williams)

-- 34 --

ALMETER

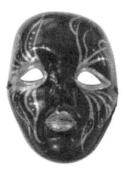

We aren't looking for Darrell's cousin Bertha Merriman when we find her. There is no reason to search. Ronnie Williams, the second oldest of Darrell's four brothers, had years before informed Darrell that Bertha was dead. According to Ronnie, Bertha committed suicide, so heartbroken she felt she could not go on living after chronic alcoholism leading both to psoriasis of the liver and an eventual major heart attack killed her husband Gene.

An Internet search of Merrimans in and around Houston, Mississippi gives us a number for a Randy Merriman. The information we find is a man at about the right age and certainly in the correct location to be Bertha's son. We want to find out from Randy whatever information about Darrell's past his late mother passed down to him.

Ironically, it turns out that Randy had passed away but his widow is more than happy to call Bertha from the trailer she still lives in on the property Randy purchased for his family.

We lean against the bright yellow countertops in our Long Beach kitchen as a voice Darrell hasn't heard in 30 years yet is instantly familiar to him comes on the line. Just the shock of finding Bertha Merriman alive is enough for Darrell, but it immediately becomes apparent there are more surprises in store.

"Is James Darrell there with you?" Bertha asks.

"Yes ma'am."

"Where is he?"

"He's standing across the kitchen staring at me."

"Well, put him on the phone."

The blood quickly drains from Darrell's face. It is lucky he is already leaning on the counter because what Bertha Merriman tells him next almost makes him pass out.

"James Darrell," she proclaims. "You ain't no James Darrell Williams. You are James Darrell Jackson!"

In fact, Bertha explains, Darrell had been named not for the doctor who delivered him as Carolyn told him, but for her uncle, a man everyone knew as Monkey, who Carolyn was cheating on R.D. with. The woman Darrell knew all his life as Aunt Bertha is actually a cousin. This was a secret her tone and quickness explained she'd wanted to tell Darrell for years.

James Darrell Jackson is a name Darrell never heard, a person he never knew existed. It takes awhile to sink in that, if what Bertha was saying is true, James Darrell Williams is really James Darrell Jackson, Jr.

As the shock subsides, the questions come. Who was this man they called Monkey? Who else knew about the affair? Why had such a life-changing secret been kept from Darrell for more than 40 years? Who is lying? Who is telling the truth?

Who is Darrell?

Enough palpable energy and excitement permeates our apartment that we could light up the complex as the phone calls go back and forth between California and Mississippi during the following weeks and months. Most calls add a little light to Darrell's history. Some conversations add dark hints at a family conspiracy. The story Bertha tells him is horrible and hard for him to hear, yet it is a tale he instinctively anticipated all his life.

Bertha has been holding this story inside for all of Darrell's 45 years. She might have told Darrell about himself sooner, but Ronnie Williams had a road block for her as well. According to Ronnie, Darrell went to Florida. But then, Ronnie said a lot of things.

No phone lines could be strong enough to hold the history cascading across the country. Bertha reveals one horrible surprise after another. To make sense of it all, Darrell feels he needs to return to the South for the first time in almost 25 years. He needs to hear this story, his story, first hand.

A diamond anniversary is rare enough in today's times, but Bertha Merriman wants to make her parents' 60th wedding anniversary particularly special. Bertha wants us to come to Covington, a Tennessee manufacturing town about an hour northeast of Memphis, for the marriage anniversary of Monkey's eldest brother Ray and his wife Almeter. Darrell is to be the guest of honor, presented to everyone in the family as Monkey's long lost son returned to the family fold. We are to stay with Bertha in her trailer in Houston, on the land that her late son Randy left. She says she wants to go with us to visit Carolyn's grave, see the places where Darrell grew up and help us with research at several libraries and municipal buildings we have staked out as necessary to our research in order to tell Darrell's story both correctly and truthfully.

Our flight booked well in advance, we plan to spend almost two weeks with Bertha Merriman. She tells Darrell that she never plans to let him out of her sight. In all the excitement of finding Monkey's son alive and well, Aunt Bertha says a lot of things.

There is a tearful reunion between Bertha and Darrell at Memphis International Airport. While they stare at each other, never once breaking gaze, Bertha's boyfriend Gerald puts our bags in his Buick's trunk and climbs behind the steering wheel. Still shivering with excitement, we get into the backseat.

"Ain't nobody here got no place for y'all to stay," Gerald curtly informs us as the doors close.

Between the two of us, we've brought what is left of our savings after buying the plane tickets: about $250 and another $100 available on one credit card. This turns out to be enough for the four days we would spend in a Covington motel plus more dinners at the McDonald's next door than we'd eaten in any fast food joint during our previous four years together.

We are told only about half of the Jacksons could make it to the celebration for Ray and Almeter. Despite their absence, the old school auditorium is packed. There's down-home pot luck, country karaoke and, though Darrell is never properly introduced to the crowd, the extended family still delivers him several surprises.

Which One Am I?

"I've been waiting for this moment all my life," the family's elderly matriarch tells Darrell when first she sees him. A Pentecostal minister, Almeter Jackson seems unduly worried that we might object to a woman holding such a position in the church. Almeter's daughter Bertha Merriman doesn't know why her mother is so concerned for our approval of her position, but it may have something to do with Almeter's Alzheimer's. After all, there are quite a few female ministers in the South and this is especially true amongst the Pentecostals.

Darrell and I find ourselves more intrigued by a different aspect of her persona. Almeter Jackson is a prophet, speaking for the spiritual or divine and serving as their intermediary with humanity. Her gifts don't seem far off those Carolyn possessed. Carolyn taught Darrell to call his powers "soul reading."

Then Betty Roland arrives. She is one of the three youngest sisters in a family that counted 13 children in all, each of them born 9 months apart from each other. Though Monkey had his own place in Memphis for a time, he would always return to Covington. Sometimes he would stay with his youngest sister Shirley, other times with Ray and Almeida and lots of time with Betty and her family. It is Betty's son Bill who looks at Darrell's eyes, notes the shape of his face and nose and first tags Darrell as Monkey Jr.

Betty knows that Bertha had invited Darrell to the party, but she is skeptical of what she will find. She has warned Bertha not to point Darrell out to her and not to tell her which one he is. "If he's Monkey's son," she says, "I'll know him when I see him."

Darrell is outside the auditorium talking to a pack of young ladies when Betty Rowland arrives. He wonders for a moment why she looks at him so strangely. He doesn't know that Betty has had her first look at him and recognized Darrell immediately as the son of her long-dead brother. Monkey's birth certificate, death certificate, the ledger signed by attendees at his funeral and the Polaroid photo of Monkey taken in the casino with the machine that paid off enough for Monkey to buy his beloved truck came home with us to California. These are highly personal mementos, not the kinds of things Aunt Betty would be likely to hand over without some serious consideration.

The morning after the celebration, Gerald and Bertha pick us up at our motel. Our return plane trip is still 8 days away, but the reunion is obviously over. "We sure did help you a lot," says Bertha, and we have to agree. We do feel the sting of being unceremoniously shuttled away much sooner than agreed to when we all planned this reunion, but we don't say that out loud. Instead, we honestly feel thankful for the time and information we did get to experience. Besides, the backseat of a Buick is no place for a confrontation, We just want to get to Beale Street in Memphis where we ask Gerald to drop us off.

As we waited for our plane several days earlier in Long Beach, we received a phone call out of the blue. It was Mary Barnick, a researcher and journalist originally contacted through Craig's List. "We sure hope to meet you when you get out here," she says. Not realizing she lives some three hours from Memphis, we phone her from the motel the night we discover we've worn out both our welcome and our bank account. Mary and her husband Bo don't think twice about coming to our rescue. We can't bring ourselves to tell Bertha that is what is happening. She has done for us than we could have expected during our abbreviated visit.

We do have one last question for Bertha before we leave her and she leaves us. Did she know Don Sinclair had been molesting Darrell? "Yes," she says. "Your mama and I talked about it."

Darrell's mind fills with questions. If Bertha knew the molestation was happening, why didn't she tell anyone; the police, Monkey, Johnny or even R.D.? Does she really love him? Does she really care for him?

Then he thinks back to how the police reacted the first time Don molested him. He remembers his mother's non-reaction. He knows Bertha is absolutely correct when she tells him, "No one would have believed me even if I told about you being molested." In the general way of thinking, things like child molestation never happen in Arkansas. As with men beating their wives or wives cheating on their husbands, even if something like that does happen, there isn't a soul who is going to admit it.

Darrell's story is particularly filled with selective memory and inadvertent admissions. The one that bothers us most is Almeter's exclamation when she first meets Darrell, "I've been waiting for this moment all my life." Bertha Merriman assures us that her mother never did know that Darrell existed and that Alzheimer's sometimes has her a bit confused these days, but we decide to question her after we return home. If she did know that Monkey had a son in the next state over, why didn't any she or her husband Ray or Monkey or any of the extensive Jackson family come looking for him? Almeter can neither confirm nor deny knowing about Darrell. Our questions seem to confuse her all the more.

"Arkansas might as well be another planet," is all she says.

Which One Am I?

– 35 –

DAMIEN

Darrell isn't much for the news. He finds it too depressing and much too repetitive. No one remembers history. No one learns from mistakes. It's always the same set of experiences over and over again. Only the faces change.

The news comes to him predigested, the story always filtered through someone else's experience. Darrell might never have known about the drama unfolding in his old home town had the History Channel not aired a well-known documentary about West Memphis. It wasn't until 1998 that Darrell heard about the West Memphis Three.

The film is *Paradise Lost: The Child Murders at Robin Hood Hills*, a 1996 documentary film directed by Joe Berlinger and Bruce Sinofsky. The filmmakers had gone to West Memphis to document a murder trial. Teenagers Jason Baldwin, Jessie Misskelly, Jr. and Damien

Echols, who was said to be the trio's ringleader, were accused and ultimately convicted of the brutal deaths of three little boys: Christopher Byers, Michael Moore and Stevie Branch. *Paradise Lost* was to be the first media to bring national attention to the case. It was also the first to cast doubts upon the veracity of the law system in West Memphis.

While out riding their bicycles one evening in May 1993, the three smaller boys had disappeared. Their bodies were recovered the next day in a flood control canal in a grove the locals called Robin Hood Hills. Their bodies were naked, savaged and drowned. Alone among the three, the Byers boy looked to have been castrated.

Darrell found himself yelling at the television. "Those poor kids! I know what they're going to do to them!" Though Darrell's case wasn't particularly similar to that against the West Memphis Three, the police methodology used in both cases was strikingly similar. Even some of the prosecutors shared both cases.

Some things had changed in the 12 years between Darrell's case and Damien's. Ever since Ronald Reagan became President of the United States in 1976 partly by marrying the Republican Party with the Religious Right, ironically the Devil was being blamed for everything. Satanic Ritual Abuse (SRA) had become the rage in the popular media, with talk show hosts including Phil Donahue, Sally Jesse Raphael, Oprah Winfrey and Geraldo Rivera devoting programs to exploring the phenomenon.

Satan's influence was pernicious, according to the talk shows. Bible prophecy predicted the Antichrist would emerge first from the sea and here was Satanism making its first presence felt in California in the upscale seaside town of Manhattan Beach. During the McMartin Preschool trial beginning in 1984, it was said that so strong was the appeal of the dark side that the Devil could even lull a grandmother, 73-year-old Virginia McMartin, into his service.

Of the journalists covering SRA, Geraldo Rivera's involvement was particularly influential. His background as a serious news reporter gave him the credibility lacked by many talk show hosts. By 1985, the former ABC News reporter was beginning to move into the more exciting and potentially more lucrative world of tabloid TV. On the episode about SRA, one of a series of special programs he hosted about the fringes of American life, he stated that there were, at the time, over 1 million Satanists in the U.S. He linked this movement with ritual child abuse, child pornography and satanic murders. He warned viewers that, "the odds are that this is happening in your town."

Soon after the special aired, it also led to a case of "Satanic Panic" described in a book of that title. Throughout Jamestown, NY, police received reports of teenagers holding a "black mass" on Halloween. The humane society received calls about pets that had been killed in ritual fashion.

None of it proved true. Some teens wearing dark clothes and strange haircuts had merely held a Halloween party. As fear continued to escalate throughout the country, Rivera found it necessary to issue a retraction and to apologize for the damage his programs had done to innocent people. To date, his is the only apology from anyone in the media.

Where education is lacking, humans historically have explained the unknown through ritual and superstition. West Memphis Juvenile Probation Officer Jerry Driver knew that there was a reason for everything. He would make bringing the city's troublemakers to justice his life's work. Until the West Memphis Three case, there had never been a criminal act attributed directly to this religious belief. Successfully helping prosecute the first case of true Satanism at work would be a nice black feather in anybody's cap.

There was little indication that Jerry Driver would be the man to make history. Driver's early career was as a commercial airline pilot. When that career ended, he and his wife opened a housecleaning service. It was only after that venture failed that Driver accepted a job with Crittenden County as a juvenile probation officer. This was the position Driver held the night he, wearing a policeman's uniform, arrested Darrell. Police saw him as something of an expert on local troublemakers. By the time of the West Memphis Three case, he had been become Crittenden County's chief juvenile officer.

When she got the chance, Carolyn Williams called Jerry Driver a lying crook. As the River Grove Townhouses went up in flames behind them, Carolyn noticed most how the officer was treating her youngest son. For his part, Jerry must have thought Carolyn hadn't seen him slap her boy, but the mark that quickly appeared on Darrell's face gave it away. Up in the driver's seat, Johnny was getting hot too. Carolyn warned him not to say a word. She knew what was coming and didn't want two of her boys in jail.

Darrell's arrest was like a practice run for what would happen 12 years later to the West Memphis Three. It was their oddness that made both Darrell and Damien Echols into targets. Darrell had his strange mannerisms and feminine bearing. Damien was always outfitted in Wal-

Mart's most mysterious solid black, his hair worn in what the Damien of today calls "stupid haircuts." Both were from lower income and therefore politically impotent families. They may have grown up in West Memphis, but they were still troublemakers, outsiders, "from off."

As became quickly obvious, the probation officer Jerry Driver had been watching Darrell for some time. Until that night, Darrell remembered that he had been seeing Driver sitting in a plain looking car pretty much everywhere he turned. This was the man he'd seen watching as he walked by the police station. The strange man showed up on multiple occasions parked near Aunt Jeanne's house. He'd also seen the car down at Wonder Elementary. Darrell had dropped out of school by then, but Jerry had no way of knowing that. Darrell just figured the creepy man he kept seeing who he would later know as Jerry Driver was just some old guy — some pervert like Robert McDeigh -- who was interested in young boys.

Jerry Driver wanted to take his Darrell directly to the police station. That was hard to do with Carolyn screaming at the top of her lungs that she wanted his captain there. With so many witnesses to the arrest, Driver could only bow to Carolyn's demands. Before he made that call to his captain, Driver made sure to wave Aunt Jeanne's car through.

Memories resurfaced. As a result, watching *Paradise Lost* was like reliving the nightmare of Darrell's own life. More faces appeared on the screen there in Robert and Darrell's Long Beach apartment. They were older than he remembered and in different roles, but their identities stood out. Chief among them was the judge assigned to the West Memphis Three case, David Barnett. He had practiced law for six years and attended Northwestern School of Law's attorney courses, before running for Prosecuting Attorney in 1974. He was elected in 1975 at age 32, the youngest Prosecuting Attorney for the Second Judicial District in Arkansas.

Darrell never met David Barnett until the day he went before the judge. Barnett was pretty sure he had a case against the boy. His entire case was to play the tape Jerry Driver had made during his second interrogation of Darrell — just not all of it. The parts where Jerry assured Darrell that if he just admitted to setting the fires he'd let him go home with his mother never made it before the judge.

This was where Darrell felt his fear mounting because it was a similar tactic also used in the West Memphis Three case. Evidence was slight, but prosecution did have a confession and accusation made by Jessie Misskelly, Jr., a boy the other two defendants admit to knowing only tangentially. The teen has been diagnosed as borderline mentally retarded, operating on the level of a kindergarten student eager to please. Though his taped confession was never introduced in court, the jury foreman has since admitted that the recording had a huge effect on the jury. What Misskelly said had received wide media attention in the local papers long before the trials. In the total absence of any physical evidence, the life sentences awarded to Misskelly and Baldwin and the death penalty handed to Echols came as a result of questionable evidence that was never legally presented to the jury. Misskelly subsequently recanted his confession.

"Arkansas will never admit they made a mistake," says victim Stevie Branch's mother Pam, now an ardent supporter of the West Memphis Three. Still, everybody loves a winner. After the West Memphis case drew to a close, Jerry Driver stayed on the job until he resigned as Crittenden County's Chief Juvenile Intake Officer in May 2008 amidst an audit of his former office. He later pled *Nolo contendere* to theft of property charges, was sentenced to 10 years probation and ordered to make restitution in the amount of $27,684.19.

Judge David Burnett stepped down from the bench in 2009. Running as a Democrat the following year, Burnett defeated Barrett E. Harrison in the May 18 primary. He then ran unopposed in the November 2 general election. He is currently the Arkansas State Senator representing District 15.

In 2012, Jason Baldwin, Jessie Misskelly, Jr. and Damien Echols were released after a West Memphis judge received an Alford plea from the defendants. According to attorney Karen Michalson, successful Alford pleas often suggest that there is an attempt to save face behind the scenes.

The term Alford plea derives from North Carolina v Alford. In this case, the Supreme Court noted that: "An individual accused of crime may voluntarily, knowingly, and understandingly consent to the imposition of a prison sentence even if he is unwilling or unable to admit his participation in the acts constituting the crime... when ...a defendant intelligently concludes that his interests require entry of a guilty plea and the record before the judge contains strong evidence of actual guilt." This means the accused defendant does not admit the act, but admits that the prosecution could likely prove the charge. In some states, a plea such as this which "admits sufficient facts" often results in the case being continued without a decision and later dismissed.

This unusual plea came at an unusual time, just as DNA testing was to be introduced. This evidence was unavailable at the time of the murders.

Its presentation at trial was expected to prove that none of the three accused men were ever at the scene of the crime.

On its face, this is a win-win situation for both sides. The state knows the DNA testing doesn't support their case and that could result in a loss at trial, but politically they can't just dismiss such a high profile matter.

The plea allows Baldwin, Misskelly and Echols to plead to a lesser crime while continuing to assert their innocence. The trio agreed to a legal maneuver that allowed them to maintain their innocence while acknowledging that prosecutors had enough evidence against them to find guilt. They were released for time served.

The West Memphis Three continue to assert their innocence from outside prison. Governor Mike Beebe has stated he will consider a pardon of the three men if someone else is convicted of the crime. The State of Arkansas has stated they will pursue no new leads generated by the DNA testing and considers the murder case closed.

The ironies of West Memphis justice were summed up best in an interview that Baldwin, Misskelly and Echols granted to the CBS news show *48 Hours* after their release. Said Baldwin, "When we told prosecutors we were innocent, they put us in prison for life. Now when we plead guilty, they set us free!"

-- 36 --

JOHN

She was just an old woman getting by on what little she had left: a card table covered with a scarf of dark purple, an empty section of Memphis sidewalk, a deck of well-used cards and the gifts passed down through generations. "Tell your fortune, sir?" Long ago she'd ceased being surprised at how few people wanted to know.

Darrell wanted to hear what the cards said because he had stopped believing that there was a future for him at all. His family had abandoned him. He had no possessions to speak of. He was with a man he did not love. Darrell knew early on that there was no future with John McGee. The man had seemed nice enough when they met in the bars. He was tall, dark-headed and slightly on the husky side, something Darrell didn't mind at all. John was also 26 years older than Darrell, who was then entering his twenties.

The age gap may have signaled to Darrell that John was mature, established and something of the father figure Darrell would search for all his life. They'd only met once before they became a couple. Not knowing any better, Darrell thought that a man like John would bring him a better life.

By the time Darrell sat down at the old woman's table, he already knew he'd been had by John. It didn't take long for Darrell to figure out that John McGee was nothing but a liar, thief and con artist. Yet this was the man whom Darrell had chosen to be with.

When Darrell and John first got together, John was employed as the manager of the Memphis apartment building in which they lived. John wouldn't keep that job any longer than he kept any other job he held, but while they were there, Darrell enjoyed being a homemaker.

John had been yearning for a home-cooked meal and so one night Darrell set out to make him happy. John left early as Darrell set about preparing an extra special spaghetti dinner. The spaghetti sauce was made in a Southern fashion as Darrell had learned through the years from watching others cook. There were fresh vegetables, multiple salads and garlic bread. Darrell had cooked it all from scratch, filling the dining room table with a veritable feast. The only thing missing from the tableau was John.

"We're going out to eat with friends tonight," John informed Darrell as he walked through the door. "I've made plans."

"We're what?" said Darrell, incredulous. "After you asked me to make you a home-cooked meal? After I spent all day in the kitchen?"

The food started flying and after that the dishes, décor and anything else Darrell could get his hands on. Darrell kept throwing until there was nothing left to throw.

Though he'd like to blame the resulting damage on someone inside, this time it was Darrell who was mad.

After losing his job at the apartment, John went to work at a restaurant. The place itself was nothing special. It was a family place where diners could dine if they wanted or order food to go. It wasn't as fancy as the average Denny's, but much classier than McDonald's.

The first time Darrell walked into the restaurant, he found, to his complete surprise, that he knew everyone working there. John McGee was managing a restaurant crew almost completely staffed by the children of Don Sinclair's first marriage.

Grown as he was, it took Don's children a bit to recognize Darrell. Though they had never been close and hardly interacted, Darrell recognized who they were right away. He remembered the Christmas during Don and Carolyn's marriage when they picked through what few toys Darrell had been allowed to possess, wrapping each one carefully. Darrell knew exactly which of these people had received which of his toys.

He told them about it as well. Darrell also told them how their father had sexually abused him. Darrell wanted each and every one of those people to know what kind of father their father had been to him.

The city of Memphis was beginning to feel no more comfortable than Darrell's relationship with John did. One day before John had run up enough overruns at the restaurant for the owners to notice their money missing, Darrell went to the nearby mall to kill time.

It was at the top of one of the mall escalators that Darrell saw him. The man was older, but looked just the same to Darrell. Beside the man was another who, judging from the body language, was likely a boyfriend of his.

Darrell recognized Robert McDeigh in an instant.

"You remember me, you son of a bitch?" Darrell accosted McDeigh. "The one you molested in the back room of the library at Wonder Elementary School in West Memphis?"

McDeigh apparently did recognize Darrell. His face turned ashen and he turned to walk back down the escalator that had been bringing him up.

"Don't pretend you don't recognize me," Darrell continued to yell at the man as McDeigh and his confused companion attempted to make their getaway.

That's when things got loud. Darrell's blood was boiling and inside him his emotions exploded to the surface, people inside assuming their battle stations: Confusion, Anger, Rage; Confusion, Anger, Rage; J.D., James, Steve; Carol, Diane, Star.

Confusion.

There were so many people around. Should he make a scene? Incite a riot? What should he do?

Anger.

What if these people had children attending Wonder Elementary? Darrell realized that he needed to let them know there was a molester in their midst.

Rage.

"If you have kids who go to Wonder Elementary in West Memphis, keep them away from this son of a bitch," Darrell screamed to anyone and everyone within earshot. "This man is a child molester!"

All around them, shoppers turned Darrell's way to see what all the yelling was about. As they did, Robert McDeigh disappeared into the crowd.

Darrell went to the Memphis police straight away after that. He wanted to file child molestation charges. He wanted justice for himself and whoever else Robert McDeigh might have hurt.

He was told there was nothing the Memphis police either could or would do. They dismissed Darrell's claims out of hand. They informed Darrell that the statute of limitations for making a claim against McDeigh's molestation had long run out.

Feeling both helpless and hopeless, Darrell hoped this old woman with her card table on the Memphis sidewalk would deliver good news. He wanted to hear that things would work out. He wanted to know that he would have the life, the normal life, which had always been denied him.

She turned the first of her cards. "This will not be a long relationship," she said as John McGee stood by listening. She turned the next. "Then you will go on a long, long journey by yourself. John will no longer be there. You will learn things along the journey about yourself that you thought you'd never be able to do."

None of this was anything Darrell wanted to hear, though really he wasn't surprised.

As the third card turned face up, the old woman told Darrell, "After your journey, you will meet the man that you are meant to be with and you will marry him. He will be your first." She described an older gentleman with dark hair who wore glasses. "You will be with him many, many years," she continued, "but he will not be the only one."

She flipped another card. And then another.

Lastly, she told Darrell he would meet another man. As she saw him then, the man was dark-headed and younger than John; someone closer to Darrell's own age. That man would be Darrell's last husband.

John and Darrell didn't stay in Memphis long after that. The owners of the restaurant began to count the over-rings, adding up the missing money that John McGee had pocketed. Before they could press charges, John did what he'd always done and moved along. Because he felt he had no alternative, Darrell always went with him.

Darrell didn't want to just run out on his family, but the only sibling he remained close to was Bobbie Lynn. She'd and her family had been changing addresses quite frequently at that point. Still, Darrell knew she was working near the airport at Babe's. Darrell knew as well as anyone else in Memphis what kind of place Babe's was, but he figured one cocktail waitress job was as good as any other.

That was the wrong assumption to make. Darrell and John had to sit in the club watching as Darrell's only sister danced her set for the customers. Stunned, he watched as Bobbie Lynn slid around the poll at the center of the stage. Horrified, he wanted to turn away from the sight of his sibling's naked breasts. Gratefully, he and John left the club as fast as they could say their goodbyes to Bobbie Lynn. Above all, Darrell was thankful that Babe's was only topless and not totally nude.

Darrell couldn't have known it then, but everything the old woman he'd met saw was to come true. Of course, It wasn't anything she told him that made Darrell finally leave the South. It was John McGee.

Which One Am I?

– 37 –

DOREECE

It could have been three months. Six months. A year. Two. The time Darrell spent with John McGee was told in changes more than constants and not a one of these was tied to anything someone might recognize as a timeline. There was all that movement inside Darrell for one thing. All those people he didn't know coming one by one to claim use of his body. They were just trying to help him, whoever they were, but they didn't realize how off-center they were making Darrell feel. Darrell was unsure of himself during the one part of his life where he needed to feel most certain about who or what he actually was.

Life with John McGee was anarchic. What Darrell had been seeking in his first real romantic relationship was someone who wouldn't lie to him, someone who he could love unconditionally and who would love him back. Darrell didn't know how to make a relationship work. During the early Eighties, there were few examples represented in the media to show young men and women how it might be done. Even today, there are fewer voices telling how to exist in a gay relationship than there are those who claim such a union should not exist at all.

Darrell may not have known what a healthy relationship was, but his family had given him plenty of examples of what one was not.

A healthy relationship was a stable one, this Darrell knew inherently, and John McGee embodied anything but that. Whatever length of time they were together saw McGee move them from Tennessee to Texas to Florida and then up to Michigan. They landed out in California for a time where Darrell got his first taste of Long Beach and twice they found themselves in Nevada living in Las Vegas.

Until Star almost killed her, Doreece came with them. An older women, heavy set and running to fat, Darrell doesn't remember how McGee's self-adopted mother Doreece got into the picture. He only knows she was well-attached to John. Doreece always said John McGee reminded her of her son and the two boys would have been about the same age. She never could bring herself to say what happened to her son or for that matter to her son's father, but she clung to John McGee as the embodiment of that lost offspring. Doreece would do anything for John McGee and the man knew it.

John certainly didn't do much for Doreece, or at least he didn't do what she most wanted him to do. It was obvious to anyone who knew them that Doreece wasn't completely satisfied with the dysfunctional mother/son relationship she shared with John McGee. She wanted John to be the one who saved her like she'd been saving him all these times he'd suddenly uprooted and moved his makeshift family. Not that John would have gone that extra mile for Doreece even if he wasn't gay. The way things were going worked out just fine for him.

Every time there was a move, it would be the dark-haired older woman who would plunk down whatever deposit their next new landlord demanded. Until they all got to Flint and things went irrevocably wrong, there were always the six of them in the house: Darrell, John, Doreece, her two dogs and a solid white cat with blue eyes and no hearing at all. Deafness had made the kitty mean. The only one who got anywhere near it was kind-hearted Doreece.

It was more the shyster than the hobo in John McGee that kept him mobile. He would always pull into town and get a job at a local fast food franchise. Such jobs never paid much, but John was less interested in the money his employers paid him than in what he could take on his own. In his Forties by this time, John was quite a bit older than most of the other employees which is likely why his employers always made him the man to close up shop. Alone in the store at night, John found it easy to write up an over-ring or two, depending on how much cash he wanted to pocket. There wasn't a business that hired him that wouldn't find a whole lot of money missing from the till after John McGee left town.

John was the worst person Darrell could have been with at this point in his life. Having just escaped his chaotic family situation, feeling anger and guilt that he hadn't had a chance to properly say goodbye to Carolyn, Darrell had unwittingly jumped from one traumatic and uncertain situation into another. Darrell was feeling hopeless and helpless, like he had nothing in the world to live for. Why was he being traumatized with no sense of permanence and the home he craved? Why didn't John love him? What could he do to make things better? Darrell had believed that this relationship would help him live a better life. Just like everyone else who came in contact with John McGee, Darrell got conned.

Unbeknownst to Darrell, the people inside were responding in their own ways. They felt angry, afraid and tormented. Unaware even of each other, they came out, did what they could to survive and went back to their rooms where alone each seethed with exasperation.

It was their fourth move in three, six or nine months that brought John, Darrell, Doreece and her menagerie to Michigan. It was a move of convenience since, according to *The Flint Journal's Journal of the 20*th *Century*, Flint gave most people little reason to come to that city during the early Eighties. The once-thriving General Motors manufacturing center was experiencing high inflation, soaring interest rates and unemployment, and increasing levels of crime. All of it was chronicled in Michael Moore's breakthrough film, *Roger & Me*.

One thing Flint did have there that John McGee needed was a place to stay. Doreece's father owned a house there which, by the time Darrell, John and Doreece got there, was every bit as devastated as Flint's economy. There was lots of clean-up and construction work needed to make the house livable and Doreece's father was way too old and physically incapable of doing any of it. Doreece could bring her friends and live rent-free if only they would help with the construction. Of course John agreed to the arrangement. Not screw was turned nor a lick of work done to the house during the time Darrell spent in Michigan.

For all the city's problems, Darrell liked living in Flint. The exodus of both business and populace left the abandoned auto manufacturing hub with a small town feel. It was quiet and Darrell thought that was nice. Quiet always gave him time to think.

His affinity for Flint was only made better by his living arrangement. Sure the house was ramshackle, but where others saw devastation Darrell saw opportunity. It wasn't much of a house but Darrell was intent on making it look the way he wanted it to look. If this was to be his house he was intent on making it into his home.

There was certainly no indication that things were about to go wrong on the day things finally did. It all started with a conversation between family members that quickly turned into a disagreement and took off from there. Darrell was talking about how he wanted the place to look, but Doreece was having trouble seeing his vision. In fact, she had ideas of her own which in no way jived with those of Darrell. Darrell had never much liked having people tell him what to do and he wasn't going to stand for it now.

Darrell got angry with Doreece. Somebody inside him got angrier still. He blacked out for a moment, coming back just in time to see a screwdriver flying through the air. The sharp metal rod was heading for Doreece. It pierced her lip. Had the screwdriver hit another two inches to the right it would have killed her.

The incident frightened Darrell just as much as it did Doreece. He had never been a violent person. He had never before performed a violent act. Darrell didn't know this person, didn't like this person, didn't remember being this person and certainly didn't want to be this person. But he was.

The person who threw the screwdriver was Star. As keeper of the rage on Darrell's feminine side, the mulatto had internalized both the sense of fierceness she had observed in their housekeeper Miss Cleo Jackson as well as the anger towards his mother Carolyn that Darrell hadn't allowed himself to confront. Star's pent-up anger was at its boiling point. It could have surfaced anywhere. It was just a matter of chance and timing that Doreece caught the brunt of it. From that moment on, Doreece kept her distance from Darrell.

Darrell and John didn't stay in Michigan long after that, though it wasn't the near tragedy that drove them away. It was the weather.

The rains were heavy during the time Darrell lived in Flint and that caused the Flint River to flood. The river had always threatened to flood its city namesake, just as the Mississippi had periodically done to West Memphis and other cities on the Arkansas flood plain. This particular flood wasn't nearly as bad as the legendary flood of 1947. That year, an ice-choked Flint River, fed by snows and rains, jumped its banks and split downtown Flint in two. Still, it was bad enough to cause damage to the home owned by Doreece's father in which Doreece and her makeshift brood were living.

Never one to pass up an opportunity, John McGee was ready when the Federal Emergency Management Agency (FEMA) opened its door to damage claims. John claimed $1,800 for damage to the house. Either there was no paperwork proving the house's ownership or the FEMA director didn't ask for any, but the check that should have gone to the elderly owner ended up in the pocket of John McGee.

Darrell had lost belongings of his own in the flood to the tune of some $800. FEMA issued him a check as well, but he never saw it. The minute John McGee had his ill-gotten gains in the mail he moved them both to Las Vegas.

Doreece didn't make the move with them. Though they would hear from her periodically whenever they had a permanent or semi-permanent address somewhere, Darrell and John would never again share a home with Doreece.

Which One Am I?

-- 38 --

ELVIS

By the time Darrell found himself living on the scary and noisy streets of Las Vegas, his relationship with John McGee was just about as dead as the King himself. It was just as well. Darrell didn't need any more reminders of his mother's relationship with Elvis Presley's father Vernon or of those Elvis-style sideburns Carrol Bevel always wore.

It had been a turbulent time for the two. John had taken them to Texas, where they lived in Houston near a theme park until the apartment above them caved in. In Florida, they'd lived near Fort Lauderdale, where they arrived just in time for Spring Break. They'd even been to California. They saw Hollywood, or at least James did, but it was Long Beach that got Darrell's attention. Darrell decided right then and there that he liked the small town feel of the thriving Navy town.

Which One Am I?

They were in Palo Alto not far from Stanford University when Darrell began to think that something had to be done. John had travelled to Northern California first, sending Darrell money to fly out that was, unsurprisingly, the same amount of cash that came up missing later from the job John was working in town. When the money came up missing, his former place of employment filed a complaint with the Palo Alto police, who issued a warrant for John's arrest. When she heard about the warrant against her beloved John, Doreece blamed Darrell for the trouble.

Elvis Presley had been in his grave for almost a decade by 1986, and the old Sin City was quickly following. The change in the city seemed to Darrell to be happening right before his eyes as the Las Vegas Strip underwent the renovation that would allow it to be the more family-friendly destination it remains today.

Off the Strip, away from its neon and gloss, things weren't looking so bright. Like many a grifter both before and after him, John had come to Nevada with no job prospects; just the dream of finding an easy leg up.

Support for the two of them fell on Darrell's shoulders. Never having held a job, he took the first he could find at a Little Caesar's Pizza outlet off the Las Vegas Strip.

For his first day on the job, Darrell was to do the restaurants prep work which was to make pizza dough by combining pre-mixed flour with water and then forming the mixture into round mounds of dough on a lightly-floured work surface. Darrell had seen his mother and the other women in his family doing just this.

By Darrell's last day at Little Caesar's not more than a week later, it became evident that someone else had been watching Carolyn in the kitchen too. As Darrell was mixing the dough and sprinkling flour on the board, he felt himself receding back behind his own eyes. "Whee!" he heard a child's voice exclaim.

Two year old Billy and four year old Jimmie had taken a liking to the task before them. For these two little boys, making up pizza dough was all play. "Whee! This is fun!" Unfortunately neither Billy nor Jimmie yet possessed the motor skills to keep control of the pizza dough. They were making quite a mess. In full co-conscious mode, Darrell could hear himself admonishing the kids. "No! "Don't!" "Stop!" "That's too much flour!" It was all for naught. Clouds of flour quickly filled the workroom, covering Darrell and everything around him in wasted restaurant resources.

"Ha ha! Whee!"

When Darrell emerged from the back room, the face underneath the mask of flour that covered him was drained of blood and white as pizza mix. Darrell was mortified. The employees at the counter must have heard the childrens' voices coming from the back, but how could he explain to his co-workers what had happened when not even he knew? He was confused but he was also frightened. It was bad enough that this strange experience had happened but it was worst not knowing when it might happen again.

Not taking a minute to dust himself off and without saying a word to anybody, Darrell sheepishly left the restaurant. He didn't think for a moment about asking for his paycheck. With the loss of what little income Darrell brought in and no money to pay for housing, Darrell and John soon found themselves living on the mean streets of Sin City.

Luckily for Darrell and John, an organization had come around amongst the homeless, offering a stint in school to teach slot machine repair. In exchange for their participation in the program, Darrell and John found themselves housed in separate hotel rooms and fed on a regular basis paid for by grants from the federal government. When Darrell got arrested for prostitution six months into the program, the organization had to return the money back to the government. Had he known at the time that he could have had the grant money delivered right to his pocket, Darrell would have used the $6,000 to leave John right then.

One day John went to work and didn't come home. Darrell didn't hear from him all that night and the entire next day. Darrell didn't know exactly where to find John, but the way John had been eyeing one of his young co-workers gave Darrell his suspicions.

The next night, Darrell went right to John's co-worker's apartment. Using his jacket to shield his hands, Darrell climbed the fence around the complex, making it to the other side over the combination of barbed wire and razor wire that topped the fence. Next Darrell climbed up the outside of the building, boosting himself up three balconies until he found the right apartment.

Darrell kicked the door hard. "I know you're in there," he yelled. "You have one hour to get home." Then he waited outside for John to come out.

There was a silent trip home, but all Hell broke loose when they got there. Darrell was hurt, angry and wanting revenge. So were the people inside, especially James, Darrell's protector. Though he doesn't remember much about the beating, Darrell knows that James broke John's glasses in a fight that left John pretty well incapacitated. Surprised at himself, Darrell vowed never to hit anyone ever again.

Darrell knew the couple's survival was all up to him. Figuring that if he had proper clothes John might be able to find a job, Darrell decided to do something to help. Since the grant money went directly to the school where he was studying, he figured he had only one option: prostitution.

Darrell had never hustled before and the way the experiment turned out convinced him to never try it again. He hadn't been standing on the Las Vegas street corner more than five minutes before what he thought was his first customer pulled up. Darrell got in the car.

Scared to death, Darrell didn't say a word to the driver until the man pulled the car into a cul de sac and parked right up against a wall.

"You're going to kill me, aren't you?" Darrell asked the man. "You're going to kill me and nobody will ever know."

"Oh no," said the man behind the wheel. "Nothing like that. So how much do you want?"

"For what?" Darrell asked him, confused as well as afraid.

"For whatever you want to do."

Darrell explained to the man that all he wanted to do was to raise some cash to buy clothes for his partner John. It was then that the other cars pulled up behind them.

Now he was really panicked. Darrell started to cry. "You guys are kidnappers! You're going to kidnap and kill me!"

"No, no," the man assured him. He opened his wallet to show Darrell his police badge.

A second man knocked at the passenger side window. "Do you know this man?" he asked Darrell.

"No."

"Then what are you doing in his car?"

Though Darrell denied to the second officer that he had ever propositioned the driver, he was told they had it all on tape. There was a recorder under the back seat, the officers told Darrell, but though Darrell asked to hear it, that's something they wouldn't allow.

The policeman who had picked Darrell up took pity on him. According to him, he would have let Darrell go had the second officer, the Police Chief in charge of the prostitution sting, not come up to the window.

They kept Darrell in jail for four days, but Darrell was glad for it. At least he hadn't gotten himself killed.

When his case came before the judge, Darrell was told the police wanted him out of Las Vegas.

"Fine by me," said Darrell. "How am I going to do it? If I hitchhike, I'll just get arrested again."

The Las Vegas Police Department ended up paying for half of Darrell's bus ticket. Travelers' Aid paid for the rest.

Darrell rode that bus as far from his past as it would take him. When it stopped in Long Beach, Darrell got off.

There was no longer any reason for him to be in Memphis. He had no home in West Memphis. And Darrell certainly didn't want to stay in Las Vegas.

After all, his family didn't want him, Darrell didn't want John McGee and Elvis Presley was dead. It was just as well. Darrell never did care much about Elvis anyway.

Robert Dann & James Darrell Williams 1st Anniversary Portrait
(Photo: J.C. Penney Portrait Studio)

Part Six

Long Beach

Long Beach is a city situated in Los Angeles County in Southern California, on the Pacific coast of the United States. The city is the 36th-largest city in the nation and the seventh-largest in California. As of 2010, its population was 462,257. In addition, Long Beach is the second largest city within Greater Los Angeles and a principal city of the Los Angeles-Long Beach-Santa Ana metropolitan area. The city is a dominant maritime center of the United States. It wields substantial influence critical to the global economy. -- From Wikipedia

Which One Am I?

-- 39 --

BEE

In 1987, Long Beach seemed like a small town to Darrell. It wasn't.

His perspective can be forgiven. After the bus from Las Vegas took him as far west as it could travel, Darrell took up lodging in the Royal Hotel. The Royal would be technically termed a transient hotel because the rooms can be had on a month-to-month basis. In fact, it is nicer than the term implies, situated as it is in the East Village Arts District, a small area filled with exclusive boutiques and upscale restaurants. The Arts District might best be called Bohemian Chic.

Long Beach was still a military town when Darrell arrived. Aerospace giant McDonnell Douglas was the city's biggest employer and the Navy had a base in the harbor. Both income streams vanished with the end of the Cold War in 1991, leaving Long Beach with primary revenue coming from the Port of Long Beach, after adjoining Los Angeles Harbor the second busiest container port in the U.S. The loss of business ultimately forced the city to modernize.

It was John who was paying for Darrell's room, food and living expenses. Darrell never did want to know where John might have gotten the cash. Otherwise, he kept himself up to date on John's activities back in Las Vegas, but he began to care less and less what his other half was up to. Darrell began to really change.

Though it was a shock to be alone in a strange place, Darrell quickly warmed to the experience. He quickly discovered the gay bars along the city's Broadway Corridor just to the east of the Arts District and made himself at home. He made new friends, even though there were always those who would claim they had met him but whom he couldn't begin to remember.

Darrell felt truly free for the first time in his life. He began to believe that he really could make it on his own. The fiasco at Little Caesar's in Las Vegas where Darrell had heard little voices and seen little hands throwing pizza flour into the air had left him afraid to apply for a job anywhere. There was no telling what would happen in a work environment and Darrell wasn't sure he wanted to find out. Still, he had spent enough time on the streets of Memphis to know gainful employment wasn't his only survival option.

Almost two months later John showed up carrying a big cardboard container of obviously stolen swimwear he obviously intended to sell. Darrell knew instantly what John was about and wanted no part of it. Having had time alone to consider their life together, Darrell had also decided he wanted no part of John. "I've got something to tell you," Darrell informed him. "I'm leaving." The lie Darrell told John was that he had met someone else. John's heart wasn't broken. He left that very night with some new boy he'd met that day in the hotel lobby.

Everything changed and nothing changed. The names were different but the heavily painted faces of the neighborhood drag queens were familiar in their own way.

Darrell made friends and began building a makeshift support system just as he'd always tried to do when he was homeless. He met Vanessa, a six-foot drag queen who had worked her way across the country since arriving in Florida five years earlier in 1980 as part of Cuba's Mariel boatlift. They both hung out with Black Robin, White Robin and Polly Fiber. Of the boys on the street, Darrell met a young straight man about his age named Wade and a young gay man about his age named Bob.

Not long after he found himself once again living among the homeless, Darrell opened his eyes to find himself standing at a table at The Americana occupied by Bob and his boyfriend Forrest. There was something strangely familiar about Bob that had drawn Darrell into the Fifties-style neighborhood diner which for many years stood between the Arts District and the gay-oriented Broadway Corridor. As Darrell learned later, his new red-headed freckled friend saw something strangely familiar in Darrell as well.

"When you wear your hair up, you're more masculine. When you wear your hair down, you're more feminine," Bob pointed out. Out of the blue he asked, "Have you ever been diagnosed with Multiple Personality Disorder?"

"Nope," said Darrell, confused by a term that he'd never heard before and wouldn't hear again until he was officially diagnosed by Dr. Sharon Higgens. "What's that?"

"Okay, I'm going to diagnose you," Bob informed him. "You have multiple personalities. Do you show up in places and wonder how you got there? Do you meet people who act like they know you but you don't know?"

Darrell had never met anyone quite like Bob. Here was another young man who not only knew what it was like to live as Darrell but also gave the condition a name. The multiples formed a crowd of two.

They shared experiences in the days that followed, especially when Bob and Forrest allowed a still-homeless Darrell to sleep on the sofa in their apartment. Bob told Darrell about an instinctive inner voice he could hear buzzing around inside his head; what Native Americans might have called a totem.

It is not uncommon for people with DID to exhibit nonhuman alter parts such as dolls, notes multiple Faith Allen on her blog dedicated to helping others with DID and those who have suffered abuse as children. These personalities may reflect objects or animals that were important to the person as a child. There is also a long tradition in the Native American population of berserker s, born shaman who became possessed by an animal as Cherokee multiple Erin Lale explains in her autobiography *Greater Than the Sum of My Parts*. Unaware of any such history or tradition, Darrell suggested Bob name his buzzing personality Bee.

Unfortunately for Bob, not all of his alternate personalities were as benign as Bee. There was a more dangerous personality who Bob called Sexual Maniac. This personality embodied one of the more common coexisting disorders experienced by men with underlying dissociative disorder as pointed out in many studies on the subject. Brought up to deny their feelings, common escapes for men are alcohol, drugs, violence and sex.

Sex for Bob's personality was compulsive. Sexual Maniac had fidelity neither to Bob's boyfriend Forrest nor to the guidelines of safe sex which by 1987 were well-known within the gay community. This type of self-destructive personality comes about, according to Kriss Erikson who moderates hundreds of posts on a popular discussion board for those with DID and their caregivers, out of despair. Sexual Maniac may well have "bought into the idea that he was worthless, that there were no boundaries so there was no need for boundaries." The last time Darrell saw Bob was when they passed in the halls of St. Mary's Hospital's Care Clinic, a Long Beach facility specializing in treatment of those with HIV.

Self destruction was something Darrell was beginning to know all too well. Since he'd been back on the streets, there was trouble within, though Darrell's interior troubles were far from obvious. With the help of local churches, he still kept himself clean enough so that few suspected he was homeless. The only difference between the churches of the South and those of the West was that those in Long Beach required Darrell to sit through a sermon in order to receive help from them. This was something Darrell didn't mind. He liked feeling that God was looking out for him.

Peace didn't come so easily to those inside. J.D., James, Steve, Billy Bill: They were all confused. Why were they back on the streets? What had they done to make their family abandon them? Would they ever have the stable home they craved? What could they do to make the ones they loved love them back? Why were they alive at all? No matter how many churches and bars they visited and no matter how many streets they walked, the answers were as clouded as the fog rolling in over Long Beach Harbor.

Had Darrell been under psychiatric care during this time, Dr. Higgens would have helped him to befriend the destructive ones and restore in them a faith in life. As the doctor would do once Darrell entered counseling, she would have helped him give value to the individual inner people and also to his overall self. For now, Darrell wasn't even sure that he was a multiple. Bob's off-hand diagnosis may have been correct, but it also may have just as likely been wrong. Even if Darrell was a multiple, he had no idea what to do about it. The only person he knew who was like himself was Bob -- and Bob was far from what the psychiatric community considers integrated. Had Bob been further along in his own treatment and had his psychiatrist been able to give Sexual Maniac a better sense of his role in Bob's life, Bob might have avoided becoming exposed to HIV.

There were no sexual maniacs inside Darrell. He and all the people inside believe in the fidelity they never saw their mother practice. Neither did they follow the typically male pattern of turning to alcohol to escape from their pain. They all remembered the promise Darrell had made to the owner of J-Wag's back in Memphis. Hard liquor would never again pass Darrell's lips and he couldn't stand the taste of wine or beer. Drugs were another matter.

The War on Drugs was in full bloom by the Eighties. The number of arrests for all crimes had risen by 28% while the number of arrests for drug offenses rose 126% according to *The 1989 NCCD Prison Population Forecast: The Impact of the War on Drugs*, a study published at the end of the decade. Arrests may have increased but supply was hardly diminished. There wasn't a drug on the street that didn't make it into Darrell's body at one time or another.

Darrell preferred stimulants. Drugs like crack cocaine, known on the street as speed, helped Darrell remain up at night when the streets were most dangerous. This also led to his interior clock becoming permanently reset. Darrell still sleeps best during daylight hours and likely will for the rest of his life. The necessity to share the needles used to inject the speed into his blood with his street brethren ultimately led to his own HIV infection.

Stimulants might have helped him during his period of street life, but Darrell quickly discovered that the available depressants of the period were a waste of time. He tried heroin and handfuls of Valium in an effort to end his life. Darrell didn't know why, but all he got for his troubles were an upset stomach and really bad headache. The people inside had apparently learned from their experience with the PCP-laced joint his sister Bobbie Lynn once provided and the passed-out episode caused by alcohol back at J-Wag's. The effect of the drugs was split between them. Even when police approached Darrell right after he had shot up speed, the officers failed to find any reason to arrest him. Shining their light in his eyes, Darrell's pupils failed to dilate and expose his state.

All the people inside wish they could split the effects of HIV. That is one trick they have yet to master.

Today Darrell is one of St. Mary's Care Clinic's longest living HIV patients. As he did with Robert, Darrell still tries to live a reasonably healthy life and keeps his appointments with the doctors who have helped him live so far. It was at such an appointment when Darrell last saw Bob. Running late, Darrell was just getting off the elevator as the door to the elevator next to his closed. The doors were just open enough that he could see a tall red-headed man inside. He thought he recognized Bob even though the two hadn't seen each other in a decade. If Darrell hadn't been running late, he might have stuck his hand in and stopped the doors from closing. That's something else Darrell regrets he didn't do.

-- 40 --

VANESSA

Of all the friends the couple had made in their 25 years in Long Beach, only Ray and Vanessa came to Robert Dann's memorial. Vanessa knew how important it was to Darrell to have someone there. More than anyone, she knew what it was like to love your loved ones.

Vanessa had landed in Miami in 1980 as part of the Mariel Boatlift. While many of the exiles sent stateside with Castro's consent were discovered to have been released from Cuban jails and mental facilities, that wasn't Vanessa's story at all. She had been raised in an anti-Castro family living in an anti-Castro town but that's not what got her to Miami.

Once her parents had passed away, the townspeople heard that, as a gay person, Vanessa was on Castro's list of undesirables. She could either abandon her home and all her belongings or be killed. Making the decision for her, Vanessa's neighbors hustled her to the boat. Her brother, the only other surviving member of her family, came as well. He stayed in Miami. Vanessa came to Long Beach.

Vanessa was one of the first people to take Darrell under her wing the night he left John. Though she had a small place of her own, Vanessa had been homeless enough to wonder how something like this could happen to such a nice young man. Vanessa and Darrell spent all that night talking at a since-closed Winchell's donut outlet where they were joined by White Robin. His jacket forgotten in the rush to get away from John, Darrell shivered both against the cold and with fear of what might come.

He needn't have worried but he did. His street family helped Darrell as much as they could assist anyone who refused to ask for help. What Darrell really wanted and needed was a secure home with someone to love him but his dreams were beginning to seem like some distant star on the horizon. Like J.D. and Billy Bill inside him, Darrell was beginning to lose hope. Long Beach streets may have been no worse than those of Memphis, but they were streets nonetheless. Darrell felt he had only one more place to turn.

The stairs still descend from the end of 8th Place down to Alamitos Beach but waves and wind have long ago smoothed out the sand dune that Darrell climbed that fateful morning.

Darrell often prayed and still does, but on this day he had a special request. There was a strap around his arm and a needle ready to supply the overdose that he hoped would kill him.

"I can't take much more of this," he prayed to the Almighty. "I'm tired of being alone. I need someone who will love me and take care of me."

That's when he heard the voice from on high. "Stop!" God commanded him. "All you need to do is tell me what you need."

"I need someone to love me and take care of me," Darrell responded. "I want someone who won't lie to me or cheat on me. I don't care if they are male or female. I just need someone to love me for the rest of my life."

"Sit on the mound," the voice told him. "And it will be there."

Darrell knew enough not to question. There had been beach work being done and the workers had left a mound of sand. He pumped the drugs into the ground and threw away the syringe. Then he looked around him.

The clothes Robert Dann wore that day are still in the closet. There is a pair of dark black jeans and a matching jean jacket hanging back in the corner. On the shelf overhead are his heavy black Harley Davidson motorcycle boots. At 6'1" and a muscular 210 pounds dressed all in black on a sunny beach day, he would have seemed anachronistic, imposing and hard to ignore.

Robert's eyes were on the ground as he approached the sand dune. "I normally wouldn't ask," said Darrell truthfully. He made it a point to never ask anyone for anything. "But you don't possibly have a cigarette, do you?"

"I don't normally give out cigarettes when people ask me," Robert answered. "But okay, you can have one."

"What's wrong?" Darrell asked Robert. "You look like you've lost your best friend. Why don't you come over and sit down? I don't bite."

Robert did sit down. The two got to talking and launched what would be a long relationship. Twenty two and a half years later, it would be over as fast as it began.

Darrell wouldn't see much of Vanessa or anybody else for the next 10 years. Though he went along with Robert whenever the older man had a job driving truck, when they were home, Darrell's history of abandonment meant he could never bring himself to leave the house. Robert tried to get Darrell to do things on his own, but Darrell was frightened that one day he would return and his key wouldn't fit. As a result, they were always together and generally alone.

Making use of their time in isolation, Robert taught Darrell some of the skills he himself had learned in life. Darrell bristles at the thought that Robert might have served as a father figure, but Robert did take on much of the role abandoned by R.D. Williams, Danny Poole and the rest of the men who had come into Darrell's life while ignoring him completely.

During his previous life in his native Rhode Island when he was married with a child, Robert had owned an antique store. He taught Darrell how to identify legitimate antiques and to value their worth. When he wasn't driving a truck, Robert made money by buying and reselling these antiques. He also did local construction renovating houses and apartments. Under Robert's tutelage, Darrell learned to swing a hammer with the best of them.

According to Robert, he'd always had everything he wanted but he knew Darrell never had the opportunity to own nice things. Robert made sure there was money so that Darrell could have what was always denied him. Their apartment filled with collectibles, toys and knick knacks. There was neither rhyme nor reason to the purchases. Some of them Darrell picked out. The rest reflected the tastes of the people inside.

What Robert was doing was preparing Darrell for a life without him. They were both aware of the 26 year age gap, though that weighed more on Robert than it did Darrell. There was also the matter of Robert's HIV status. Both had tested positive yet for different strands of HIV. Today it is known that HIV is a highly variable virus which mutates readily. There are many different strains of HIV, even within the body of a single infected person. Robert's HIV was found to be fast acting. Darrell's strain is slow.

Vanessa didn't see Darrell much during this time. She had met Ray, a laid-back and caring man who had dated his share of females, about the same time Darrell met Robert. Ray likes to say he had never before met a woman quite like Vanessa. The two settled into a long and caring relationship that continues to this day.

Sometimes Vanessa would see Darrell riding with Robert in their truck and she took solace in knowing that Darrell had found someone who was willing to give Darrell everything he craved. To Vanessa, Robert looked like a good man and sounded like a good man. "You look at someone and you can read the person," she said. "It was a blessing. Darrell was in good hands."

Though they never knew him well, Vanessa and Ray though highly enough of Robert Dann to come to his memorial. They were surprised at both at what was going on and what was not. Robert had friends of his own, that much they knew. He liked to go down to the gay bars on Broadway and play pool with his buddies, both male and female, who Darrell eventually considered his friends as well. Not a one of them came to the house to share their memories of the man and the good times they shared with Robert.

The house instead was filled with Robert's relatives. They had brought food, though no one seemed concerned that Darrell wasn't eating a bite of it. In fact, Darrell hadn't wanted the memorial to take place at all. He was confused and suicidal, far from being ready to say goodbye to the man he loved.

It was the family matriarch, Robert's sister Joan, who had insisted on the get-together. Joan had been pushing for it to happen ever since the day she heard about Robert's death, originally insisting that it happen that very next day. Darrell was able to stall her for a week.

When she might have been concerned with Darrell's well-being, Joan seemed more interested in Darrell's possessions. The memorial was Joan's chance to case the house. That was the day she began to specify which of Robert's belonging she felt should be given to her and her family. Joan wanted Robert's clothes, tools and his collection of beer steins for starters. She never did ask if there was anything Darrell might need.

Fulfilling Darrell's immediate needs fell on the shoulders of Ray and Vanessa. Darrell most needed to talk. The couple stayed with Darrell long after the family had left, letting him vent his sadness and feelings of loss well into the night.

Few of Robert's old friends came around much after that. It is just as well. Darrell wouldn't allow them into his house, much less his life, if they did. Neither does he talk anymore to Robert's family, though he did give them both the tools and the beer steins. Ray and Vanessa, on the other hand, are always welcome. Those two are family.

Which One Am I?

– 41 –

RABBIT

In 1925, economist Stuart Chase wrote in his work *Tragedy of Waste*, "For those who believe, no proof is necessary. For those who don't believe, no proof is possible."

He might as well have been writing about DID.

Truddi Chase (no known relation to the economist) brought the people inside her collectively called "the troops" to Oprah Winfrey's Baltimore talk show in 1990 and later was one of the first guests on Winfrey's national TV show. Chase talked about her memoir, *When Rabbit Howls*, titled after possibly her earliest personality split, Rabbit, a child without language who howls with the memory of being raped at the age of 2.

By the time of her appearances with Winfrey, nothing Chase could have said could change the popular perception of DID. The public and psychiatric community had together entered what Angela Lansbury sang about in the 1971 Walt Disney film *Bedknobs and Broomsticks*, "The Age of Not Believing."

This new attitude was first evidenced in the reviews of Chase's memoir. Some reviewers doubted the tale's authenticity, as well as that of DID in general. "It's a lot easier to discredit than it is to defend," Christopher Lehmann-Humpt wrote in the *New York Times*. He went on to do just that, even using quotes in his report to passive-aggressively dismiss "mental health professionals."

Not nearly as damning was Elizabeth Stark's review of Chase's life story in *Psychology Today*, though she throws in her doubts. "Its symptoms are so bizarre," she wrote of DID, "that even some mental-health professionals doubt its existence and attribute the behavior to accomplished acting."

Taken together, these two reviews set the tone for how DID would be perceived by "mental health professionals," as Lehmann-Haupt referred to them in America's Newspaper of Record, for decades to come.

"Misdiagnosis is a very significant problem," wrote David M. Reiss, M.D., a psychiatrist who pointed out that having evaluated or treated over 10,000 patients, he has never encountered a case of what he calls "pure" DID. That is to say, the older diagnosis of "multiple personality disorder" in which the person manifests totally separate identities unaware of each other that only become evident through hypnosis.

"Pure" DID is not listed in the *DSM-5*. The proposed changes for the American Psychiatric Association's *Diagnostic and Statistical Manual of Mental Disorders (DSM-5)* are fairly straightforward. The upcoming updated manual proposes a DID diagnosis if: There is disruption of identity; Inability to recall important personal information; Clinically significant distress and impairment in important areas of functioning; and a disturbance that is not a normal part of cultural and/or religious practices nor due to the effects of a substance.

Blame the change on *Sybil*. The book originally launched a flurry of reported DID cases but may now derail any further cases being named. Most recently, author Debbie Nathan interpreted a cache of letters at the John Jay College of Criminal Justice to present *Sybils's* subject Shirley Mason as a patient who was easily persuaded to contribute to what became a particularly lucrative ruse. In *Sybil Exposed: The Extraordinary Story Behind the Famous Multiple Personality Case*, Nathan presented the world's most famous multiple as a woman who was coaxed and perhaps drugged into admitting to the existence of her multiple personalities.

Doctors today tend to make the *DSM's* standards even tighter. No one wants to fall victim to a criminal faking an excuse or, for that matter, for the crimes of *Sybil*. "The over-diagnosis of DID has led to a negative 'push-back' which has discounted the significance of the dissociative phenomena that does occur quite often," noted Dr. Reiss in his paper on DID. Still, Reiss limits his diagnoses of "pure" DID to those who demonstrate "clear evidence of identifying themselves at different times with different names and different personalities – while being…unaware of this phenomenon."

It is not likely that Darrell would have been properly diagnosed following such a proscription or purity, nor would have Cameron West, author of *First Person Plural*. It is fairly safe to say that in pursuit of a "pure" diagnosis many patients with DID, an d particularly those who experience co-consciousness, will continue to fall through psychiatry's cracks.

A principle goal of avoiding the push-back of diagnosis has led many doctors to develop a fall-back plan. Borderline Personality Disorder (BPD) is today's diagnosis of choice. Infuriating to DID patients, those who are "deliberately manipulative or difficult," are termed to have BPD. That someone whose complaints are being dismissed or downplayed might be angry about it and therefore "difficult" is not a consideration.

It is true that some patients prefer a diagnosis of BPD in order to avoid the stigma of a DID diagnosis, as Dr. Reiss pointed out. For others patients, it is the other way around. Either way, the patient receives a diagnosis that the medical community considers controversial.

As with DID, there is no consensus in the psychiatric community as to what symptoms constitute BPD. "Borderline personality disorder (BPD) is an emotional disorder that causes emotional instability, leading to stress and other problems," according to the Mayo Clinic. *The International Statistical Classification of Diseases and Related Health Problems, 10th Revision* (known *as ICD-10*) renames BPD as Emotionally Unstable Personality Disorder. The diagnostic criteria leave a lot of wiggle room.

This tendency to favor the safer of the two choices has left a lot of what would otherwise be DID patients misdiagnosed and believing that their very existence is denied. As DID patient Stephanie Lee said, "It's easier for someone who is successful in the psychiatry business to deny that which is not well understood. One has to play by the rules big time to get through the medical education system. They become mostly very middle-of-the-road, cooperating citizens."

Lee, a multiple who spent 15 years as a Crisis Intervention Paraprofessional, pointed out, everyone who has been identified as mentally ill has spent some portion of their life having their reality denied, a social crime in the name of psychiatry both in her opinion and her life experience. It is enough to make anyone "difficult."

"Several (more than three) psychiatrists have told me that 'Borderline Personality Disorder is the diagnosis one uses with any patient on whom they can't get a clear handle with another diagnosis,'" she said.

It is not unusual for patients and therapists to view DID in quite different terms. For every DID patient who views their "T," as therapists are referred to on Dissociative Identity Disorder discussion boards, as indispensible, there is likely another whose "T" has misdiagnosed them. For those two, there is likely at least one more pair who fail to be diagnosed at all.

It would not be fair to the diagnostic community to blame these failures of diagnosis solely on The Age of Not Believing. Cases of DID are spread worldwide while experts in the field are not. Still, even in countries where research is most advanced, there remains a need within the psychiatric community to diagnose DID as almost anything but what it is.

This leaves DID survivors, as Rob Spring, Director of UK-based monthly publication Positive Outcomes for Dissociative Survivors (PODS), calls multiples, feeling that they are rare. "In studies of the general population a prevalence rate of DID in 1% to 3% of the population has been described," Spring noted in a recent article, quoting from a 2009 article by Nijenhuis and van der Hart in the *Oxford Handbook of Psychopathology*. Nijenhuis and van der Hart argue that this means DID is at least as common as schizophrenia, yet in 2009 there were 25,421 papers on PubMed relating to schizophrenia but only 73 relating to DID.

The number of citations, or rather the lack of same, is astounding considering that the online research module PubMed contains more than 21 million citations for biomedical literature from MEDLINE, life science journals, and online books.

With little consensus on the existence of DID, it is not surprising that there is not much agreement about what to do about it. While Marlene Steinberg, M.D., writing with Maxine Schnall in *The Stranger in the Mirror*, a 2001 handbook on the subject of DID as it appears in everyday life, stated that hypnosis can be useful for those with dissociative disorder, this approach has been since discredited. A negative example of the effects of hypnosis in this situation is Truddi Chase, the subject of *When Rabbit Howls*. Treated by hypnotherapist Dr. Robert Phillips, her core personality was taken over by those inside and in effect ceased to exist. While Chase is not the only multiple whose core has either vanished or been vanquished, and not all of such DID patients were subject to hypnosis, it is the belief of professionals, including Darrell's doctor Sharon Higgens, that the loss of the first born is often a result associated with hypnotizing a DID patient.

More typical is the use of medication in conjunction with psychotherapy. Medication on its own is never a substitute for psychotherapy, Dr. Steinberg cautions in *The Stranger in the Mirror*, and both must be utilized by a therapist who understands DID and accepts it as a valid diagnosis. The goal is integration, a result only achieved after working through what could be many phases of therapy. The over all process is designed to comfort and communicate with the patient's separate parts, to help them communicate and cooperate as a team.

The timing of integration varies with each patient's insight and ego-strength as Dr. Reiss put it. It may also be a simple matter of correct labeling. "Integration" is commonly confused today by both patients and medical professionals with "fusion." Even Leah Petersen, the multiple who advised the first major television show to focus on DID, Showtime's *The United States of Tara*, confused the two terms.

The process of fusion which Dr. Cornelia Wilbur tried with both Shirley Mason and Billy Milligan, in which interior personalities give up their sense of self and are coaxed into merging into a new personality, is long discredited but still sometimes tried. Many in the International DID community discount fusion to the point of avoiding any doctor who suggests it as a possible "cure."

Petersen can be forgiven for her mistake. Even Truddi Chase confuses the terms in what is arguably the seminal representation of life with DID, *When Rabbit Howls*. Though it was said in many reviews of her book that Chase refused integration, the truth was that, like many DID patients today, she refused fusion. At one point in the text, she answered her hypnotherapist when Dr. Phillips suggested it, "Whom would you choose among us to live beyond that integration? Whom would you kill?"

-- 42 --

RONNIE

We find Velma McDermott outside Heber Springs. She and the rest of the remaining Williams clan of her generation purchased their own mountain about 50 miles north of Little Rock, the Arkansas state capitol. There lived most of R.D.'s siblings, possibly as many as 10 or 12. Darrell isn't sure how many brothers and sisters R.D. had. Only R.D. and Kitty had the senior Richard Williams as their father. The rest were by a different man and Darrell never really got close enough to remember them. Of the four surviving siblings, Bruce Larry is living on the mountain after leaving Memphis, visiting Los Angeles and finally deciding the gay scene was a little too fast for his liking. R.D. was supposed to join his sisters and brothers in Heber Springs, but he never did.

Darrell's Aunt Velma is as reliable a source as anyone we've talked to. Though Darrell remembers her primarily as the family Black Widow, watching what would be her second husband wheeling her wheelchair-bound first husband into a family gathering, like the Joshlins on the other side of Darrell's bloodline she has traded one addiction for another. Velma doesn't think of sex much these days. It is God who fills her time.

Now a devout Jehovah's Witness, Velma's history has been as reborn as her soul. In between admonitions to "accept the Lord" and "have faith in Him" she tells Darrell what really happened to R.D.

It's a long story unfolding like a sad country ballad but Velma isn't missing a beat. People always remember slights more than favors and there is a reason humans do so. According to the article "Bad is Stronger than Good" published in *Review of General Psychology*, a text book put out by Educational Publishing Foundation, humans do this because of our evolution. Human brains are more attuned to picking up on negative information because it is the bad things that can kill or harm. The way Velma tells it, Darrell's brother Ronnie caused a lot of people lots of harm.

Velma's story didn't come as much of a surprise. Darrell suspected somebody was planning something back in Mississippi ever since the calls began coming. His phone started ringing not long before his 10th anniversary with Robert. If only Darrell would come home to Houston, Ronnie told him, the family would take care of him. Darrell had no doubt that Ronnie had the finances to feed another mouth though he was unclear and uncomfortable considering what Ronnie meant when he told Darrell he would be "taking care" of him.

Ronnie had received a large settlement because of a bad accident at his work. The surgeon charged with correcting the original damage to Ronnie's legs had never reattached the nerves after the operation. Ronnie's legs atrophied. In the following malpractice lawsuit, Ronnie Williams had been awarded a $2.2 million settlement. What Darrell didn't know until Velma let it slip was that all of that money was just about gone by the time the calls began.

By the time Ronnie began his onslaught, Darrell knew where his home was. By that time, Darrell hadn't lived in the South for over 20 years. Home was in Long Beach with Robert. Darrell also found the notion that he had to return to Houston to be with family insulting to the family he had built for himself with Robert and their cat Boo.

Darrell decided to go, but not for the reasons Ronnie gave him. The boy R.D. called "my youngest" but never "my son" wanted to confront the man. Darrell packed up a suitcase full of photos to show his siblings what family really was. The case, light blue with an angel print, was filled with photos of some of Darrell's favorite memories and also photos of events he couldn't remember at all. There were pictures of Boo as a kitten, portraits of Robert and himself exchanging wedding bands, Robert's family pictures from the days before Darrell, photos R.D. had sent and snapshots of a visit to Disneyland Robert made with Billy, a trip Darrell still doesn't remember at all.

Things went badly from Darrell's first morning in Houston. "Do you want to talk to Darrell?" he heard Johnny asking somebody. "I don't have anything to say to him right now," came the answer. It was a voice Darrell hadn't heard in many years, his brother Allen. Darrell took that is a slight that his brother didn't want to talk to him. Ronnie made him believe that's exactly what it was.

Darrell did spend one of his two nights in Mississippi at R.D.'s bed side. Despite asking R.D. directly whether or not he was Darrell's father, the words "yes" and "no" didn't seem to be in R.D.'s vocabulary. Instead, R.D. made sure Darrell knew that he'd taken out a life insurance policy just as Carolyn had before her death. Each sibling was to receive $50,000. The money he'd been awarded after an injury on the job — more than $1 million -- was in a safe deposit box. R.D. never did trust bankers.

Instead, R.D. trusted his son Ronnie. That safe deposit box he was so proud of, the one that held all his money in the world and would ensure that he could pay for his own funeral and headstone when the time came, was in both their names. R.D. might have suspected that he would never join his siblings up on the mountain, but he never had inkling that Ronnie would betray him.

At the time of Darrell's visit, R.D. likely didn't know that his safe deposit box was almost empty. He wouldn't find out until near his death that the money he'd been so proud to have saved to pay for his own funeral and headstone was being used for something else. Eventually, he'd have to sell his trailer — the one that was supposed to be moved from West Memphis over to Heber Springs and up the mountain — to one of his sisters in order to get the money for his own burial.

Everyone knew that Ronnie had blown through his own settlement, but they didn't suspect that he'd go through R.D.'s as well. When he got the money, Ronnie did what most people who never had money do when they get it: he bought things. At one point, he had two homes and bought cars for himself and Lisa. What he didn't do was pay taxes on the money he'd received. It didn't take the Internal Revenue Service long to catch up with him. They took everything he had.

After the dust settled, the only things Ronnie Williams had to show for his troubles were two legs he could barely stand on and an increasingly dangerous addiction to OxyContin. Known as "Hillbilly Heroin" on the street, OxyContin is used to treat moderate to severe pain that is expected to last for an extended period of time. It is an opoid pain reliever, a narcotic, similar to morphine and it can be extremely habit-forming.

Unlike the situation with any of the drugs Darrell uses, OxyContin abuse is a huge problem in the United States and particularly in the South. The drug is easily purchased from clinics in the Florida panhandle and resold on the street for 10 times its purchase price. Florida's Lt. Gov. Jeff Kottkamp wrote in an op-ed published in Florida newspapers, "Nearly all of the top 50 prescribers of oxycodone (an active ingredient in OxyContin and other pain relievers such as Percoset) in the United States are in Florida." In a recent survey, only 7% of OxyContin users got the drug from a doctor and 13% bought it from a drug dealer or other stranger. Nearly two-thirds got the drug from a friend or relative.

According to a 2003 study by the Government Accountability Office, OxyContin's warning label warns to not crush the controlled-release tablets because of the potential for rapid release of oxycodone. Ironically, it is hypothesized that this may have been what led to many people crushing the tablets and snorting or injecting the drug. Injecting it into his arm is what Darrell saw Ronnie doing the day Darrell decided he needed to go home.

Darrell phoned Robert back in Long Beach. When he got Robert on the phone, Darrell's husband told him he hadn't wanted to mention it, but their good friend Clayton had passed away just the same time Darrell's plane hit the heavens on its way to Memphis.

Would Robert like Darrell to come home for the memorial? Of course he would. Cutting his visit as short as he could, Darrell informed his siblings that he had to go back. It was only then that R.D. told Darrell of his impending death.

The kids inside were upset that they couldn't stay to help take care of the only man they knew as their father. They wanted to help him through his last days, offer their support and be there to say goodbye since they regretted not having a chance to do so with their mother. As yet undiagnosed, Darrell knew none of this. He had yet to meet any of the people living inside him and it would still be a few years before he was diagnosed with DID. Darrell only knew that this was no family dynamic he wanted to be part of. He didn't like drugs. He hadn't felt particularly welcomed by his family. Darrell had to get home to Robert just as soon as he could.

It was Johnny who drove Darrell back to Memphis International. The sudden change in flight schedule went on the credit card Ronnie had put down to pay for Darrell's round trip.

This extra charge must not have gone down with Ronnie any better than did the shortened visit itself. Ronnie wanted Darrell to stay, though the reasons are anyone's guess. It could well have been that he really did want the family together this one last time preparing for the imminent death of their father. It could also have been that, with money running low, Ronnie saw the check he thought Darrell was receiving from Social Security as much-needed income. Oxycontin is expensive.

Darrell sees his brother now as someone who is controlling and wants to have leverage. Also and interestingly enough, Ronnie wants to deny what happened within the family as much as possible. As our friend Kriss Erickson pointed out, this is common enough. Some people want to hold the answers, yet want to remain unaware of them.

Ronnie still holds Darrell's blue case with its heavenly artwork and its precious cache of photos. In his haste to get back to Robert, Darrell inadvertently left behind those reminders of his past life. Not only did the case stay behind but so did a dragon with a watch that Darrell had purchased at the local Wal-Mart to give to Robert for his birthday. Repeated requests and entreaties made to other family members have yet to get Darrell's prized possessions into the mail. Ronnie refuses to acknowledge he has the case and watch. The rest of the family is too afraid of Ronnie to confront him.

It was plain that Ronnie appointed himself the Keeper of Memories. Unable to control the family, Ronnie controls the narrative; the stories family members are allowed to tell. It is he who ran into Bertha Merriman on the streets of Houston shortly before our visit. Both he and his wife Lisa called the woman who raised him and his siblings "a bitch" for daring to spoil R.D.'s good name by telling Darrell about Monkey. In Ronnie's mind, the honor of a proud Southern man – and that of his family – must be protected above all.

Dead men have no honor, so perhaps R.D. isn't the only family member Ronnie is trying to protect. By reading between the lines and lies and by listening intently to what nobody will say, history is reconstructed. In the safe deposit box Ronnie once shared with R.D. are two more tales Ronnie keeps from the light of day. In this dark and forbidden place are the letters Carolyn mailed to Darrell shortly before her death.

Susan and Lisa originally placed the letters, double wrapped in an effort to protect them from the elements, into the hole in a tree that once stood in front of the home where R.D. once lived. Shortly before the Mississippi home just outside Houston burned down, Ronnie removed the letters to someplace both safer and easier to protect.

He has read the letters yet Ronnie can't bring himself to believe them. Full of shame and blame, the letters discuss a lot of terrible things; a family's horrible history. These messages from beyond Ronnie saw as a burden. At first, he wanted to burn the letters but to do so would have destroyed their power. They can change minds. They can change destinies. For these and so many other reasons, the letters remain locked away in the bottom of Ronnie's safe deposit box. Only he controls the family history.

Ronnie has no idea that Darrell has figured out where Carolyn's letters are hidden. Neither does he have the slightest notion that his Aunt Velma McDermott has joined Bertha Merriman in finally allowing the truth about the Williams family to come to light. This is the story they each must tell so they can live with themselves. This is the story Darrell tells himself.

– 43 –

TOM

It has been years since someone asked me to play piano. Yet here I am, up in the Ozarks where a small crowd waits for me to put my hands to the keyboard. We have been invited into the studio Bo Kirgis and Mary Barnick have built next to their house. The house itself sits far away from any neighbors, as seems to be the custom here in Arkansas. There are woods behind the house providing food and hiding places for deer. Our first night, Mary apologizes for her four-legged neighbors, which can reportedly raise quite a ruckus rubbing against the trees. The only critter that wakes us our entire week there is an armadillo that has tried to burrow under the house. Not even the ticks in the grass bother us.

The room isn't all that far removed from the nature outside. It is full of guitars, wind instruments, recording equipment and expectation. Bo has strapped on a guitar and is ready to jam. Not far from him, Mary sits smiling and waiting for the music to start. Off my left hand is Darrell. Naturally, he is waiting to hear me play for him for the very first time.

Music means different things to different people. It is one of society's most efficient ways to communicate, bringing with it both meaning and emotion. It can be used for dancing, reading or jumping around joyfully like a child. It can be used as a tool for remembering life's good times. It can travel great distances. It can be used as a reminder of life's regret.

My songs were always about my loves and life written with the assumption that never was I alone in what I was experiencing and feeling. I always sought in my lyrical content and musical style to let others know they were not alone. Years ago I called my songs cathartic. Now I just think of them as sad.

To Darrell, music meant more than it did to an average child. For him it was an escape, the songs bringing stories that were more believable than anything happening in his young life. He would listen to the words, feel the music and cry. He would hear people telling him in the songs of the Seventies and Eighties what true love should be. Darrell cried because he knew he did not have that kind of love.

Darrell and I have very likely heard the same songs. What we shared in the experience is the need for love, community and to be part of something bigger than ourselves. We have come looking for a connection with family and with history. That we find what we're looking for here in a studio in the Ozarks is the big surprise.

The songs I want to share and to make part of this unexpected and moving bonding experience here in Bo's studio are the ones to which I can't remember the chords. It would be a long wait for the others if I were to waste the moment reconstructing my own work. The worst thing I could do would be to shatter the crystal clarity of the connection, setting the magic free like fireflies released from a bottle.

When my memory banks run dry and when my fingers will no longer allow me to follow Bo's lead on guitar to continue our impromptu jam session, I suggest that we'd rather just hear them play. I turn away from the keyboard.

None of us know it at the time, but the music has beckoned another new kid from behind Darrell's eyes. Robbie is here, a 10-year-old making his own debut. It's Mary who sees him first sitting there beside me perfectly mimicking every move his Uncle Bo is making on the guitar. Robbie is smiling. Mary is amazed that Robbie knows where to place his fingers on the imaginary guitar he holds. Until this moment, Darrell has never held a musical instrument in his life.

Tears come to my eyes because no one other than me has ever really seen the kids, at least not as individuals. We form a family here in the music room: Bo, Mary, Darrell, me and whoever else inside cares to make themselves known.

That Robbie would pick this time and this place to appear shouldn't surprise us. "No one has ever treated us like people before," says Robbie, the one Mary calls "Beautiful Brown Eyes," a name that embarrasses him as it would any kid his age. "People just ignore us." That Mary named him at all is the part that he really loves.

Darrell and I have never felt as safe and happy as we did during our week in the travel trailer someone left parked on the other side of Bo and Mary's house. It is a pretty standard trailer of the type people use when camping. Devoid of the bric-a-brac that crowds our house in Long Beach, we find our worries are also gone. It strikes us that perhaps we don't own all those collectibles. They own us.

Except for missing our little dog Tigger, who hates music and would have barked throughout the entire evening, we have never been happier than when we spent a week with nothing except two people who loved us. When Darrell and I are happy, the kids inside are happy.

We feel relieved after our stay in Tennessee. While it was wonderful meeting the Jackson family for the first time, things hadn't happened as planned. With every moment a surprise, we remained on guard. The kids never surfaced. We never mentioned the kids to Bertha. We never let Bertha Merriman and the Jacksons know much about us. Nothing went the way we expected it to go and we suspected that there was some disappointment that we weren't the people they expected to show up. It wasn't until we met Bo and Mary that we got to accomplish what we'd really come to Arkansas to do. The couple had kept someone else's promises.

In a cartoon version of DID, which is how people view just about every depiction of it in pop culture, Robbie would be only the first to surface that evening. There would have come his doppelganger Dot, the little ones Billy and Jimmie, the older boys and the girls. It would be a kaleidoscope of faces and a cacophony of voices; a parade of personalities all vying for attention like a troupe of clowns tumbling out of a tiny car.

This is not how we live. This is how everyone else thinks we live. They know we do. They've learned all about DID on television.

"How can you stand it?" one old friend asks me. "Stand what?" I answer. Living with Darrell is no different than living with, say, a musician or an actor, a politician or anyone who spends time in front of a camera, behind a microphone or speaking to large groups of people. Dr. David M. Reiss in San Diego calls these characters people create to use on the public stage "dissociation in the service of narcissism." It is a form of dissociation where something like an alternate personality is developed purposely. The short version of that is the old showbiz saw of "staying in character," something not every performer is able to turn off – or wants to -- once they leave the stage.

We all wear masks. Tonight, though, we're all being ourselves in more ways than even Bo and Mary realize.

Bo chooses an appropriate guitar and Mary picks up her concertina. They begin to play a song for us. We don't remember what song they chose, but it might as well have been "Mary's Song." Their original composition is a lovely and lilting instrumental. It might be called a sea chanty except that the Ozarks are way too far inland for that. We haven't even seen many ambers waves of grain on our expedition. If they were there at all, they've all been plowed under in exchange for the government subsidy for growing the soybeans and rice that we've seen no one here consume.

I close my eyes. The wistful melody coaches me gently to imagine places far, far away. The irony is that I don't want to be anywhere else but here. I want to remain in this place, this time forever. I want to stay here with Bo and Mary and Darrell and Robbie and Tigger too if we could get someone to ship him to us. I am comfortable with small herds of deer, noisy armadillos, even the ticks in the grass. Of course I can't stay. Our return plane to Long Beach leaves in three days.

I open my eyes again and there is Darrell. I've never seen him happier and that makes me as happy as I can be.

This is what music is supposed to be. This is what music means to me. This is a language we can all understand, one that just crosses borders, heals transgressions and unifies us all as human beings. Music is about understanding and acceptance. We bring both emotions home with us.

We still play "Mary's Song" on the CD Bo and Mary gifted us before we left Arkansas. It takes us back to the Ozarks, to the studio that special night and it makes us sad that we aren't living there still. We were all "from off," yet the music brought us to a place we all could share. "Mary's Song" became not just Bo and Mary's song but ours too.

I end the evening fulfilled and surprised. Could it be that I wasn't being myself anymore than was Darrell? Bo and Mary, through their kindness and through their music, have opened my eyes.

I think about the people who loved my music once. I think about the people who tell me they love my music and the memories my songs invoke. I think of the joy it brings me to bring joy to others. It reminds me that not everyone was just waiting for my playing to stop. This feeling of unbridled joy is one I want my husband to experience always. That smile on his face assures me that I'm pretty good at bringing him exactly that.

We both love Bo and Mary for saving us in so many ways. I will always love them for accomplishing the impossible. They have reminded me not just who I am but also why.

Which One Am I?

-- 44 --

TARA

No matter what day of the week or time of the day, somewhere on our cable service it is time to air an episode of *Law & Order*. It seems there are always crimes to be solved, missing persons to locate and motives to be determined.

On this morning's episode, Sam Waterston in the character of Prosecutor Jack McCoy was tasked with trying to discover the identity of a murderer. This is not a rare thing for Jack McCoy to have to do in a normal *Law & Order* story line. Neither is it uncommon to find my button hopping cable search has turned up yet another episode where the alleged perpetrator is also an alleged multiple.

This episode will evolve like most others where DID is used as a surprising plot twist. There will be a discussion of DID: Does it exist?

What are its traits? How can the prosecutor trip up the multiple's story on the witness stand? And what if DID is real? Who will Jack McCoy prove guilty if the body is unaware that someone inside him or her committed a crime? Somewhere, Billy Milligan is smiling, proud that his trial continues to have such a lasting influence yet probably angry that he isn't getting paid for it.

Law & Order isn't the only show on television where DID propels a plot or two. There were story arcs on *Criminal Minds* and episodes of *Psych*, *ER* and *Nip/Tuck*. As a plot device, DID has shown up in the movies, books, pro wrestling and even Anime. This style of saturation marketing has its strong points, but it is still television that holds the greatest influence with about 60% of Americans using television as their largest source of information.

In some ways, television portrayals of DID are no different than the literary portrayals from the days when Americans still chose to read. *When Rabbit Howls* or *Sybil* "focus only on the drama, not the misery. They look for the theater, not the quotidian," multiple Stephanie Lee told us.

Sometimes television producers just go for the comedy. The first season of *The United States of Tara* is an award-winning cable series that ran for three seasons on the cable network Showtime. Starring Emmy-winner Toni Collette in the title role and based on an idea by Steven Spielberg, *Tara* was the first series to use DID as a primary theme for a continuing series. By going off her meds, Tara hopes that the people inside will help her reclaim her past. Most psychiatrists believe this is a medical impossibility, though there are exceptions. Kriss Erickson was a DID person with over 200 inner ones. Without medication or standard psychological treatments she tells in her book *Sky Eyes* of becoming cured from DID using her own intuitive/energetic nature. Her story, though, is a particularly exceptional exception to the rule.

We were watching *The United States of Tara* to see how DID was being portrayed to the layman. We were watching *Tara* to see if the quotidian might finally triumph over the theater. It didn't take long to realize we were just watching to count the mistakes. They come fast and furious.

Darrell was the first to turn away from the screen. He found *Tara* "repulsive, downgrading and insulting to people with this disability." The show's producers weren't completely tone deaf to complaints like that. Leah Petersen, the multiple who served as an advisor to the series, wrote in *The Huffington Post* that. "If we just focused on the serious we would be doing a great disservice to the DID community, where there is a lot of people who need that humor to get through it all….Being able to laugh with others about strange behavior helps relieve tension and actually brings you closer together."

As a consultant to the series, Petersen had nothing to do with the actual writing, editing or directing of the show, which gave her a certain distance from whatever messages producer Diablo Cody chose to portray. "I simply gave them my opinions and answered questions," she said.

This lack of attention to DID makes *Tara* seem to us a one-note-samba, a joke that was repetitive no matter how many personalities the producers gave Toni Collette to portray. The actress won an Emmy for her role in *Tara*, but Darrell wasn't the only multiple who didn't laugh at Collette's portrayal.

This may be because laughter is, at its heart, not much of a laughing matter. "Laughter is based on shame," actor and comedian Hal Sparks explained to us when we asked about the nature of modern comedy. "Something that is socially awkward generates shame. Telling a joke takes the audience off the hook. What we're looking at is a reflection of ourselves."

Collette's depiction of Tara is a reflection from a fun house mirror, disappointing but not surprising. The first portrayal of any minority in the major media proves painful. Before there are characters, there are caricatures.

Cartoons are easy to find. We watch *The Boys in the Band*, the first major film to deal with exclusively gay content. A group of frenemies threw a birthday party in the film, based on a successful play of the same name, to admit how much they hate themselves, hate each other and particularly hate being gay. Released in 1970, a year after the Stonewall Riots, the characters are all stereotypes: the swishy queen; the young, dumb hustler; the closeted bisexual; the unfaithful couple.

Stereotypes were all the public could digest in 1970 and it would take until 1998 before there was any character resembling a "normal" gay on national TV. The show was Will & Grace, the "normal" gay guy was played by heterosexual actor Eric McCormack. No matter how far the public's perception of gays had come, the series still had to present a swishy queen as comic relief. The role of Jack went to Sean Hayes who, through the entire eight years the series was produced, never would divulge his own sexuality.

The poster child for caricatures on screen is harder to find. *Amos 'n' Andy* was, set in the black community but was written and voiced by

Freeman Gosden and Charles Correll, both of whom were white. The show remained very popular in the United States from the 1920s through the 1950s, first on radio and then on television. The television adaptation ran on CBS-TV from 1951 until 1953, with Gosden and Correll providing the voices for the black actors on the screen according to a 1950 article in *The Pittsburgh Press*. *Amos 'n' Andy* continued in syndicated reruns from 1954 until 1966.

The mention of *Amos 'n' Andy* is still a sticking point within the black community. Though *Amos 'n' Andy* was one of the first radio comedy series and almost certainly influenced *I Love Lucy*, which also debuted on television in 1951, the difference between the two series is less about style than it is about symbolism.

"Lucy was a full person, however broad her performance," according to Frances Callier and Angela V. Shelton, the duo who make up the comedy and political commentating entity Frangela. "She was not in any way meant to be nor did anyone seem to think that she represented "white" women in America at all, she was just the one married to Ricki Ricardo. Amos and Andy are not full people in the literary or dramatic sense if you will, they were one dimensional cultural constructs."

Amos 'n' Andy was the first and for a long time the only representation of the black community that most people heard or saw. Blacks would not see themselves represented as something more than caricatures until *The Cosby Show* made its debut in 1984. With new episodes produced until 1992, the hit NBC series focused on the Huxtable family, an affluent African-American family with a doctor as father and lawyer as mother. That the Huxtables would not come to television as the blue collar family originally envisioned by former ABC executives Marcy Carsey and Tom Werner was changed at the insistence of series star Bill Cosby.

When and if the DID community gets to see itself portrayed to the world as just another piece of society may be a long time coming. There is a lower percentage of people with DID in the United States than there are black people (12.6% according to the 2011 United States Census) or gays (3-8% according to The National Gay and Lesbian Task Force). As a smaller percentage of the population, the DID community has less power to organize as a group.

The principal difference between those with DID and other minorities is that DID itself is seen as a disease and one that society in general is very uncomfortable discussing. "Society generally wants to deny the darkest aspects of itself, just as the individual wants to deny the dark aspects of the personal self," Kriss Erickson wrote us. Erickson found a way to help the DID community by becoming a counselor and mastering Reiki, a Japanese technique for stress reduction and relaxation that is said to promote healing. "Issues like abuse, DID and difficult to diagnose illnesses all will come up and keep coming up until society 'gets' it and is willing to be more open and accepting."

When that time will come is anybody's guess. Likely it will take more than just occasional pop culture depictions on *Law & Order*, *Criminal Minds* or *Beavis & Butthead* for DID to enter the popular lexicon. It may well be a comedy, a more scientifically-sound successor to *The United States of Tara*, that helps the world to take DID seriously. It may also take something more.

James Darrell Williams & Robert Dann 10th Anniversary Portrait
(Photo Credit Unknown)

– 45 –

ROBERT

"Hello," came the voice on the telephone. "You don't know me, but I'm James Darrell Williams."

Of course I knew him. We'd been hanging out for two weeks by the time Darrell called. I'd come to know a fair amount of his recent history and even reached the point where I could almost reproduce his Arkansas accent.

"My psychiatrist says I need to tell you I have multiple personalities," this odd new person said. "You've been dating one of them. His name is J.D. and he's only 15 years old. "How could you?"

The initial shock wore off quickly as I assured Darrell that this J.D. person sure didn't look like a teenager. Then came his questions. What had we done? Where did we go? Most importantly, what had we done with Robert's ashes? We decided a coffee meeting was in order.

Which One Am I?

Darrell didn't recognize me. It took him a bit to warm up to who to him was this stranger J.D. had been seeing. I told him what I could. J.D. and I met in The Brit, the same neighborhood gay bar where Robert Dann had liked to shoot pool. J.D. told me that Robert Dann, who he considered his husband, had recently passed away. He missed Robert dearly and regretted that Robert's health hadn't allowed them to go many places or see many new things. Having just come out of an abusive relationship myself, I was looking for someone to go to places with me. We agreed that neither of us was ready for a relationship but were wide open to a friendship.

The whirlwind started the very next day. We started at The Abbey, the largest gay bar on the West Coast where they offer any combination of dining, dessert, drinks and dancing. We snacked on taquitos on Olvera Street, the historic Mexican landmark in downtown Los Angeles. J.D. really wanted to pick out which Hollywood stars' names he could recognize among those inscribed in the terrazzo and brass stars along Hollywood Blvd. He also wanted to visit Graumann's Chinese Theater to attempt to squeeze his own feet into John Wayne's surprisingly petite boot prints. We closed the night at Miceli's, Hollywood's oldest Italian restaurant where the ceiling is covered with autographic Chianti bottles and the wait staff sings show tunes. By the time we drove back to Long Beach, we were both spent. Still, we were more than ready to do it all over again.

J.D. confessed to Darrell what he had done with Robert's ashes before Darrell and I ever met. He had taken a walk down Alamitos Beach, J.D. told Darrell. Taking the steps down from 8th Place, he had walked the beach where Robert had been and past the parking lot where the lifeguards watched Robert collapse. J.D. had asked Robert to let him know where he wanted to be. When his leg went into the sand, he dispersed Robert's ashes into the sea.

At my first meeting with Darrell, he told me he thought I was going to hit him for dragging me into the world of DID and for J.D. having potentially led me on. There was no problem and still isn't. Having spent most of my life in the entertainment world, I am acquainted with people who have one personality in public and another in private. Besides, I'd never dated anyone who didn't seem to have at least two personalities. I call it the "Six Month Rule" because that's how long it generally takes for someone new to be comfortable enough to allow me to see who they really are. That never happened with Darrell. He's the most stable and consistent person I've ever dated.

Robert likely hadn't meant for his life with Darrell to end where it began. It was Darrell who knew something was wrong that morning. Robert was getting ready to leave to take his metal detector down to the sand searching for the drop coins and lost jewelry he sold to help the couple get through each month. From combing his hair to brushing his teeth, Robert seemed more methodical than usual. Everything seemed to be in slow motion and Darrell saw that Robert was bathed in a faint glow. "I love you," the stoic Italian uncharacteristically called to Darrell as he moved towards the door.

It was mid-afternoon when the call came into the house from the Emergency Room at St. Mary's Hospital. On the line was one of the nurses who would only tell Darrell that Robert had been in an accident. After he picked up the phone from the floor where the shock of the news made him drop it, Darrell got Robert's room number from the nurse. He hurried to the hospital as fast as a man who doesn't drive can hurry. Darrell remembers walking into Robert's hospital room. After that, he remembers nothing.

The kids inside knew Darrell couldn't handle the stress of seeing Robert die. For 22 ½ years Darrell had defined himself by his marriage. Robert might have planned for Darrell's life after his passing, but for Darrell the future was a blank. Had Darrell not worried about Boo the cat being left alone in the world, he would have wished to die with his beloved. Despite his worries about their pet, Darrell was suicidal. He refused to eat, could barely sleep and spent days and nights doing nothing but walking the streets of Long Beach. Within a two month span, he had dropped from a 46 inch waist to a 27.

That was when J.D. stepped up. As the dominant personality among the older kids, J.D. embodies less anger than most of the others. Unthreatening and personable, it is he who is most able to "pass" in society at large. The story of what happened the day Robert died was entirely told by J.D. It had to be. Darrell wasn't there.

The lifeguard at Alamitos Beach said later that he watched Robert as he left the sand and went to his car. He saw Robert unlock the door, sit down in the driver's seat and immediately slump against the steering wheel. It was a heart attack that hit him unexpectedly. Both the lifeguards and the hospital staff assured Darrell that Robert's death would have been both quick and painless. Robert Dann died the minute he sat behind the wheel.

In reality, there had been plenty of unheeded warnings that something was wrong with Robert Dann. Just three weeks before, paramedics had been called because Robert couldn't breathe. He was admitted to the same Emergency Room at St. Mary's Hospital in which his life would eventually end.

"When was your last major heart attack?" the nurse wanted to know. Darrell and Robert would have liked to know that too.

They knew there were problems. Robert had previously had stents placed in his neck where his veins were collapsing. Stenting involves placing flexible mesh tubes to prop open blocked blood vessels. It is a commonly used to clear plaque-clogged heart arteries which cause heart attacks.

Not only were Robert and Darrell unaware of Robert's heart attack, they didn't know about the four previous attacks either. Robert's autopsy revealed the signs that they had occurred. If he had known about the heart attacks himself, Robert certainly never told Darrell. Neither did his clinic seem concerned about those earlier attacks. Had they known, they would have prescribed Lasix, a medication that helps to decrease blood volume by increasing the amount of salt and water that the kidneys remove from the blood. Robert had received no such prescription from the clinic. The Emergency Room doctor wondered why Robert hadn't.

Robert was always having trouble getting in to see his doctor. There were appointments made, but the clinic always had an excuse. The doctor was always in surgery, out for the day or generally unavailable. No one else thought to check his chart to make sure what needed to be done was getting done.

After Robert's death, Darrell had wanted to sue the clinic for wrongful death and medical malpractice. Because in the State of California Robert and Darrell could not be considered legal spouses, such a lawsuit would have had to be brought to court by Robert's family. For her own reasons, Robert's sister Joan refused to do so.

Darrell may never fully be over his anger at losing Robert. Consolation for Darrell comes these days in knowing that he's done almost everything Robert asked him to do. Not everything in the house has been sold, though enough has been removed so that there are fewer memory-raising mementos. We haven't moved from the house they shared, just changed it enough so that the interior looks somewhat new. It isn't only their lack of attendance at the memorial that keeps Darrell from seeing his and Robert's family and old friends. It was one of Robert's wishes that Darrell find a new relationship, one that would help Darrell begin his life again.

Robert Dann continues to live here. There are his clothes in the hall closet and the cherished recollections Darrell shares, sometimes longingly and sometimes accidentally.

Above all, Darrell is happy. He knows Robert is in a better place sharing the afterlife with his personal trinity consisting of God, Jesus and Boo the Cat. Darrell knows this because J.D. told him so.

The last night I spent with J.D. before Darrell banished him to his bedroom there behind Darrell's hazel eyes for using Darrell's name without permission, J.D. asked me to drive him to the end of 8th Place. He needed to be alone, he told me. Of course I respected his wishes.

In my rearview mirror I watched him as he sat at the top of the landing of the stairs leading down to the beach. I watched him light a cigarette which helped me see his hands moving through the air. It was quite a lively discussion with someone only he could see. J.D. might have been talking with God or more likely Robert. There was no way of knowing. What I did know was that J.D. was enjoying whatever words were floating on the late night sea breeze because I could tell that who I still thought of as Darrell was smiling.

The last mental image I have of J.D. is this: His silent conversation ended with a wave of his hand and a nod of his head. With that he walked to the car and got into the passenger seat for the short drive back to the white house in which we live now, the one with the rust-colored trim. I wouldn't see J.D. again for months. Instead, I'd get to know Darrell.

This is where our story begins.

Tom, Tigger & Darrell
Upon their return from Arkansas, Thanksgiving 2010
(Photo: Thomas Smith Sr.)

AFTERWARD

There are more than 15 people living inside James Darrell Williams. But who is he really?

Who are any of us?

Who am I?

I am a Californian because my grandmother brought my father here from Arkansas. Lillie Mae Stewart brought the senior Thomas Stewart Smith, named for my grandfather's father who died young, to California's Central Valley because word had gotten back to her in Fort Smith that my grandfather Ernie Edward Smith was out on the West Coast chasing more than one of the get-rich-quick schemes he would pursue all his life. A professional wrestler during the time before wrestling went Hollywood, my grandfather was also known as something of a ladies' man. "Lady" wasn't a word my grandmother would likely have used to describe what my grandfather was chasing out in California.

I am a Californian because my mother worked her way across the fields of the continental United States after her parents died within a year of each other in her native Puerto Rico. Gloria Ester Arizmendi's eldest sister Susanna married a man who brought my mother, her three sisters and brother to work their way to the coast picking whatever crops needed to be picked. Susanna's husband decided after the family left the island that they should all convert from Catholicism to the Seventh Day Adventist sect. He made sure everyone in the family adhered to a severe interpretation of Old Testament Laws. Even buttons on clothing were seen as sinful adornments. These Biblical laws applied to everyone except him. Upon reaching Northern California, my mother and her youngest sister Carmen tired of the man's abuse and separated from their siblings. Gloria found a job at my grandmother's doctor's office in the tiny Central California town of Corcoran.

The original plan was for my father's parents to adopt my mother, but that changed when my father returned to Corcoran from an off road motorcycle race he had ridden in on Catalina Island.

I am a Californian because I am a product of my family's history, its psychology, sociology, geography and, to a certain extent, fantasy. I am not so different from Darrell. My destiny was determined long before I was conceived. Neither am I so different from anybody else. It is what we make of our opportunities, or lack of same, that makes us individuals.

Which One Am I?

I am Darrell's husband as of June 20, 2011 because he is the first man I've ever been with who gives me more than he takes. We haven't the paperwork, but are doing what we can to help California join the rest of the civilized world in allowing gay marriage.

This book has proven a very difficult journey for both sides of our couple. Darrell's memory of events has been questioned and we expect they will be questioned still. History bears this out. On *Oprah*, Truddi Chase told how a *Washington Post* reporter had tracked down her family, including her stepfather following the publication of *When Rabbit Howls*. Unsurprisingly, Chase's family denied any abuse had taken place. There is also a widespread effort to discredit the story told in *Sybil* and, by extension, all memoirs about DID.

Some doubt that Darrell could recall in explicit detail events from his childhood, not to mention those from before. Family members, former family members, Southern authorities: they all deny everything we've spent more than a year trying to document. Yet no one can -- or will -- deliver alternate versions of the incidents Darrell remembers only too well.

A suspicious fire burns down a large apartment building in a small town. A mother of five suffers a near-fatal car accident. A house burns down taking with it some highly-valued animals. A sibling is abused, molested and abandoned. These are the moments that have escaped people's memories. They dismiss each incident with the same alacrity someone would if he or she simply misplaced a set of car keys.

The question for us has never been how Darrell can remember these experiences, but rather how anyone could forget. A statement we both heard recently on television struck a chord with us: "Hidden in your greatest trauma is your greatest gift."

Forgetting is Darrell's gift. During daylight hours, he can will away his memories. It is at night that his mind is most vulnerable. When he closes his eyes, he sees most clearly: abuse, abandonment, betrayal, danger.

It became very clear early on that it's not that people can't remember. It's that they won't. "If you find out R.D. isn't your father, then you aren't my brother. Know what I'm saying?" Darrell's brother Allen, out of prison and back in Mississippi, tells us when we ask the local police to track him down for us. "Just let it go," his brother Johnny tells him by phone from West Memphis.

Darrell can't "let it go." The people inside won't let him. It is in those traumas that they exist. It is with the assistance of every last person inside him that Darrell keeps the pain at bay, allowing him to survive and thrive from day to day. These are the people who help us live.

I worked under the name Tom Kidd when I started performing. In the interests of maintaining the character and promoting my music, that became my pen name. That persona I created followed me later into the world of publicity.

As do the people inside Darrell when they decide to come around, Tom Kidd takes a lot of energy to maintain. Unlike Darrell's experience, I can choose to turn him on and off. I haven't been Tom Kidd for a very long time now.

A person does not have to be a performer to have moments of dissociation, a point driven home by Marlene Steinberg, M.D. and Maxine Schnall in their book *The Stranger in the Mirror*, a guide to DID recomended to us early on by Dr. Sharon Higgens. In fact, this point should be clear to anyone who has had a dream. In dreams we all dissociate.

Our dream is to let others with DID know they are not alone. Our dream is to help correct the science and scuttlebutt that leads to so many DID patients being either misdiagnosed or not diagnosed at all. The science is particularly important. Too many people will disbelieve our story and neither will they believe memoirs about life with DID told by anyone else. They don't believe in DID. Science doesn't care what someone believes.

The truth is that what happened to Darrell is almost certainly happening to someone, somewhere right now. This is what we need to tell.

This is who we are.

I am the dark-haired man the old woman foresaw long ago at her card table on the sidewalks of Memphis. My hair was darker back then and I am still quite a bit younger than was Robert Dann.

I am the luckiest man alive.

I am Darrell's last husband.

And he is mine.

Questions for Further Discussion

1. Is James Darrell Williams a reliable narrator of his own life story? Why or why not? Given their history of secrets, denial and obfuscation, are the narratives told by others in Darrell's family reliable?

2. The concept of shame appears several times in the book though used in different contexts. How does the idea of shame change and evolve in the world around us? Is the concept of shame still important to people today?

3. In her introduction, Mary Barnick calls this book a "love story." Do you agree with her statement? Why or why not?

4. In the Foreward, the authors state that "We took alternate versions into consideration, but Darrell's experience always remained primary." Is this a valid approach taken to tell someone's life story? Why or why not?

5. How does the format of multiple timelines help the reader better understand what it is like to have Dissociative Identity Disorder (DID)? Does it help the reader understand what it is like being Darrell?

6. Did a remembered incident actually occur if official records contradict that memory, have been destroyed or were never created at all? What might have happened instead to generate the same outcome?

7. What influence does location have on someone's life history? Would Darrell's life have been any different had he been born in a different town or region of the country? Would anyone's?

8. Some of this book's themes include the search for both identity and family. At its core, what is identity? What is family? On this expedition through the South and through history, does Darrell find either? Does Tom?

9. Darrell's presumed aunt Almeter Jackson tells the authors, "Arkansas might as well be another planet." In what ways does she mean this? How far would people have to travel to find themselves on "another planet"?

10. What role does Darrell's sexuality play in how his life unfolded? How might events have been different had he been heterosexual instead of gay? Would these events have been different at all?

11. Is history really constructed of "scribbled notes, selective memory and inadvertent admissions"? Is there a definitive source for any historical event? If so, where is it?

12. *Which One Am I?* ends with the phrase, "This is where our story begins." To which entities does "our" refer? Darrell and Tom? The authors and the reader? Somebody else?

References

'18-yr, Old Brinkley Boy Dies of Self Inflicted Gunshot', *Brinkley Argus* (1971). (p. 1). Brinkley: River Publishing.

'AIDS: The End of the Beginning', *New York Times*. (1987, Dec. 30). Retrieved from http://partners.nytimes.com/library/national/science/aids/123087sci-aids.html.

Alden, B. (1998). *Will & Grace*. Television series. Los Angeles, CA & New York, NY: NBC.

Allen, F. (2008). "Dissociative Identity Disorder (DID): Animal Alter Parts and Other Nonhuman Alter Parts", *Blooming Lotus: Journey to Recovery from Childhood Abuse*. Retrieved from http:// http://faithallen.wordpress.com/2008/10/23/dissociative-identity-disorder-did-animal-alter-parts-and-other-nonhuman-alter-parts.

Allison, R. (2004). 'Dual Personality, Multiple Personality, Dissociative Identity Disorder - What's in a Name?,' *MultipleMinds.blogspot.com*. Retrieved from http://multipleminds.blogspot.com/2004/12/dual-personality-multiple-personality.html

Aloe, M. & Rivera, C. (1988). 'Devil Worship: Exposing Satan's Underground', *The Geraldo Rivera Show*. Television broadcast. New York, NY & Los Angeles, CA: King World Productions.

'Amos And Andy Name Subs for Television Roles', *St. Petersburg Times*. (1951, Jun. 18). Retrieved from http://news.google.com/newspapers?id=jncxAAAAIBAJ&sjid=Yn0DAAAAIBAJ&pg=3569,1199892&dq=freeman+gosden&hl=en.

Arkansas Department of Health, State of Arkansas. Death Record for Carolyn Alberta Bevel. (1983, Nov. 8), File # 2709829.

'Arson Not Indicated in 12-Apartment Fire,' *West Memphis Evening News*. (1981, Jan. 14).

'Arson Possibility in $300,000 Apartment Fire,' *West Memphis Evening News*. (1981, Jan. 13).

'Arson Ruled Out in Apartment Fire,' *West Memphis Evening News* (1981, Jan. 14).

'Banishment', *West's Encyclopedia of American Law*. (2005).

Baumeister, F., Bratslavsky, E., Finkenauer, C. & Vohs, K. (2001). 'Bad is Stronger than Good', *Review of General Psychology*. (Vol. 5. No. 4. pp. 323-370).

Belton, J. (2008). *American Cinema/American Culture*. Columbus, OH: McGraw-Hill Humanities/Social Sciences/Languages.

Berendt, J. (1994). *Midnight in the Garden of Good and Evil*. New York, NY: Random House.

Berlinger, J. & Sinofsky, B., (1996). *Paradise Lost: The Child Murders at Robin Hood Hills*. Television broadcast. New York, NY: Home Box Office America Undercover.

'Blaze Damages Apartment Units', *West Memphis Evening News*. (1981, Jan. 11).

'Borderline Personality Disorder,' *PsychNet.UK*. Retrieved from http://www.palace.net/~llama/psych/bpd.html.

Bowie, M. 'Driver resigns; audit starts Tuesday', *West Memphis Evening Times*. (2008, May 26).

'Brief History of Carnival Memphis', *CarnivalMemphis.org*. 2012. Retrieved fromhttp://carnivalmemphis.org/Carnival_History.html.

Carlin, D. (1995). 'Trauma, Testimony, and Fictions of Truth: Narrative in *When Rabbit Howls*', *Texas Studies in Literature and Language*. (Vol. 37). Retrieved from http://astraeasweb.net/plural/truddi-narrative.html.

Central Delta Historical Journal (1998). Central Delta Historical Society. (Vol. Two, No. 1, p. 25).

Cloitre, M., L. R. Cohen, L.R. & Koenen, K.C. (2006). *Treating Survivors of Childhood Abuse: Psychotherapy for the Interrupted Life*. The Guilford Press: London.

Cohen, D., Nisbett, R., Bowdle, B. & Schwarz, N. (1994). 'Insult, Aggression, and the Southern Culture of Honor: An "Experimental Ethnography"', *Interpersonal Relations and Groups Processes*. Washington DC: American Psychological Association.

Connor, S. 'Brain changes at puberty 'help to develop intellectual machinery", *The Independent*. (2006, Sept. 8).

Chase, T. (1987). *When Rabbit Howls*. New York, NY: Jove Books.

Crowley, M., Utt, K., Dunne, D., Jiras, R. (1970). *The Boys in the Band*. Los Angeles, CA: National General Pictures.

'Discover Main Street', *BroadwayWestMemphis.com*. Retrieved fromhttp://www.broadwaywestmemphis.com/what_002.html.

'Dissociative Identity Disorder – Two Famous Cases', *Psychology.jrank.org*. Retrieved from http://psychology.jrank.org/pages/189/Dissociative-Identity-Disorder.html.

Doyle, P. 'West Memphis Three Finally Freed', *Rolling Stone*. (2011, Sept. 15). P. 20.

Eisendrath, S. J. (1997). "Psychiatric Disorders", *Current Medical Diagnosis and Treatment, 1998*, edited by Stephen McPhee, et al., 37th ed. Stamford: Appleton & Lange.

Erickson, K. (2009). *Sky Eyes*. Seattle WA: AKW Books.

Fausset, R. "West Memphis Three' freed in '93 slayings', *Los Angeles Times*. (2011, Aug. 19). Retrieved from http://www.latimes.com/news/nationworld/nation/la-na-west-memphis-3-20110820,0,5874148.story.

Foman, D. (2011). *Only I Can Define Me: Releasing Shame and Growing Into My Adult Self*. Ft. Lauderdale FL: CreateSpace.

Foster, D. & Cerissa (2009). 'The Oxycontin Express', *Vanguard*. Television series episode. New York, NY: Current TV.

Garland, K. 'Arson Charge Dropped in River Grove Fire', *West Memphis Press-Scimitar*. (1981, Feb. 11).

Garland, K. 'West Memphis Apartment Fire Ravages Townhouse Complex', *West Memphis Press-Scimitar*. (1981, Jan 12).

Geidd, J. (2002). 'Inside the Teenage Brain', *Frontline*. Television series episode. Boston, MA: WGBH educational foundation.

'Geraldo Rivera: Satanic Ritual Abuse & Recovered Memories', *ReligiousTolerance.org* (1998). Retrieved from http://www.religioustolerance.org/geraldo.htm.

Gillis, C. (2010). '1970-1979', *American Cultural History*. Lone Star College-Kingwood Library, Kingwood, TX. Retrieved from http://wwwappskc.lonestar.edu/popculture/decade70.html.

Hansen, C. (1998). 'Dangerous Therapy: The Story of Patricia Burgus and Multiple Personality Disorder', *Chicago Magazine*. (June 1998). Retrieved from http://www.chicagomag.com/Chicago-Magazine/June-1998/Dangerous-Therapy-The-Story-of-Patricia-Burgus-and-Multiple-Personality-Disorder/index.php?cparticle=2&siarticle=1.

Hathaway, B. (2011). 'Past abuse leads to loss of gray matter in brains of adolescents', *Yale News*. New Haven, CT: Yale Daily News. December 5, 2011.

Haughton Place. Undated brochure for Haughton Place. Amory MS.

Hewlett, J. (1998). 'Kentucky art teacher was 'Sybil,' scholar confirms', *Detroit Free Press*. December 23.

Hilgard, E. (1988). 'Professional Skepticism about Multiple Personality,' *The Journal of Nervous and Mental Disease.* (#9, Vol. 176, p. 532). Philadelphia, PA: The Williams & Wilkins Co.

'History of Schizophrenia,' *Schizophrenia.com.* Retrieved from http://www.schizophrenia.com/history.htm.

James, D. *Multiple Personality Disorder in the Courts: A Review of the North American Experience.* Retrieved from http://www.astraeasweb.net/plural/forensic.html.

Johnson, N. (1957). *The Three Faces of Eve.* Los Angeles CA: 20th Century Fox.

Kennett J. & Matthews S. (2002). 'Identity, control and responsibility: the case of Dissociative Identity Disorder', *Philosophical Psychology.* (Vol. 15, Num. 4, 1 December).

Keyes, D. (1981). *The Minds of Billy Milligan.* New York NY: Random House.

Kirgis, B. & Barnick, M. (2011). "Mary's Song." (Bo & Mary Kirgis with the Czecrish Moronic Orchestra). Audio CD: Czecrish Records.

Lale, E. (2011). *Greater Than the Sum of my Parts.* Seattle WA: Amazon Digital Services.

Lehmann-Haupt, C. (1987). 'Books of the Times: *When Rabbit Howls',* New York Times. July 6. Retrieved from http://astraeasweb.net/plural/nytchase./html.

Leveritt, M. (2002). *Devil's Knot.* New York, NY: Atria Books.

Mangione, M. (2006). "America the Blue". (Michelle Mangione). On *Life Beneath the Sun* (Audio CD). Long Beach, CA: 101 Distribution.

Martin, B. & Winbush, D. 'House-Fire Victim Been there Before,' *West Memphis Press-Scimitar.* (1981, Jan. 12).

McIntyre, K. (2007). 'Haven Theater,' *CinemaTreasures.org.* Retrieved from http://cinematreasures.org/theaters/21050.

McLeod, S. A. (2008). *Information Processing.* Retrieved from http://www.simplypsychology.org/information-processing.html

Miller, M. 'Litany of troubles left Flint's foundations cracked', *The Flint Journal presents: Journal of the 20^h Century 1980-1989.* Retrieved from http://www.flintjournal.com/20thcentury/1980/1980main.html

Morton, J. (2012). 'Memory and the dissociative brain', *Trauma, Dissociation and Multiplicity.* Valerie Sinason (Ed). Abingdon, Oxon, UK: Routledge.

'Multiple Personality Disorder,' *Gale Encyclopedia of Medicine* (2008). Retrieved from http://medical-dictionary.thefreedictionary.com/multiple+personality+disorder.

Munro, K. (2000). 'Incest & Child Abuse: Definitions, Perpetrators, Victims & Effects', *KaliMunro.com*. Retrieved from http://kalimunro.com/wp/articles-info/sexual-emotional-abuse/incest-and-child-sexual-abuse-definitions-perpetrators-victims-and-effects.

Nathan, D. (2011). *Sybil Exposed: The Extraordinary Story Behind the Famous Multiple Personality Case*. New York, NY: Free Press.

Nathan, D. & Snedeker, M. (1995). *Satan's Silence: Ritual Abuse and the Making of a Modern American Witch Hunt*. New York, NY: Basic Books.

Nguyen, M.T. (1999). 'Civil Rights – The History of Gay Rights', *Enderminh.com*. Retrieved from http://www.enderminh.com/minh/civilrights.aspx.

Nordqvist, C. 'No Fear Felt By Woman Without Functioning Amygdala', *Medical News Today*. (2010, Dec. 17). Retrieved from http://www.medicalnewstoday.com/articles/211972.php.

Nuss, J. (2011). 'Ex-Death Row Inmate Enjoys First Night of Freedom', *SignOnSanDiego.com*. Retrieved from http://www.signonsandiego.com/news/2011/aug/20/ex-death-row-inmate-enjoys-first-night-of-freedom/.

Pendergrast, M. (1996). *Victims of Memory: Sex Abuse Accusations And Shattered Lives*. Hinesburg, VT: Upper Access Books.

'Personality Disorders,' American Psychiatric Association *DSM-5* development (2012). Retrieved from http://www.dsm5.org/proposedrevision/pages/personalitydisorders.aspx.

Petersen, L. (2010). 'Mismatched Boots', *Huffington Post*. Retrieved from http://www.huffingtonpost.com/leah-peterson/mismatched-boots_b_584738.html.

Petersen-Crawford, L. (2010). *Not Otherwise Specified*. Santa Barbara, CA: Leah Petersen.

Pierce, R. 'Missing $28,000.00 Puts Youth Probation Office Under Prosecutor's Eye', *Arkansas Democrat Gazette*. (1998, Jan. 13)

Pope, H., Barry, S., Bodkin, A. & Hudson, J. (2006). 'Tracking Scientific Interest in the Dissociative Disorders: A Study of Scientific Publication Output 1984–2003', *Psychotherapy and Psychosomatics*. (Vol. 75, No. 1).

'Portions of Brain are Smaller in Children Born Prematurely, Researches at Stanford and Packard Find,' Stanford School of Medicine (2004). Retrieved fromhttp://med.stanford.edu/news_releases/2004/august/reiss.htm.

Prendergast, C. & Swan, P. (2011),'Painting outside the lines,' *Mental Health and Social Inclusion*, Vol. 15 Iss: 3 pp. 138 -142.

'Preserve America Community: West Memphis, AR', *PreserveAmerica.gov*. Retrieved from http://www.preserveamerica.gov/ARwestmemphis.html.

'Prosecutors Will Delay Pursuit Of Arson Charge,' *West Memphis Evening News*. (1981, Feb 11).

Ramsfield, K. & Kuter, R. (2011). 'Multiple Personalities: Crime and Defense', *TruTv.com*. Retrieved from http://wwwtrutv.com/library/crive/criminal_mind/psychology/multiples/index.html.

Reinhold, R. 'The Longest Trial - A Post-Mortem. Collapse of Child-Abuse Case: So Much Agony for So Little.' *The New York Times*. (1990, Jan. 24). Retrieved from http://www.nytimes.com/1990/01/24/us/longest-trial-post-mortem-collapse-child-abuse-case-so-much-agony-for-so-little.html.

Reisel, P. (2006). 'Life After the Movies: Former Film Stars Transition into 1950s Television'. *AmericanPopularCulture.com*. Retrieved fromhttp://www.americanpopularculture.com/archive/film/former_film_stars.htm.

Reiss, M. (2012). 'Dissociative Identity Disorder.' San Diego, CA: DMRDynamics.

Rudgley, R. (1998). *The Encyclopedia of Psychoactive Substances*. New York, NY: St. Martins Press.

Saks, E. & Behnke, S. (1997). *Jekyll on Trial: Multiple Personality Disorder and Criminal Law*. New York, NY: NYU Press.

Sharockman, A. (2010). 'Florida's drug problem: 49 of top 50 oxycodone prescribers are from state', *Tamba Bay Times*. (March 18). Retrieved from http://www.tampabay.com/news/politics/stateroundup/floridas-drug-problem-49-of-top-50-oxycodone-prescribers-are-from-state/1080672.

Schreiber, F. R. (1973). *Sybil*. New York, NY: Warner Books.

Sizemore, C. C. & Pittillo, E. S. (1977). *I'm Eve*. New York: New York: Doubleday & Company.

Spielberg, S., Falvey, J., Frank, D., Cody, D., Junge, A. (2009). *The United States of Tara*. Television series. Hollywood, CA: ShowTime Networks & DW Studios.

Spring, R. (2012). 'Denial: a personal and societal journey', *Multiple Parts: The Magazine of PODS*. Huntingdon, Cambridgeshire, UK: PODS. Retrieved fromhttp://www.pods-online.org.uk/denial-ajourney.html.

Stark, E. (1987). 'Inside the Mind of a Multiple,' *Psychology Today*. Retrieved from http://altraeasweb.net/plural/ptchase.html.

Steel, F. 'The West Memphis Three,' *TruTV.com*. Retrieved from http://www.trutv.com/library/crime/notorious_murders/famous/memphis/index_1.html.

Steinberg, M. & Schnall, M. (2001). *The Stranger in the Mirror: Dissociation – The Hidden Epidemic*. New York, NY: HarperCollins.

'Steve Joshlin Fatally Shot', *West Memphis Evening Times* (1971). West Memphis, TN: Crittenden Publishing Co.

Stumbo, B. (1989). 'Colorado Killings : Split Egos: Trendy Alibi or Disorder?', *Los Angeles Times*. (1989, Oct. 8). Retrieved from http://articles.latimes.com/1989-10-08/news/mn-329_1_ross-carlson/3.

Sussman, A. (2007). 'Mental Illness and Creativity:A Neurological View of the "Tortured Artist"', *Stanford Journal of Neuroscience*. (2007, Fall) Vol. I, Is. 1.

Tennessee Department of Health, State of Tennessee. Death Record for James Darrell Jackson. (1998, Mar.3), File # 001738.

Teram, et al, (2006). 'Towards malecentric communication: Sensitizing health professional to the realities of male childhood sexual abuse survivors', *Issues in Mental Health Nursing*, 27, 499-517.

The Encyclopedia of Arkansas History & Culture. Little Rock AR: Central Arkansas Library System. Retrieved from http://www.encyclopediaofarkansas.net.

Tustin, K., & Hayne, H. (2010). Defining the boundary: Age-related changes in childhood amnesia. *Developmental Psychology*, 46, 1049-1061.

Van Arsdale, S. (2001). 'Sybil,' *Ace Weekly*. Lexington KY: Ace Weekly. (Cover)

Weitz., K. 'Kim Noble: A woman divided', *The Independent*. London UK: The Independent. (2006, Aug. 27).

West, C. (1999). *First Person Plural*. New York, NY: Hyperion.

Whitaker, E., (2009). 'The Origin of the Cotillion', Suite101.com. Retrieved from http://www.suite101.com/content/the-cotillion-a88136.

Winfrey, O. (1990). 'The Woman with 92 Personalities,' *Oprah Winfrey Show*. Television series Episode. Chicago, IL: Harpo Productions. Retrieved from http://www.oprah.com/oprahshow/truddi-chases-multiple-personalities.

Wong, Y. J. and Rochlen, A. (2005). 'Demystifying men's emotional behaviour: New directions and implications for counselling and research'. *Psychology of Men and Masculinity, 6,* 1, 62-72.

'Youth Charged with Arson', *West Memphis Evening News.* (1981, Jan. 19).

Zaidi, H. (2012). 'Multiple Personality Disorder,' *HealthMad.com.* Retrieved fromhttp://healthmad.com/mental-health/multiple-personality-disorder/.

Which One Am I?

Made in United States
North Haven, CT
31 July 2025

71214407R00173